ESSENTIAL WISDOM
from a
SPIRITUAL MASTER

ESSENTIAL WISDOM
from a
SPIRITUAL MASTER

SADHGURU
Yogi, Mystic and Visionary

JAICO PUBLISHING HOUSE
Ahmedabad Bangalore Bhopal Bhubaneswar Chennai
Delhi Hyderabad Kolkata Lucknow Mumbai

Published by Jaico Publishing House
A-2 Jash Chambers, 7-A Sir Phirozshah Mehta Road
Fort, Mumbai - 400 001
jaicopub@jaicobooks.com
www.jaicobooks.com

© Isha Foundation

ESSENTIAL WISDOM FROM A SPIRITUAL MASTER
ISBN 978-81-7992-882-0

First Jaico Impression: 2008
Tenth Jaico Impression: 2013

No part of this book may be reproduced or utilized in
any form or by any means, electronic or
mechanical including photocopying, recording or by any
information storage and retrieval system,
without permission in writing from the publishers.

Printed by
Repro India Limited
Plot No. 50/2, T.T.C. MIDC Industrial Area
Mahape, Navi Mumbai - 400 710

Contents

	Preface	vi
	Introduction	viii
1.	Seeker's Predicament	1
2.	With the One Who Knows	63
3.	The Only Bondage	130
4.	Body's Plight	205
	Afterword	296
	Glossary	303
	Index	327

Preface

There often comes a moment in people's lives when full stops fall away. Question marks surface. And commas. Vast yawning commas. It feels like the life sentence can no longer be parsed by an inherited system of punctuation.

This is the point at which the individual becomes a seeker.

The questions are old ones. They have been asked since the dawn of time. But old answers won't do. The old answers have fossilized into scripture, into spiritual artefact, into glorified hearsay. What the seeker wants is breathing, vibrant, pulsating answers. Answers from a live source, a deep-sea diver who has plumbed the depths of existence and returned with an eyewitness account. Answers, in short, from a living master.

This is a book for seekers. It encompasses the gamut of questions – restless, fevered, desperate – that have arisen in every seeker's mind at some point or the other. Questions about fear, desire, suffering, commitment, free will, determinism, God, faith, love, morality, self-deception, doubt, karma, the spiritual path, the mind, the body, disease, healing, madness, death, dissolution. And more.

The answers are by Sadhguru Jaggi Vasudev, a living master and mystic of our times. Unshakably anchored in inner experience, he remains unaffiliated to any organised religious, sectarian or ideological tradition. Forthright, witty, unconventional, provocative, but deeply compassionate, these answers were shared with close disciples over a period of ten years on various occasions. Spanning a variety of subjects that he seldom addresses otherwise in public, these words were spoken to foster the growth of a few who had been with him for a long time.

The tone is intimate, the cadence conversational, the context specific. And this is the book's strength. Seekers of every culture and persuasion will find themselves turning from eavesdroppers to participants from the very first page. For the answers carry the unmistakable ring of authenticity, the deep clarity and wisdom of one who knows what it means to seek. And to know.

And just how to map the arduous, often interminable, journey in between.

If approached with openness and receptivity, the answers can initiate a powerful inner journey. A pilgrimage to the very core of one's being.

* * *

The book includes an introduction to Sadhguru as well as short prefatory notes to each chapter by Swami Nisarga. Short poems by Sadhguru serve as entry points to each chapter.

— Arundhathi Subramaniam

Introduction

Even at a time when there is great versatility in people's understanding of the word spiritual, it is hard to fit Sadhguru into the category of a Spiritual Master in an established sense of the word. If you think he is someone who walks on water, materializes things out of thin air, reads people's minds, looks into a crystal ball and tells people what they did and ought to do, you are in for a surprise. And if you think not, you are in for a bigger surprise!

For those of us who have had the good fortune of being a witness to all the contradictions, paradoxes, compassion and Grace – sparks and thunders apart – from a million other things that he is, attempting to describe him is certainly not an enviable task. Yet, the possibilities and promises for the layman and the world, in this most blessed phenomenon of our time are so rich and plenty that it would indeed be criminal to not make an attempt, however clumsy.

I first met Sadhguru sixteen years ago, when I had just finished my schooling and was in college. A particular teacher in my school had enthralled us to seek a spiritual master – actually the more sacred version of it – a Guru – and be initiated by him, like he himself was. My imagination, fired by books like *The Autobiography of a Yogi* and other similar works

Introduction

led me to yearn for a similar esoteric opportunity. For a couple of years, the picture of a sagely being with a long, flowing, grey beard sitting under a banyan tree and teleporting a handful of disciples into the other worlds was deeply imprinted in me.

So, when I first met this man, clean-shaven and clad in blue jeans and T-shirt, speaking flawless English and riding a motorcycle, as Sadhguru was in those days, I did not in the least think that I had met the Guru. However, the forty minutes that I spent in his introductory talk temporarily distracted me from the sage under the tree and made me look forward to his teachings and practices with the hope that it would help my near-sightedness and my studies – my most pressing problems then.

As years passed, and I got to spend a little more time with this person, unknown to me, bit by bit, little things in me began to align and orient themselves to seek the higher realms of knowing and living and to not settle for the mundane and the mediocre. Ever since then, in scarcely detectable ways, undeterred by my own undoings, Sadhguru's Grace and unseen hands continue to transform my life, taking me beyond my limitations to a destination unknown and undreamt of.

To find a real Guru, a true Guru, or the best Guru, is the most common quest of the seeker. Especially in this culture, where the spectrum of spirituality spans from the devout to the atheist, from the pious to the aghoras – the gory and the unsightly – from the ascetic to the emperor, from the selfless, industrious karma yogis to the academic Vedantins; obviously, getting one's prescription right is of paramount importance.

Sadhguru's response to the predicament has been, "You cannot choose a Guru. Deepen your longing and the Guru will choose you," – a reality from his own life.

Sadhguru's ways are very unorthodox, if not wild, totally

devoid of conformity and other tell-tale marks of one who has been through the garadi[1] of a Guru. So it was only natural to assume that Sadhguru evolved by himself, an example that one wished to emulate. Sadhguru takes utmost care as to how he deals with each person he encounters. Somewhat like the famous saint who threw a volley of stones at the visitors to his ashram taking care that not one stone ever hit anybody, Sadhguru's abrasive ways have always fostered growth. Yet being with such a person meant there was no knowing what could happen next. This always kept us on tenterhooks.

So one morning, at a sathsang in the ashram when Sadhguru spoke for the first time about his Guru who graced him three lifetimes ago and the Dhyanalinga, the reactions were mixed. For many, it was reaffirmation of their secret belief and wish of Sadhguru being connected to a sacred and ancient lineage of Masters, but for clumsy novices like myself who were bumped and bounced often on this roller coaster ride with him, it was like an insurance policy. "Despite his wild ways," I distinctly remember thinking, "this man is actually accountable..."

Of all the wonderful traits of Sadhguru, the one that endears him to one and all is that of being a friend. As one who abhors the seriousness that people on the spiritual path often get into, Sadhguru often imparts the most profound teaching with utmost nonchalance. His uncanny sense of humor not only delivers the message, but also gives the seeker the much-needed break from the monotony that often sets in.

To a disciple who lamented in a poem that he sought to become an eagle in the sky, but only managed to become a hen looking up to the eagle, pat came the reply:

The hen that you are, how will you know what deceptive ways Grace will descend. It is Grace that brought you here and it is Grace that will deliver.

Introduction

I prefer the hen that looks up to the sky than an eagle that flies but always looking down.

How high is not the question, but how intense is your longing for the sky.

May you always be in Grace.

— Sadhguru

To print in the form of a book the Master's words about the sacred, spoken to carefully prepared disciples and to make it available to the uninitiated and the indifferent alike, is definitely a sacrilege at Isha, where 'live transmission of the experience' is the mantra.

However, this book is not to create another mirage in the harsh deserts of life, but to spread the sacred fragrance of bounty and abundance of an Oasis of a Living Master and an invitation for one and all to come, drink, dive and dissolve into it. Those of us who have been blessed by being involved in making this book happen, bow down in gratitude to Sadhguru for enabling us to make this priceless offering to the world.

In history and lore we have heard of many Blessed beings who strive to enlighten the world in their own ways. Some from the solitude of the mountains, some from their palaces, some from their hermitages, some in the battlefields and some in the marketplace. Sadhguru, whose abode once was the peaks of the Velliangiri Mountains, in symbolism that is true of His own life and work, now has descended to the foothills to inspire and infuse the seeking into the beings of the plains.

At a time when we are overwhelmed by the innumerable calls all around by leaders of sorts exhorting the masses to follow them, these verses from a poem by Sadhguru summarize what is typical of him:

…I was born like you, I eat like you,
sleep like you and I will die like you

but the limited has not limited me
life's bondages have not bound me
as the dance of life progresses
this space, this unboundedness has become
unbearably sweet
become love and reach out
become me!

— Swami Nisarga

Seeker's Predicament

From muses and mystics you did hear
Seeming to be the sounds of phantom lands
In ignorance's bind, lifelike phantom seems
Oh, creatures of surface, the depths of life will you ever seek.
— Sadhguru

Knowing not where he comes from, knowing not where he is bound, the seeker's predicament is indeed pathetic. Trapped in layers of ignorance that bind more tightly than any cement or concrete, the seeker's pain is known only to those who have lived it.

Starting his journey from an obscure point in evolution, where life chooses to bestow awareness and conscious seeking in him, the seeker is confronted with a plethora of choices and uncertainties on the path. Without proper guidance and the necessary Grace, like a rudderless boat, the seeker goes in endless circles in a boundless ocean, alternately chasing some glimmer of light on the horizon and plugging those self-destructive leaks his ignorance keeps punching into himself.

Like a solitary shepherd in the mountains, lovingly resting his flock under the moonlit skies between two hard days of a long journey, whose course and outcome are known only to him, these interactions with the Master reflect a rare kind of intimacy, understanding and compassion that spring from the Master's deep urge to share and deliver.

He knows that the kindness, the insights and the wisdom, which he so generously shares, soothe the bruises and the wounds of the day and firm up the resolve of the flock to walk with him one more day. Thus, day after day, the Master charms his flock, infusing an ethereal lightness into those he can, while numbing the pain and biding his time with those he cannot.

SEEKER: *Sadhguru, as I walk this path, I am becoming aware of the many fears and insecurities I have within me. How do I leave these behind and move ahead?*

SADHGURU: You don't have to leave your fears and insecurities because they don't really exist. You keep creating them unconsciously. If you don't create them, they don't really exist. Why you create them and how to stop creating them, that's your question. The fundamental reason why fear has arisen in you is – one way of looking at it is – in this vast existence of which you don't know the beginning or the end, you're just a little human being. Being the small entity that you are right now, naturally fear is there. It's overwhelming; there is fear and insecurity about what will happen to you.

As long as you're identified as a physical body, as long as your experience of life is limited to your physical and mental faculties, fear and insecurity are inevitable. It's just that different people may be at different levels of fear and insecurity. Today, if your life is happening well, you might have forgotten your insecurity. Tomorrow, if your life is turned upside down, you will be reminded because it's always within you. Only when a person begins to experience himself beyond the limitations of his physical body and mind, then this person can become free from insecurity and fear.

Experiencing yourself beyond the physical is what we're referring to as spiritual. When I say spiritual, don't think it is about going to a temple. Don't think it is about praying for this or that. If you look at your prayers, ninety-five percent of the prayers in the world are all about either asking for something, fundamentally asking for protection, or for being taken care of. There's nothing spiritual about it; it is plain basic survival. In most people, the very basis of prayer is fear and insecurity. If prayer exists in your life as an act only, it is obscene, being reverential towards one aspect and not being so to everything else. If you become prayerful, that's wonderful, and if you're using an act of prayer towards becoming that quality, that's fine. Now if you're routing your survival through the heavens, that's very stupid; even worms and insects take care of their own survival. So when I say spiritual, I am talking about you beginning to experience that which is not physical. Once this spiritual dimension is alive, once you start experiencing yourself beyond the limitations of the physical and the mental, only then there's no such thing as fear. Fear is just the creation of an overactive and out-of-control mind.

SEEKER: *But Sadhguru, isn't it very natural and human to become anxious when things don't go the way we expect them to?*

SADHGURU: Why are you making all your incapabilities natural and human? Now if a few things aren't going smoothly in my life and if I don't become anxious about them, if I retain my sense of balance and continue to do what I have to do, would you call me inhuman? Is that what you're saying? When things aren't going the way you want them to go, that's when your capability is most needed. When you become anxious, do you become more capable or less capable? Less capable, isn't it? When you most need your capability, you're forsaking it; would you call that an intelligent way to act? So what you're saying is to live unintelligently is human; that's a very wrong idea. To live intelligently is what being human is all about.

SEEKER: *Much of the anxiety I experience comes through my relationships. Isn't it reasonable to expect some understanding from other people?*

SADHGURU: When you live in this world, there are various types of complex interactions happening. As your field of play increases, the complexity of interaction also goes on increasing. If you're just sitting in a cubicle, working on your computer with only one other person, you need only a little understanding; but if you're managing a thousand people, you need a vast understanding of everybody. Now suppose you're managing a thousand people and you want all these people to understand you, then you're not going to manage anything. You need to understand the limitations and the capabilities of these thousand people and do what you can; only then will you have the power to move the situation the way you want it to go. If you're waiting for these thousand people to understand you and act, it is only a pipe dream; it's never going to happen.

SEEKER: *Suppose somebody is in a close relationship with me and is very important to me. Shouldn't I expect better understanding from them?*

SADHGURU: That's the point; the closer the relationship is, the more effort you should make to understand them, but that's not what's happening in your case, Ram. It so happened, once there was a man who had been slipping in and out of a coma for several months, with his wife staying at his bedside night and day. When he came to, in those few moments of consciousness, he motioned for her to come closer. As she sat beside him, he said, "I've been thinking… you have been with me through all the bad times in my life.

When I got fired, you were there to support me. When my business went down the tubes, you were there working overtime and doing night shifts. When I got shot you were by my side. When we lost the house in that legal clash, you were right there beside me. Now my health is failing, and you're still by my side. Now when I consider all this, I think you only bring me bad luck!" This is exactly what you're doing to yourself and to your relationships. Somebody becomes closer and dearer to you only as you understand them better. If they understand you, they enjoy the closeness of the relationship. If you understand them better, then you enjoy the closeness.

SEEKER: *This is easier said than done. It is difficult to always be there...*

SADHGURU: See, it's not that the other person is totally bereft of understanding. With your understanding you can create situations where the other person would be able to understand you better. If you're expecting the other to understand and comply with you all the time while you don't understand the limitations, the possibilities, the needs and the capabilities of that person, then conflict is all that will happen; it is bound to happen. Unfortunately, the closest relationships in the world have more conflict going on than there is between India and Pakistan. India and Pakistan have fought only three battles.

In your relationships, you have fought many more battles than this and are still fighting; isn't it so? This is because your line of understanding and theirs is different. If you cross this L.O.C., this Line of Control, they will get mad. If they cross it, you will get mad. If you move your understanding beyond theirs, their understanding also becomes a part of your understanding. You will be able to embrace their limitations and capabilities. In everyone, there are some positive things and some negative things. If you embrace all this in your understanding, you can make the relationship the way you want it. If you leave it to their understanding, it will become accidental. If they are very magnanimous, things will happen well for you; if not, the relationship will break up.

All I am asking is: do you want to be the one who decides what happens to your life? Whether they are close relationships, professional, political, global or whatever, don't you want to be the person who decides what happens in your life? If you do, you better include everything and everybody into your understanding. You should enhance your understanding to such a point that you can look beyond people's madness also. There are very wonderful people around you, but once in a while they like to go crazy for a few minutes. If you don't understand that, you will lose them. If you don't understand their madness, you will definitely lose them. If you do, then you know how to handle them. Life is not always a straight line; you have to do many things to keep it going. If you forsake your understanding, your capability will be lost. Whether it's a question of personal relationships or professional management, in both places you need understanding; otherwise, you won't have fruitful relationships.

SEEKER: *Talking specifically about the work situation, there's a company we have been approaching for business and they're taking their own sweet time in letting us know if we've got the deal. It's extremely frustrating and de-motivating. I'm tempted to just curse the client and move on. Now if our understanding encompasses the client's difficulties, we may be more at peace, but wouldn't that dull the edge we need to pursue and close the deal?*

SADHGURU: If you really want the best deals in life, don't try to make deals. You must be in such a way that your client should fall in love with you in every way. This is not a trick. The deal will happen if it's necessary; it won't happen if it's not. The deal is for both people's well-being, so it must be needed by both of you. Once we live in the world, there are transactions. Some are of a personal nature, others are different. All of them affect your life. Whether you talk to a taxi driver for a minute, or you talk to your boss, or speak to your client, husband, wife or child; every transaction is affecting your life. Now the problem with you is that you hold one transaction above the other. You involve yourself more with one and less with the other. It won't work like that. All these things are needed for you to have a fruitful life. Why don't you just fall in love with the whole situation? As long as you wish to be in that situation, make it happen like a huge love affair. Why not? That's how it should be. Only then work becomes effortless. What is it you're calling a love affair? It's unconditional involvement and doing whatever is needed. If you don't have that sense of involvement, you will always try to get the best deal out of somebody. That means you must meet the dumbest people in the world. Intelligent people will never bite your dumb deals. There once was this almost confirmed bachelor who for months had been pursuing an attractive lady and became her most devoted admirer. At long last he collected sufficient courage to ask her the most momentous of all questions. "There are quite a lot of advantages to being a bachelor," he began, "but there comes a time when one longs for the companionship of another being. A being who will regard one as perfect, as an idol to be worshiped and treated as one's absolute own, who will be kind and faithful when times are tough and hard, who will share one's joys and sorrows." To his delight he saw a sympathetic gleam in her eyes. She nodded in agreement and then said, "I think it's a great idea! Can I help you choose which puppy to buy?"

So do you see that for you to make a deal, you should only meet people who are more stupid than you? If you meet people who are more intelligent than you, there's no way to get the deal to your advantage. If you just give yourself and see how both of you can be benefited from the deal, then whenever it is possible, it will happen. Of course, deals are subject to many other conditions such as market situations, economic conditions or the world situation, but if you establish your inner way of being and are doing the best you can do, then what has to happen, according to your capability, will happen. What you can't do won't happen anyway. Even if you break your head it won't happen, but that's okay. You need not be a super human being capable of doing everything. If you don't do what you're capable of doing, that's when it's not okay, that's when you have failed. So don't worry about always pulling off deals, deals and more deals. Just learn to offer yourself, which is the best possible thing that you can offer to the whole situation. Then naturally people will take it if it's what they need.

God didn't intend this. You have become a disciple of the devil if your whole life is about making deals. The devil is always making a deal with somebody. God never made a deal with anybody. Once it so happened that a priest was walking on the street and he saw a man who had just been stabbed. The man was lying face down on the street, struggling for breath and writhing in pain. The priest had always been taught that compassion was the highest thing, love is the way, and all that stuff. Naturally, he ran to the man. He turned him over and saw that it was the devil himself. He was shocked and horrified and quickly backed away. The devil begged him, "Please take me to the hospital! Do something!" The priest hesitated and thought, "Why should I save you, the devil? You're against God. Why should I save you? You should die. The whole priesthood is about somehow banishing the devil, and it looks like somebody has almost done a good job of it. I'll just let you die." The devil said, "Don't do this. Jesus told you to love thine enemy, and you know I am your enemy. You must love me." Then the priest said, "I know the devil always quotes the scriptures. I'm not going to fall for that." So the devil said, "Don't be a fool. If I die, who will come to

Seeker's Predicament

church? Who will seek God? Then what will happen to you? Okay, you won't listen to the scriptures, but now I am talking business; you better listen." The priest understood that this was true. With no devil, who would come to church? This made business sense. He immediately put the devil on his shoulders and took him to the hospital.

So don't go about making deals for selfish reasons. Maybe you haven't attained to your full Divine nature, but at least in this case let us imitate God for a while. God doesn't make deals. Deals will be offered to you in so many ways. In a way, everybody is just a businessman. Everybody is trying to pull off some deal: some in the market place, another maybe at home, another maybe in the temple, and a few maybe even with their spiritual process, but everybody is trying to pull off some kind of a deal. When you get a good deal, you are all very civilized and nice but if a deal goes bad, you will yell and scream. All priorities in life will change. Deals may sometimes boomerang in your face. One day Shankaran Pillai's barn burned down. Shankaran Pillai, feeling dejected and deflated, refused his lunch and set off for the bar to drown his misery. His wife, taking things into her own hands, called the insurance company and boomed into the phone, "We had that barn insured for five lakh rupees and I want my money NOW! My husband is so upset he's missed his meals!" The agent replied, "Hey, Mrs. Pillai, hold on a minute. Insurance doesn't work quite like that. We will need to ascertain the value of what was in the barn and provide you with objects of comparable worth." There was a long pause before Mrs. Pillai very gravely replied, "Then I'd like to cancel my husband's life insurance."

SEEKER: *Oh my God...*

SADHGURU: Who wants something of comparable worth, especially a husband of all things! (Laughs). Wouldn't you agree Joyce? There's something called vasanas. Do you know what vasana means? They are certain old qualities and flavors within you. However much you may try to pretend that you're a very nice and loving person, when deals are offered, suddenly old vasanas will take control of you. There's an urge to bite the deal. That's why on the spiritual path we talk about setting a goal. If you set a goal for yourself, you don't bite any deals on the side and you don't go off the path. The goal itself doesn't take you anywhere. In fact, it's a barrier. It has to be dropped somewhere in the process of growth. The goal is only there to ensure that you don't make any more deals. It's not there to get you bound. It's there to release you from the temptation of deals.

SEEKER: *Sadhguru, how does yoga help me perform better in this environment?*

SADHGURU: When we say 'yoga', probably for many of you it means some physical postures, twisting yourself into some impossible postures. That's not what we're referring to as yoga. Yoga means to be in perfect tune. Your body, mind and spirit and the existence are in absolute harmony. When you fine-tune yourself to such a point where everything functions so beautifully within you, naturally the best of your abilities will just flow out of you. When you're happy, your energies always function better. Do you see that when you're happy you have endless energy? Even if you don't eat, if you don't sleep, it doesn't matter; you can go on and on. Have you noticed this? So just knowing a little happiness is liberating you from your normal limitations of energy and capability.

Now yoga is the science of activating your inner energies in such a way that your body, mind and emotions function at their highest peak. If I don't sleep for two days, you won't notice any difference in me. I can still have a full day of activity. When your body and mind function in a completely different state of relaxation and a certain level of blissfulness, you can be released from so many things that most people are suffering from. Right now, you come and sit in your office, and you have a nagging headache. Your headache isn't a major disease, but it takes away your whole capability for that day. Just that throbbing takes away everything. With the practice of yoga, your body and mind will be kept at their highest possible peak.

There are also other dimensions to it. When you activate your energies, you can function in a different way. As you're sitting here right now, you consider yourself to be a person. You're identified with many things, but what you call as 'myself' is just a certain amount of energy. Do you know, modern science is telling you that the whole existence is just energy manifesting itself in different ways? If this is so, then you're also just a little bit of energy functioning in a particular way. As far as science is concerned, this same energy which you call as 'myself' can be here as a rock, lie there as mud, stand up as a tree, bark as a dog, or sit here as you. Everything is the same energy, but functioning at different levels of capability.

Similarly among human beings, though we're all made of the same energy, we still don't function at the same level of capability. What you call capability or talent, what you call your ability to do things in the world, your creativity, is just a certain way your energy functions. This energy, in one plant it functions to create rose flowers, in another plant it functions to create jasmine; but it's all the same energy manifesting itself. If you gain a little bit of mastery over your own energies, you will see, things that you never imagined possible, you will do simply and naturally. This is the experience of any number of people who have started doing these practices. It's the inner technology of creating situations the way you want them. With the same mud that we build such huge buildings, initially people were building little huts. They thought that's all they could do with it. With the same earth, haven't we built computers? What you call a computer is dug out of the earth.

Do you understand what I am saying? We thought we could only dig mud and make pots or bricks out of it. Now we dig the earth and make computers, cars, and even spacecrafts out of it. It's the same energy; we have just started using it for higher and higher possibilities. Similarly, our inner energies are like that. There is a whole technology as to how to use this energy for higher possibilities. Every human being must explore and know this. Otherwise, life becomes very limited and accidental; you get to do only what you're exposed to. Once you start activating your inner energies, your capabilities happen in a different sphere altogether.

SEEKER: Master, there are so many different kinds of yoga. How do I know which type of yoga is best for me?

SADHGURU: Right now, the only things which are in your experience are your body, your mind, and your emotions. You know them to some extent, and you can infer that if these three things have to happen the way they are happening, there must be an energy that makes them happen. Isn't it? Without energy all this can't be happening. Some of you might have experienced it; others can easily infer that for these three things to function, there must be an energy behind them. For example, this microphone is amplifying the sound of my voice. Even if you don't know anything about the microphone, you can infer that there's a source that powers it. So these are the only four realities in your life: body, mind, emotion, and energy. These are the only four realities. So whatever you wish to do with yourself, it must be on these four levels. Whatever you wish to do you can only do it with your body, your mind, your emotions or your energy. If you use your emotions and try to reach the ultimate, we call this bhakthi yoga; that means the path of devotion. If you use your intelligence and try to reach the ultimate, we call this gnana yoga; that means the path of intelligence. If you use your body, or physical action to reach the ultimate, we call this karma yoga; that means the path of action. Now if you transform your energies and try to reach the ultimate, we call this kriya yoga; that means internal action.

These are the only four ways you can get somewhere: either through karma, gnana, bhakthi or kriya – body, mind, emotion, or energy. These are the only four ways you can work with yourself. "No, no, no, I am on the path of faith. I don't need to do anything else." Is there anybody here who is only head – no heart, hands and energy? Is there anybody here who is only heart – not the other things? You're a combination of these four things, isn't it? It's just that in one person the heart may be dominant, in another person the head may be dominant, in yet another person the hands may be dominant; but everybody is a combination of these four. So you need a combination of these four. It's just that, only if it's mixed in the right way for you, it works best for you. What we give for one person, if it's given to you, may not work well for you because that person is so much heart and this much head. Only when it's mixed in the right proportion it works for you. That's why on the spiritual path there's so much stress on a live Guru; he mixes the cocktail right for you, otherwise there's no punch.

There is a wonderful story in the yogic lore. One day, one gnana yogi, one bhakthi yogi, one karma yogi, and one kriya yogi were walking together. Usually these four people can never be together, because gnana yogi has total disdain for every other yoga; it is the yoga of intelligence. Normally, an intellectual person, a thinking person has complete disdain for everybody else. A bhakthi yogi, full of emotion and love, thinks all this gnana, karma and kriya yoga is just a waste of time. Just love God and it will happen. The karma yogi thinks that everybody is lazy and that they have all kinds of fancy philosophies; what needs to be done is work. One must work and work and work. The kriya yogi just laughs at everything. The whole existence is energy. If you don't transform your energy, whether you long for God or you long for anything, nothing is going to happen. So they can't be together, but today they were walking together. Then it started to rain. They were in the forest and it started raining. They started running, looking for shelter, and there they found an ancient temple which just had a roof, no walls on the sides. In the center, there was a Linga. So these people went inside the temple for shelter. The storm became more and more furious and it started blowing in torrents. The fury of the storm was getting into the temple so they went closer and closer to the Linga. There was no other way to be because it was just blasting them from all sides. Then it became very furious. There was no other place; the only way they could get some protection was for all four to hug the Linga. Suddenly they felt something enormous happening. A huge presence, a fifth presence was there. Then all of them said, "Why now? For so many years we have pursued You and nothing happened; why now?" Then Shiva said, "At last the four of you got together. I have been waiting for this to happen for a long time."

SEEKER: How does one always remain young in spirit, Master? Life somehow seems to be catching up with me.

SADHGURU: A seeker is always young. Whatever the physical age of the body, it doesn't matter. You have to be eternally young. The day you become old, it's over. Anyway, how can you become old in spirit? Only by carrying the past, isn't it? If you carry sixty years of burden with you, you're sixty years old. If you don't carry anything, you're like a newborn. The physical body may develop limitations, but the way you are has no limitations. It simply has no limitations. You are this many years old or that many years old simply because you carry that many years of garbage with you; and this whole thing about celebrating birthdays and remembering that you're that old is making sure that you fix milestones. I used to have a farmhand working for me, a very simple chap. His innocence was most touching. He was nearly fifty years old. If you would ask him his age, he would say, "Maybe I am twenty – twenty five." He had no sense of years. He didn't know. When the rain came, he would plough, then he would throw the seeds. When food came, he would eat. Life went on like this for him and he didn't know his age. Maybe he was unintelligent, but when an intelligent person lives like this, he becomes a sage. He was a saint, not knowing, not carrying the burden of the past. Moment to moment, just see the weight of the load you're carrying. Your face has become squeezed up. The burden is evident. It's there and it shows.

SEEKER: *Sadhguru, all of human life on this planet is always revolving around good and bad. The very basis of right and wrong is good and bad, but I have heard you say many times that there's no such thing as 'good' and 'bad'. Can you speak more about this, Sadhguru?*

SADHGURU: People always believe that they are good and somebody else is bad, isn't it? That's the only way they can carry on their missions in the world. Right now, we're on this part of the Himalayan road, from Pipal Koti – actually, from Rudraprayag to Badrinath – they are making it into a two-lane highway. Every year, so many people die here because of landslides and vehicles going off the road. Driving here on these curves, one mistake and you've had it. When you travel here, you give an enormous responsibility to the driver. Just one mistake of his and you're finished. Every year, so many people make those mistakes. If you don't know this, when you see a small heap of scrap metal on the side of the road, it's usually a salvaged vehicle. I can tell you this now since we are at the end of the trip (laughs).

So they are laying a two-lane highway. Is it good or bad? It's good, because people like you can travel in more comfort, with less risk; so that's good. Today, a lot of people may tell you to stop building roads, disfiguring the mountain, and disturbing the creatures on this planet. So for them, this is bad. Just because those in power, or the majority, think something is good, it won't become good. Maybe it would be better to take a person as an example. Now whatever a terrorist is doing, is it good or bad? You tell me.

SEEKER: *It's bad.*

SADHGURU: Why? What is he doing?

SEEKER: *He's the source of suffering for many people.*

SADHGURU: You can look at it that way. In the same situation, who is good and who is bad all depends on which side of the border you're on. Is India good or is Pakistan good? You're on this side of the border, so obviously Indians are good; Pakistanis are evil. If you were on the other side of the border, you would be arguing for the other side. It all depends on what you're identified with. Accordingly, you have your 'goods' and 'bads'. You can't think beyond that. Your thinking itself is limited to your identifications. Your identifications are always limited, so your thinking is also limited. With this limitedness, why do you get into this nonsense about deciding what's good or bad? The moment you say something is bad, you can't stop disliking it, can you? Can you say, "This is a bad person, but that's okay with me"? On the surface you may say it, but if he gets closer to you, though initially it is just dislike, later it will turn to hate. The moment you identify something as good or bad, you're just dividing the world.

Now somebody comes and says they want to walk the spiritual path. So I tell them, "Okay, stay here for a week. Let us see what we can do." Then he says, "No, no, Saturday is my cousin's birthday; I have to go. I can be here only for three days." So I ask, "All right, but how far would you like to go with this?" He says, "All the way." Then I say, "So in three days, all the way? Anyway, you do these few things when you're here, then let's see what to do next." He will say, "No, I don't like this." Then I tell him, "Okay you give me a list of things that you like. We will do only that." He sits there, thinks seriously for a while and writes down half a dozen things. So I ask, "What? In this vast existence, you like just about half a dozen things, and with that, you want to be spiritual?" Where is the possibility?

The moment you create good and bad, you're dividing the world. Once you divide it, where is the question of inclusion? Where is the question of yoga? Where is the question of becoming one with everything? Where is the question of knowing truth? Your division is because of your stupidity; it has got nothing to do with reality. Good and bad are always according to your ego requirements. If you go by this, you enslave yourself to the dualities of life; you divide the existence. So the question of turning spiritual never arises.

SEEKER: *Sadhguru, most of the time, in any given moment, I don't seem to know what's required of me. I am clueless in thought, emotion and action. How does someone truly know what's needed in any given moment?*

SADHGURU: If you are sitting here as a bundle of thoughts, opinions, and emotions, you will never know what's needed. Most people are like this. What you call a human being is not really a being; it is just a bundle of thoughts, emotions, and opinions that were gathered from elsewhere. If you're in this condition, you will never know. If you simply sit here as life, you always know. You will always know what's needed. You don't need to think about it. You don't have to educate yourself to know. Any human being who is able to sit here as life will simply know what the other beings around him need; but if he's sitting here as a bundle of thoughts, emotions, and opinions, his whole perception will be distorted and he will never know. He will always come to the wrong conclusions about life. When you don't know what's happening with life, you will only drive your life with your thoughts, opinions and emotions. This can lead to a whole calamity within yourself and, if you're a powerful person, to the whole world. This is happening right now. People are highly opinionated, isn't it?

SEEKER: *Master, there seems to be a correlation between being open to possibilities and being educated. Being educated seems to impose a kind of logic which prevents openness. There also seems to be an inverse correlation between economic prosperity and being open to spiritual possibilities. Is this so?*

SADHGURU: Let me put this question the other way around. The question that's being asked is: "Do uneducated people have better possibilities of spiritual Realization, or do poor people have more possibilities of being spiritually Realized?" Am I right? Fundamentally, the word 'education' means to cultivate your mind, to constantly imbibe new possibilities; that's what education means. Now can education become a barrier for these new possibilities? Yes, it can. Anything can become a barrier, for that matter. You already mentioned yours, education and wealth. Not just education and wealth – power, fame, position – anything can become a barrier, but anything can also become an access. It's not education or wealth which can open or close you; it's just how you relate to them. If you have seen education itself as a possibility, which it is - in certain dimensions of life education is a possibility which opens up many vistas – it's the same for wealth. If you have money or wealth it can open up many possibilities in the world around you and also within you. Let's say one day you want to stay at home to meditate, so you don't go to work. You can do that. If your condition is such that you have to work for every meal, then that possibility is closed. Even if you wish to meditate, your hunger will take you to work. Now you have money, so if you wish, you can sit; that possibility is open.

So are education and wealth, in some way, working as a barrier for spiritual growth? It could be, and it is so for a lot of people, unfortunately. This is not because there's something wrong with money or with education; it's just the way you relate to them. If you have seen them as a means, then there's no problem; but if your whole sense of who you are has come to you only from your qualifications, or from your bank balance, then yes, education and money are barriers, not only for your spiritual growth, but also for your physical and mental well-being. If you're seeing them only as a means, only as tools for access, then they are in no way barriers. In fact, they can be very useful because they bring you so much understanding and so many possibilities and in many ways your life is more free. So by themselves they aren't barriers, but you can make them into barriers if you wish.

SEEKER: *It has happened that they have become barriers, if you look around the world. Why have they become barriers? That seems to be a statistical observation today.*

SADHGURU: If you go by statistical comparison between cultures, between the East and the West, the distinction isn't just in terms of education and wealth. There are a whole lot of cultural differences. For example, if you take India and the United States, India is considered to have a strong spiritual tradition and the U.S. is seen as an economic culture. Everything is fundamentally economics in that culture.

So the difference is cultural. Individually, if you look at them, there isn't much difference. Here, there's a whole spiritual tradition, so people have taken to that possibility because it has always been available. There, when a young person grows up – let's say when he's twelve or thirteen years old – all that he knows is what's available to him in that culture. So that's how he goes. It takes a little extra intelligence for a person to look beyond what's available in his culture.

In India, whether you like it or not – even if you have an allergy for it – spirituality gets lobbed into you one way or the other. In your families, in the society, wherever you go, some of it will touch you. It didn't happen because you were longing for it. Naturally, it touches you because it was everywhere. So if you look at the statistics, it's not fair to just take economic well-being and educational background as the basis; there's a whole cultural equation. The reason why there's so much spirituality in this land and has always been is because it has always been a very stable culture. It has remained steadily in one place for thousands of years. If any culture remains steadily in one place for many years, then definitely spirituality will become a huge force in that land; but when the cultures are new, naturally economics will be the most important aspect of that culture.

Wherever the culture is very old, the mystical will be very active. Wherever the culture is new, economics and social well-being will be most active because those are the first things that you will attend to in your life. Only when your economic and social needs are well taken care of, then – as an individual or as a culture – you start looking beyond for other dimensions. Until this is taken care of, you will only be thinking of settling these things. You can't talk spirituality to a man who is hungry on the street; it won't mean anything to him. There are many spiritual aspirants, sadhus and sanyasis who have chosen to be hungry, they're different. But you can't talk mysticism to somebody who is hungry due to life situations. In many ways, a culture which is new is hungry, hungry for life and well-being, because the people still remember the difficulties that their forefathers had gone through to build it.

A culture that has matured for thousands of years has developed an understanding of renunciation, giving up well-being and taken up walking on the street in pursuit of Realization. Nowhere else in the world will you see this, but in India we know it. So many kings and emperors have dropped their kingdoms – their wealth, their comforts, their pleasures – and walked the streets as beggars. Nowhere else in the world has such a thing happened. It can only happen in a culture that has been steady for a long period of time, where slowly other dimensions of life have become more important than physical survival. So your psyche is going beyond survival instincts. When survival is still important, all you seek is well-being.

Just now, Doug was mentioning this: it seems that in India people aren't bothered by danger. It's not that they aren't bothered about danger. It's definitely true that the longing to survive, the need to survive and the conscious urge to survive are stronger in the West than here. Here, if death comes, people take it so much more easily than people there do. Since Western cultures are young, the survival instinct there is strong. After ten thousand years, they will also be this way, because by then physical well-being and social well-being won't mean as much to them; they will be looking for other dimensions. It's unfortunate that cultures have to take so long to realize this. Generally cultures may take a long time, but individuals need not take that long. Out of your intelligence you can see it right now, and the spiritual process is always individual.

SEEKER: *Master, will the teachings and practices you've given to me help me break my rigidity and flower?*

SADHGURU: I am glad you understand that it is your rigidity which has prevented your flowering. You can become rigid in many dimensions. During the practice of yoga asanas you realize how rigid you are physically. It takes a little more awareness for you to know the rigidity in your mind and emotions. Somebody who's very rigid in his thoughts and emotions believes that he's perfect because he doesn't allow room for any other way of looking, thinking, or feeling. When you meet this man, you think he's pig-headed, but he thinks he's perfect. Similarly, there can be rigidity in your energy. For someone whose energy is very fluid, the very first day of the simplest yoga kriya, and the energy will start moving and transforming, whereas for another person, even after practicing it for a long time, nothing seems to happen. This simply depends on how malleable the energies are. The rigidity in all these dimensions isn't really separate, they're all interconnected. The rigidity in one dimension manifests itself into the others.

On Patanjali's path, yoga is a system where it doesn't matter what kind of a fool you are, what level of unawareness you're in, what kind of karmic bondages you have; there's still a way for you. If you're willing to at least bend your body, you have already broken one karma. If your forehead touches your knee, then you have broken a physical karma. This is not a joke; it's quite an achievement for a person who has never done it before. This simple limitation would have increased with the passage of time. Even the little flexibility that's there in you today will become less as time goes by. A day will come when you're totally rigid, both physically and mentally. This is happening to everybody. Look at your own life; see how flexible you were at the age of ten or twelve, both physically and mentally. At the age of twenty, the flexibility is considerably less and at the age of thirty, most of it has gone. Not only physically; mental rigidity has also set in very severely as you progress on this path; it's not progression, rather it is regression. Life is just a regression for most people. They are not growing; they are going backwards. Even what little assets they have come with, they don't grow; they just go backwards, unfortunately. Whatever advantage you were born with, you haven't enhanced it; you have only taken it backwards.

Every advantage that comes to most people only ends up as a curse. Money, influence, comfort, intelligence become only curses to most people. They actually come as blessings but you turn them into curses. You're not using your intelligence to reach the peak of your consciousness, to become peaceful and loving. You're using your intelligence to drive yourself crazy. For example, you think it would be very nice to be a peasant. They seem to be very simple. It looks romantic to you, but if suddenly you become a peasant, you would curse the whole world. If you were sent to earn your living for three days, everyday you would curse the whole world. When you have that, you dream of this and when you have this, you dream of that. Maybe you call it romantic, but it's just plain stupidity. It destroys life.

Anybody who goes against life, anybody who goes against that which is the source of life is plain stupid. He's an utter fool, and all I am asking of you is to watch, just watch whether you are for the Creator or against the Creator, every moment in your life. If you see this, everything will be settled. If you can't think of your Creator, just think of me. Every action that you do, just see whether you're for me or against me. If you do this, things will be settled. Your mind will be settled if you just do this sadhana. It needs diligence. Otherwise, it's not going to happen. With every moment and with every breath, just see. If you have the diligence to see, this sadhana is enough for you. It will clear up your mind totally. Tomorrow you will be ready for samadhi.

SEEKER: *It sounds so easy, so close, but is it really that simple, Sadhguru?*

SADHGURU: It is actually very simple, but because of you it has become extremely complicated, because of your personality. The path by itself is not complicated. The complexities that one encounters on the spiritual path aren't because of the path. The complexities are only there because of the mess that is your mind. The path is very simple, but because you're there, it becomes extremely complicated. Nothing moves within you. You become rigid, as if rigor mortis has set in. You need the Master's Grace to quell the madness of your mind. If you allow this, then the path is too simple, as the path is the destination. If you simply sit here now, everything will pulsate with the existence. If you just sit here, your whole being will pulsate with the existence. There's no other way to be, unless you make an effort to be some other way. How can you be away from the existence in which you live? How is it possible? It envelops you in every way, inside and out. Nobody can ever be away from it. It's just that you're doing everything to stay away, maybe unconsciously. Just stop doing that and everything will be okay. Now just to get you to stop doing all that nonsense, we have started you on these kriyas.

In one way if you look at it, all of this isn't necessary. If you ask J.K. how long to hold kumbhaka to get Enlightened, he will just throw you out of the place, because it is not so. It is true that this is not so, but unfortunately it's needed right now. You have kept your energies suppressed to such an extent, the mind has become so oppressive that it suppresses life to the point where nothing moves except what's needed to support the ego. Your energies are moving only to the extent that is convenient for your ego; a little more energy and the ego will burst. The moment energy rises within you, everything is dissolved. The ego knows it very well. That's why it has kept it suppressed. If you don't have any energy, then again the ego will become very weak. When all energy is cut off, the ego will feel very weak and it doesn't like that. So it just allows the amount of energy which supports and feeds it well. If the energy becomes too much, the ego will be shattered. If Kundalini begins to rise, everything will be shattered and nothing will be left. You will be just a force merging with everything around you. You won't have a will of your own anymore. Since you're not willing to surrender your will, we're prodding you through this sadhana to provoke your energies.

That's why the path of asana and kriya. Since you're not able to do it by yourself, just activate creation itself in a certain way. If it begins to move, it settles everything. It's like a flood. Have you ever visited a place just after a flood? If you have seen the place before and after, the change is incredible. People think it is sad; people generally think it is a tragedy. Yes, naturally it is a tragedy if you see what it leaves behind or what it takes away – your homes, your crops or your centuries-old world are wiped away in only a few hours of fury. So your sadhana isn't about getting somewhere. It's just a way, a method to unleash a flood so enormous that it wipes away your petty creations and leaves you as the Creator intended you to be.

SEEKER: *Master, can anybody get Enlightened by practicing simple yogic practices? Are there other means towards Enlightenment? How will I know if I become Enlightened? How does one identify an Enlightened being?*

SADHGURU: Senthil, what do you mean, can anybody get Enlightened? The question is whether every human being is capable of Enlightenment. If you're capable of ignorance, you're also capable of Enlightenment, isn't it? An animal isn't capable of ignorance, please see that. An animal is never ignorant, nor is it Enlightened, but a human being is capable of being ignorant. You are, aren't you? If you're capable of ignorance, you're also capable of Enlightenment. The question is, when will it happen to you?

Now you ask me, "How will I recognize it? If I get Enlightened, how will I recognize it?" When it happens, there will be no question about it, because it will pervade every dimension of who you are in such a glorious way that there will be no question about it. There will never be the question, "Am I really Enlightened or not?" There will be no such thing; it won't give room for any such doubt. It depends on what your idea of Enlightenment is. There are many Enlightened beings, but you will never know who they are or where they are, because they never declare it. They have no need to do that. Only when a person has to do a certain type of work, he goes through the shameful process of declaring his Enlightenment, because people can't see it. He has to declare it and by doing so, many people will question and probe it. Many people will say it is false. It's quite a shameful thing to declare I am Enlightened.

Most Enlightened beings will never declare it, and you will never know. You need not know whether somebody is Enlightened or not. What's your problem? If it happens to you, it's wonderful. Whether somebody is Enlightened or not, what difference does it make to you? So, "If it happens to me, how will I know?" You don't worry about that. If you're capable of missing such an event, Senthil, don't worry, I will tell you.

SEEKER: *Sadhguru, I can accept you as my Guru, but to become one with all the participants here…*

SADHGURU: The ego is always like this; it is not seeing how to be in tune with what's surrounding it. It's always trying to stick out. Among people, you want to stick out like a sore thumb, and a sore thumb always hurts. Maybe it sticks out, but it hurts. Sticking out always hurts. Once, after returning from London, Shankaran Pillai – who was decked out in new tight denim pants, body-hugging satin shirt and was sporting a new hairdo – went to the nearest park to show off his new look. He approached an old man who was sitting on a bench and sat down next to him. The old man stared at Shankaran Pillai, looking him up and down. His stare finally focused in on the six inch multicolored spikes coming out of his head.

The spikes were all flashy colors – orange, purple, green, yellow, blue and pink. Shankaran Pillai looked over at the old man and said sarcastically, "What's the matter, old timer? Never done anything wild in your life?" Without batting an eye the old man replied, "Well, I got drunk once and had a date with a parrot and I was just wondering if you were my son." These days, you're making a whole culture of trying to stick out. The more exclusive you try to be, the more excluded you're getting from life and existence, hence the hurt.

The more you try to be special, the more you get hurt. Just be, just melt and become part of the wind around you, the earth around you, become a part of everything. You're here only for a while. At least when you're in a place like this, where nobody is going to trample on you, let your defenses down. Let it be. Forget your comforts, your sensibilities, your likes and dislikes. Leave all that nonsense and be with me. Live like the snakes. Just crawl around, eat and if you feel like curling up under a tree, do it; at least for a few days, it's worthwhile. I am telling you, a lot of barriers can be removed by going out and living in nature. That's the reason why, when one begins a spiritual journey, they go to the Himalayas or to some other mountain. By merging with nature and living there, the ego will be destroyed, just by doing that. That itself is half the sadhana.

I met some Naga Babas in a place just above Kedar, in the Himalayas, and stayed with them for two days. They had run out of money; they were hungry and cold. For two days I took care of their food and spent time with them. I only had on a little woolen in-shirt and a T-shirt. Fortunately, somebody had given me a shawl which was a big blessing. If the shawl hadn't been there, I would have frozen. It was so cold that even my insides were shivering. I could literally feel the stomach bag shiver. These Babas are naked sadhus who aren't supposed to wear anything that is stitched. They wrapped something like a shawl over themselves, because it was too cold. They weren't even wearing footwear and they didn't even have money for tea. They were saving the little they had to go to the Kumbha Mela.

That was more important for them than having something to eat. When I asked them what their sadhana was, they said they were doing nothing. They just roam about like the nagas, the snakes. Their Guru had told them to spend twelve years in the Himalayas and then he would initiate them. When one is so uni-directional that he can wait twelve years, being oblivious to harsh weather and difficult living conditions and just wait for his initiation, reaching the highest can't be denied to him.

There's not much for the Guru to do; whether he has something to give or not, these guys will get it anyway because of the very way they have made themselves. They don't need a Guru. If a man has that much patience and stamina that he can stay twelve years, not knowing when or if the next meal is going to come, just waiting in that terrifying cold in a queue to be initiated, he will get it anyway. That itself is a sadhana. The Guru knows that if he initiates someone the same day the person comes to him, it will be wasted on the man. He will waste the whole opportunity. So he sends hundreds of people to the mountains like this every year. Maybe only some of them make it – many run away because it's a very difficult path. It's very tough to stay in such conditions. When a person is willing to do this, whether he does it or not, that's not the point. If he's willing to go to any length, that man gets it. It is that simple.

When people are calculating how much to give, and how much to hold back – like Jesus said, "You can't serve me and Mammon at the same time." When Jesus used the word 'Mammon', he used it to be almost synonymous with pleasure. So Jesus said, "You can't serve me and Mammon at the same time. If you want to be my disciple, you have to leave Mammon." If you're seeking comfort – it's not that you shouldn't be comfortable; it's not about having comfort or not, but if you're seeking comfort, forget it. This path is definitely not yours. What he said is very true.

The very purpose of putting a group of people together like this is to help you understand your likes and dislikes, which are the basis of all the limitations you have set for yourself as a person. Take a careful look at your personality; you will see it is just a bundle of likes and dislikes. These likes and dislikes have risen from your enslavement to the duality of life, which is the bedrock of ignorance. The very word 'yoga' means to transcend this duality and know the oneness of existence. Various devices have been used to help people go beyond this enslaving duality. You like or dislike something simply because somewhere deep down you have identified it as either good or bad. Whatever you identify as good you can't help liking and whatever you identify as bad you can't help disliking.

This is why the Hindus created the personality of Shiva as a complex amalgamation of all that's beautiful, ugly, terrible, pleasant, good and bad. They made him the highest so that in accepting him, you accept everything. You transcend the limitations of your likes and dislikes and in turn, your dualities. Here you see all the varieties of human beings. If you can accept the likes of a few of those who are here, who are going about like self-appointed messengers of the Divine, you have transcended. Do you see the weirdest of the weird? (Laughs, pointing toward a few participants).

SEEKER: *If I am on the spiritual path, how do I deal with family members or friends who are making it very difficult? There seems to be a fine line between comforting them and telling them to grow up, or just to open their eyes, or even to just bang them on the head. How can I deal with a situation like this? They're not in total acceptance even though they say they are, and they continue to demand too much out of me.*

SADHGURU: Everyone has to handle the reality according to their choices. For whatever you may choose, there is a consequence. Don't be in a fool's paradise and believe that you can get away without paying a price. For everything there's a price. The spiritual path is never in anybody's way. It's just your choices about where you go, what you do, how much time you spend here or there that cause the conflict or the disturbance. This is not new; it has always been so, whether you're going to a party or the cinema. Someone in your family wants to go to the mountain; you want to go to the beach. The same problem will be there. Isn't it? So it's not about your spiritual path, it's just incompatibility with where you want to go, and where you don't want to go. Your spiritual path isn't in conflict with anybody. The conflict is in your choice about doing things in your life. These need to be handled as usual; you see how much of what is most important to you and act accordingly so that life goes on.

If your spiritual longings are taking you completely away from the situations in which you live, then there will be a certain amount of disturbance and conflict. Not really conflict, because conflict happens between two people; there will be some disturbance. It is always bound to be there, unless people around us are so mature that they're willing to accept things they can't understand, which is rare. Now, the question comes from a certain sense of guilt and discomfort. "What am I doing to the other members of the family?" These kinds of thoughts may come, but enshrining one's limitations isn't a great thing to do, either for you or for the other person. It may be painful to break your limitations. However painful it is, it's worth breaking them. How do you do it? If you can administer it gently, it's wonderful. Sometimes it can't be done so. It's not that it can't be done gently, but the other people refuse to make it gentle. They feel that if it happens gently you will escape the guilt of doing it. Somewhere there is an intention that, if you get to do what you want to do in your life, you must suffer. So they will do everything to see that you feel guilty about it. On the day Gautama, the Buddha, who was just seeking — not even knowing what, but just seeking — left his kingdom, his wife and an infant child, and like a thief, walked away in the night, probably his family saw him as the most terrible man, but how glad we are that he did those terrible things, aren't we? If he hadn't done those terrible things, the world would have been poorer, and those people who lived with him wouldn't have been any better. Anyway, maybe they would have found some other misery after some time.

SEEKER: *So when you're in a relationship, that's a commitment too. The family and children come first. You have spoken about commitment, and how people should be committed. So why doesn't this hold true on the path of spirituality? When it comes to spirituality, doesn't it seem like you're abandoning your family and walking away from social structures just to pursue your spiritual interest?*

SADHGURU: For your spiritual path, there is no need to walk out of anything. It's just that, when the family structure is made in such a way that it doesn't allow for any other possibility except for breeding and brooding, then it becomes a breaking point; not otherwise. In what way is spirituality breaking up any family? The family breaks up because of its own intolerance, because of its own immaturity, because of its own limitations that people are trying to set upon each other; not for any other reason, not because of spirituality.

SEEKER: *Sadhguru, how do I deal with being so obsessed with the spiritual path?*

SADHGURU: Once you are on a spiritual path, if you're genuinely on the path, you're not just obsessed; you are possessed. If you want to hit the peak of your consciousness, all the energy that you have has to be focused in one direction. If you're throwing it in ten different directions, it's obvious you're not going to get anywhere, isn't it? Even if you throw all the energy that you have in one direction, still it may not be sufficient. That's why the Master fills in that space of lifting you up when it's needed; but if you want to distribute your energy in ten different directions, then definitely it will be futile. So don't be obsessed; be possessed by the path. There's nothing else for you; everything else is just to get you there. Only when it becomes like this, your spiritual path means something.

If it's not so, if it's a side interest in your life, that you like spiritual entertainment – different people seek different types of entertainment and some people dabble with spirituality – that's up to you. I have nothing to say for such people, but if you're really seeking to know, then your whole being should be focused in one direction. You're completely possessed by it. This doesn't mean you will become unreasonable. This doesn't mean you can't run a family. This doesn't mean you can't fulfill your social responsibilities. Just use them as a spiritual process for yourself. Every breath, every step, every act that you perform in your life becomes a spiritual process. Only then there's no conflict. When you say, "This is my spiritual path, this is my family, this is my profession, this is my club, these are my drinking friends," then you have a conflict. If you eat, you eat only because you want to know. If you drink, you drink only because you want to know. If you work, you work only because you want to know. Then there is no conflict.

SEEKER: *Sadhguru, sometimes I feel dull and sluggish. Can you tell me how to become more energetic and more alive?*

SADHGURU: There are many ways to look at this and understand it. One level of energy that you know is the food that you eat, the water that you drink, the air that you breathe, the sunlight that you receive. These things are becoming energy in your system, the day-to-day energy that you experience, to some extent – in different people to different extents. Another way of looking at it is that what you call 'life' or what you call 'yourself' is energy. How alive you are, how wakeful you are, is how energetic you are. So your ability to convert the food that you eat, the water that you drink, the air that you breathe, whatever else you consume, whatever inputs go into the system; to convert them into active, productive energy in you – is different in different people.

It's not just about digestion and assimilation. The conversion of energy happens in different states, depending on how alive or how awake your own energies are. You might have seen, once you start certain spiritual practices, your level of energy is totally different. Your ability to stay awake, your ability not to be tired, your ability to just go on with life, is so much better once you start these practices. If you practice these kriyas daily, you can see that if you don't do them for one day, there's a distinct difference. In a way, all spiritual practices – when I say 'spiritual', I am talking about the kriyas or even dhyana – are fundamentally to make your energies more awake than what they are now.

Whether we're talking about Kundalini or simple plain energy as in the English language, it's basically about raising ourselves to a higher level of energy. What you call 'life' itself is energy. So if you want to function on a higher plane of life, you need a higher level, a higher quality of energy. There are many methods to do it, and most of you have already started with some simple methods. There are other ways to energize a person which can be more dramatic; but dramatic methods of energizing need proper preparation, balance and control over life. That requires much more awareness from a person, to know what he's doing and not doing with himself. Most people, even the so-called spiritual people, ninety-eight percent of the time don't know what's happening within themselves. When it comes to their body or their energy, they don't know at all. Even when it comes to their mind and emotions, most of the time they don't know until it becomes acute.

Right now you're sitting here and a certain emotion may be building up within you in a very small way and you're not aware of it. If somebody comes and calls you an idiot, you explode. Now you think you're angry. This has been building up, probably for days, weeks, or months, but it's not in your consciousness or awareness because of your state of energy or the way you are. Many factors are involved. So what's happening within you isn't in your awareness. When what's happening within you isn't in your awareness, the whole process of life is accidental, your energy is accidental. When it is accidental, you see one day you're energetic, the next day you're not. It's like this.

You definitely would have noticed, on a certain day you're very happy; you seem to be very energetic on that day. Another day you're not so happy; you have no energy. So one reason we're always talking about being peaceful and happy is not for the sake of being peaceful and happy, but because only if a person is peaceful and happy, his energies begin to become alive in a certain way. Otherwise the system is simply blocked up. Only if these energies are alive, you can activate them towards a higher possibility. So when you talk about being energetic – for different people being energetic means different things. In a sense, for a school kid, being energetic means being able to go to school, play games, come back home and fall asleep. For a laborer on the street, it means to be able to perform his activity all day. Maybe for an executive it means to sleep less, to travel more, to be more productive. For a yogi, he doesn't want to sleep or eat. He wants to be that way for many days – just being alive by his own contact with existence, not by putting something into him.

Being energetic means different things to different people in different areas and different perspectives of life. Right now, when you say 'energetic', if it's just about being a little more energetic in performing your day-to-day activities in the world, the practices that you're doing will definitely take care of it. If that's not enough, there are ways to upgrade that a little bit so that it can be taken care of. For me, being truly energetic means that when you sit here, the physical body is no more a limitation for you. If your energies are really active, the physical body is no more a limitation. Energy becomes the main contact. Right now, your body, mind and emotions are the main contact that you have with the rest of the world.

That's how you communicate, that's how you reach out. You can touch somebody either physically or mentally. With your thoughts, you can communicate or emotionally you can convey something. This is how you are.

Once you're truly energetic, you can communicate with everything in the existence energy-wise. When you start communicating energy-wise, there's no distinction between this and that. Once the barrier is broken, that's ultimate nature. When you start a spiritual process, being energetic means going beyond all limitations, because in energy there is oneness. In the physical body there can never be oneness. In mental thought there can never be oneness. We may talk about oneness, but it's never going to happen. With our emotions we may think we're one, but we're still separate. No two people can feel exactly the same way. You may believe so, but if you have any sense, within a short time you will realize that it's not so. Some people may take years to realize; a few people will realize quickly, but everybody will realize. No two people are exactly alike physically, mentally, emotionally; it's not possible. When you become truly energetic, oneness is just natural. That's the way it is.

SEEKER: *Sadhguru, at your gatherings or sathsangs people are transported to states of extreme ecstasy. Are these people specially blessed? Am I condemned to a state of rock-like yoga?*

SADHGURU: You first decide what's important to you. Now that you refer to me as 'Sadhguru', is being with your Guru more important, or having what somebody else has in their pocket more important to you? "No, no, no, I don't want what they have in their pocket. I want what they are having in their heart, or their head, or wherever." It's not any different. You aspiring to be as rich, as beautiful or as ecstatic as somebody isn't any different. When you sit with your Guru, you just sit with him. Don't worry about what's happening to somebody or what's not happening to you. Your whole life will be wasted. First of all, why did you look at somebody else? You were supposed to be with me in the sathsang. Why are you even noticing somebody else? If you're totally with me, you shouldn't even notice what's happening to somebody.

There was a beautiful incident which occurred in Arjuna's life. It's of a totally different nature, but it is relevant. The royal tutor, Dhronacharya, was teaching all those brothers – one hundred and five of them – the artistry of archery, how to shoot an arrow. He himself was a great archer; there are many legends about him. One day, Dhronacharya set a little toy parrot upon the topmost branch of a tree. Then he told his whole class, one hundred and five princes, "Now we will go out. There's a parrot on top of the tree and you're required to shoot this parrot. Let's go." He took them outside, pointed out where the parrot was and, one by one, asked them to set their arrow to the bow and aim. When they aimed he said, "Wait." He kept them in the position of aiming for a few minutes, and then asked them, "What do you see?" They said, "Oh, we see the leaves, the branches, the parrot," this and that, everything, including the whole sky. When it came to Arjuna, he aimed and Dhronacharya asked, "What do you see? What all do you see?" Arjuna said, "Just one point on the neck of the parrot. That's all I see." And that was all he saw. That's why Lord Krishna chose Arjuna to give the teaching to and nobody else, because the man was set. He sees only what he has to see and nothing else. This man will make it.

Now when you sit there, I ask you to close your eyes. If somebody makes a little noise, you want to open your eyes and see what's happening behind you, what's happening around you, what's happening everywhere. Sathsang is about you simply being with me. Don't worry about what's happening with somebody. It's not even your business to notice what's happening to somebody. You just be with me. Then there will be no problem.

Seeker's Predicament

SEEKER: *Sometimes I get the feeling that people create so much trouble in their lives, so much suffering, simply because they're not sensitive enough to see that what they sow is what they reap. For example, when they get angry, jealous or hateful… In such situations, what's possible for people to do? I wish people were more sensitive. I feel that if I somehow try to interfere, I will just create more trouble.*

SADHGURU: You're asking about your ability to make somebody's life – it's actually about this that you're asking – to make his future and his liberation. If you have to make it, first of all you have to earn his trust, which doesn't come easy. It takes an enormous amount of work, responsibility, energy, wisdom and simple sense to earn that trust from people. Even if you can earn this trust, it's different for different people. There are a dozen people sitting here. I can't interfere with their life to the same extent. Isn't it? There are some people, if they are going the wrong way, I can just hold them by their hair and turn them around and say, "This is the way." No problem, they will go that way. With somebody else I have to say, "Please, go this way," but they're not going to go this way, they're going to go that way, an in-between way. I have to just allow that to happen, even though I know it's not the best for them. So with each individual your ability to interfere with their life and do what's needed is different, depending upon how much trust you have earned from that person. To earn this trust you need time, you need energy, you need effort; so many things are involved. Otherwise, trust doesn't come. On the surface, everybody will bow down to you. Everybody will say this and that; that's not the point. When it really comes to the crunch, how far you can interfere is a wisdom and a simple sense that you need to have. You can't interfere to the same extent with everybody. Certainly that man who's going on the street, even if he's walking to his death, I can't stop him and say, "Don't go there. Go here." I can't say that. I will allow him to walk to his death because there's nothing else to do. Most of the time there's nothing else to do, because he wouldn't be available.

How much you can do and what you can do with a certain individual is always limited, depending on how open and how willing he has become. For ages, spiritual masters have always been talking about willingness, trust, surrender, these kinds of things, not because they want somebody to surrender to them, but because that's the only way they can truly interfere with somebody's life and set his life on a different track altogether. Otherwise, you have to always work within the limitations of the other person's understanding. If I do something which isn't within the realm of your understanding, immediately you will leave. So I am constantly working only within the limitations of your understanding, not in totality. If I interfere in totality, you will leave. That's why I said being a yogi is wonderful, fantastic, but being a Guru is frustrating.

SEEKER: *Master, the more I seek the spiritual path, the more confused I become. Yet at the same time there seems to be a kind of clarity – a confused clarity. Will a time come when there will be clarity without confusion, and if so, how do I create that?*

SADHGURU: The more you seek the spiritual path, the more confused you're becoming. That's a good sign, because confusion is always a better state to be in than living in stupid conclusions. With the stupid conclusions that you had made in your life, there was comfort, there was solace, and there was convenience. There was a false sense of security in these.

Now you step onto a spiritual path and everything becomes turmoil. All the things that you were comfortable with look stupid now. Things that you valued and cherished suddenly look so insignificant and not worthwhile. Everything has turned upside down. There's a very beautiful Zen saying: "When you are ignorant, mountains are mountains, rivers are rivers, clouds are clouds, trees are trees. Once you enter the spiritual path, mountains are no more just mountains, rivers are no more just rivers, clouds aren't just clouds, trees aren't just trees. But once you arrive, once you are Enlightened, once again mountains are mountains, rivers are rivers, clouds are clouds, trees are trees." From ignorance to Enlightenment, it is a full circle back to the same place, but a huge difference, a world of difference, a difference which is indescribable.

Once you enter the spiritual path, everything is in turmoil, everything is in question. You don't know where you stand. You don't know anything. Before knowing anything about spirituality, you were at least comfortable, self-satisfied. You ate pongal in the morning, drank coffee, and you thought that was the ultimate. Whatever your breakfast was, you thought that was the ultimate pleasure. Now, nothing matters. You don't feel like eating, don't feel like sleeping, don't feel like doing anything, because nothing is really worthwhile anymore. It never was worthwhile. You just deceived yourself into believing that it was. If it was truly worthwhile, how could it go away? If you truly knew what's what, how could you get confused? The very fact that you're confused means you didn't know, isn't it? You had made wrong conclusions, just for the sake of comfort and security.

If comfort is all you're seeking, you must psych yourself up to believe you're perfect, that everything is okay with your life. "My house is good, my husband is wonderful, my life is great, my children are fantastic, even my dog is fabulous. This is it; this is life." You must tell yourself this every day, and go on with it. It will be quite good, nothing wrong with it. It's just that it is limited, and this being will never settle for anything limited. It doesn't matter in how many ways you try to fool yourself; somewhere there's a longing. Carefully look at all the happiness that you have known in your life. On the surface there's happiness, but somewhere deep inside, there's a certain suffering in everything. The suffering is just because the suppressed being is always longing. To even become conscious of this suffering, people take lifetimes.

Entering the spiritual path means you have become conscious of your suffering. You were suffering unconsciously; now you have become conscious of it. Conscious suffering is always deeper than unconscious suffering, but it is good, at least you're conscious about it. As long as you haven't become conscious, the suffering will always remain. Once you have become conscious, it need not remain forever. There's a possibility, isn't it? Entering the spiritual path is a possibility, being with a Guru is a possibility, that's all it is. If the possibility has to become a reality, the first thing is that you're willing to see everything the way it is. You're at least willing to recognize your limitations. If you want to hide your limitations, where's the question of liberation? Where is the possibility? You have destroyed it completely, isn't it?

If you're chained right now and if freedom has to come some day, the first and foremost thing to see is that you're chained. If you're refusing to see that you're chained, the question of liberating yourself never arises. So when you realize that you're chained, there will be pain, there will be suffering, there will be struggle, there will be confusion. Now old memories will say, "I was better off before." This is the way of your mind. When you were in high school, your mind told you, "Oh, kindergarten was so fantastic." You know how you went to kindergarten. When you went to college you said, "Oh, my high school days were so wonderful," but we know how you went through high school also. When you were done with your education, you said, "My university days were the most blissful days!" We know how you struggled to write your assessments, to find the book that you wanted in the library. We know how you suffered all those classes and those professors; but now that it's over, you claim it was fantastic.

So as a part of your survival technique, memory has a way of erasing certain unpleasant things and making the past always more pleasant than what's there right now. This is a trick of survival. Otherwise, psychologically, you will crack up. You always have something to fall back on and say, "Oh, it was wonderful." Now there's a confused clarity. Isn't that good? You're confused and still clear. On a certain day, a farmer with a truck full of animals is on his way to the market for auctioning. He comes upon a hitchhiker, and gives the man a lift. On the way to town, the farmer starts sipping on some home brew, swerves off the road and crashes in a big ditch. The hitchhiker is thrown out of the truck and into the ditch, with shattered ribs, a busted leg and a smashed arm – he's totally in pieces. The farm animals are also seriously messed up. The farmer is the only one with only a few cuts and bruises. He gets out of the truck and inspects his animals. The chickens have broken legs and wings, and can barely move. "These chickens are useless now," the farmer explodes. "Nobody will buy them!" He grabs his shotgun from the truck and shoots the chickens. Next, he sees that the pigs are all busted and bleeding. "These pigs are worthless too!" So he reloads the gun and shoots them, too. The farmer then looks at the sheep that are in the same state as the chickens and the pigs, and screams, "Worthless sheep!" He reloads his shotgun and blows away the sheep. The injured hitchhiker witnesses all this carnage in great horror. The farmer then moves over to the ditch, peers inside, and shouts, "Are you okay, down there?" Instantly the hitchhiker, crawling up really fast, says, "Sure, I've never felt better in my whole life!"

That means even if we throw you into hell, it doesn't matter; you will be clear. Now I am not interested in sending people to heaven. I am interested in making people in such a way that, even if they go to hell, nobody can make them suffer. That's freedom, isn't it? "I want to go to heaven, I want to go to heaven," is a huge bondage. Suppose you land in the wrong place. Suppose someone hijacked your airplane on the way to heaven. He didn't crash it; he just landed it in the wrong place. You're finished, aren't you? You're always living with something that can be taken away from you by somebody or something. True liberation is when nobody can take away anything from you; and that which can't be taken away from you is your blissfulness, your inability to suffer. "I want to go to heaven", means you're still capable of suffering. That's why you want to go to a good place, isn't it? Gautama repeatedly said, "I don't want to go to heaven. I want to go to hell." People thought he was crazy, but that's how a liberated man will be. "What's my problem with hell? Anyway they can't make me suffer, so I will go to hell." This man is free, isn't he? So if you're confused and clear, that's good. "When will all my confusions go away? When will absolute clarity come?" I don't want to fix a date, but I bless you, let it be today. Why tomorrow? It's twenty past ten; there is one hour and forty minutes left of today. That's a lot of time, you know? An hour and forty minutes is not little; it's an enormous amount of time. Let it be today.

SEEKER: *After a long time I have just learned to let go and let things happen. Then yesterday you told me that I had to work towards it. I am very confused, Sadhguru!*

SADHGURU: Now Marie-Christine, now that you're confused, that's good. That's the intention, to keep you always confused. Confused means you're still looking. Confused means you still don't know. Please understand: there are only two ways for your mind to be right now. There's no such thing as 'let go' in your mind. Either it's confused or it has made some conclusion. I always prefer to have you confused rather than being in some stupid conclusion about what it is. So now talking about letting go – I know this 'let go, let go' thing has been talked about too much, written about everywhere – "You must let go." What is it that you want to let go of? You don't even know what you should let go of. So right now 'let go' is also another idea, another opinion of yours about life. As long as you are alive, you're not really able to let go. At the most, if you're fortunate, you may place your life in somebody else's hands with trust. That's the biggest thing you can do. Letting go is just a phrase that never happens. It's just that your mind has acquired a new formula: 'Let go, let go'.

I have never really asked anybody to let go, if you haven't noticed this. Though I know thousands of people misinterpret me as, "You asked us to let go," I never asked you to let go. I just asked you to look at life simply the way it is, not because it is my teaching, or my idea, or my opinion as to how to live well; it is simply because that's the way it is. All I am asking you is to get involved. This 'let go' has become a mantra for all kinds of people, for drug addicts, for sex maniacs, for fatalists, and for people who are afraid of taking their life into their hands and creating what they should. For all these people, 'let go' has become a good formula. "Oh, we have let go." You have left your lives in the hands of the planets and stars. That's the 'let go' for you. This kind of 'let go' will let you down. Once a hypnotist bombastically said he would take everybody in the hall together into a 'let go' state of hypnosis all at once. "I want you each to keep your eye on this antique watch. It's a very special watch. It has been in my family for six generations," he said. He slowly began to swing the watch gently back and forth, while quietly chanting, "Watch the watch, watch the watch, watch the watch…" The crowd became mesmerized as the watch swayed back and forth, back and forth, light gleaming off its polished surface. Hundreds of pairs of eyes followed the swaying watch. Suddenly, it slipped from the hypnotist's fingers and fell to the floor, breaking into a hundred pieces. "Shit," said the hypnotist. It took three weeks to clean up the theatre!

This is what will happen with your 'let go' philosophy. It's not a 'let go'; it is just a convenience that you have chosen. So don't bother about this 'let go' business. Not once did I ever tell you to let go. I noticed that you were getting into this frame of mind, into this frame of deception within yourself of letting go and believing that you had let go, but you still haven't gotten into that state. I know many people around me who are in 'let go' philosophy and doing irresponsible things. If somebody asks them, "Why are you doing this?" They will say, "It's all Sadhguru's will. Only Sadhguru makes me do everything," for all the idiotic things they do. See, the line between devotion and deception is very thin. Why I am constantly attacking devotion is not because I am against it. It is the most wonderful thing that can happen to you, to become devoted, but I am always attacking it because the line between devotion and deception is so thin that most people will remain in deception for a lifetime, believing they are in devotion. If you really let go, if there's such a thing, devotion is a real 'let go'. If you're truly devoted, you are an absolute 'let go,' but you can't do it. You can't try to become devoted; it won't help. You can't practice devotion. When your experience of something becomes so overwhelming, helplessly you become devoted.

I have many devotees around me. When I say I have devotees around me, don't think that all the people you see bowing down, clutching at my feet, are my devotees. No, they are different (laughs). Devotees are people – in many ways, they don't know why they are here, but they are helplessly with me; they are the true devotees. Devotion has entered them. Their mind rebels against it, their mind tells them, "This is stupid. Why are you doing everything that this man says? Leave him and go," but helplessly they are here. They can't go anywhere, not because they are held by somebody or hypnotized, but simply because they have been so overwhelmed by the experience of someone that they are in devotion. The mind doesn't agree with devotion, but they have become devoted. People bow down because they believe that if they bow down they will get something. That's not devotion. You have asked this question as if there was a contradiction between letting go or being devoted and

Seeker's Predicament

working towards something. A devotee is somebody who can work twenty-four hours of the day without feeling that he has done anything. If you give him twenty-four hours of activity, still he doesn't feel that he has done anything. He's a devotee; that's a true 'let go'. If you think letting go means that you don't have to do anything, that somebody is going to take care of you all the time; that's not 'let go'.

That amounts to deception, because now you haven't completely given up your likes and dislikes, your personality, what you consider as 'myself'. It's not totally gone. Yes, there have been moments of experience, but it's not totally gone. At the same time, talking about letting go won't work. Right now, you're sort of preparing yourself with a 'let go' philosophy. You have been strengthening this philosophy for some time now, especially in the last six weeks, because the time to go home has come. New situations and old situations will confront you. You already know what those situations are. You already know how you will react to them, but you need an excuse as to how you will react to them. So 'let go' is a good excuse. That's why I told you, you must work towards it. If you don't work towards it, it won't happen.

SEEKER: *Master, is it true that on the path of liberation much effort has to be put in by the sadhaka, but finally it is Grace that takes you there?*

SADHGURU: Your effort is to defeat all your efforts.

SEEKER: *After that, one becomes effortless and finally it is the Grace?*

SADHGURU: The Grace is also you.

SEEKER: *How?*

SADHGURU: All the effort is to demolish the structures that you have built. What's true can't happen with effort. The ultimate reality can never happen with effort because it is beyond all that. The effort is always to demolish what you have already built with effort. With your own effort you have built so many structures; so with your own effort you clean up your mess. Truth is not something that you do. It's in the lap of truth that you exist. There is no question of you doing it, and if you do it, it must be a lie. Isn't it? So the moment you use the word 'Grace', you will always start looking up, wanting to receive. Don't worry about that. Your business is to demolish the structures which you have built. Grace is not something that you ask for, that you crave. If you demolish the blocks that you have built up, Grace will happen.

SEEKER: *Are you talking about conditioning?*

SADHGURU: Conditioning is only one part of the structure. You have built so many other structures. Okay, you can call it conditioning; we call it karma though. Karma is a more complete word. Conditioning tends to describe only certain aspects of life. Karma includes all of it.

SEEKER: *We're so helpless because we try and the trying is of no use. Things happen, but on the spiritual path there comes a point when you just have to let go, to stop trying.*

SADHGURU: That's what most people have done in the world. See, most people have even stopped aspiring for anything. You can't let go. How can you let go? If you let go, it is still an effort, isn't it? Like yesterday somebody was trying to say, "You know we can't do anything. We just have to go with the flow of things; that's surrender." The moment I said it is succumbing, he got mad. Somebody who's talking about surrender, if you as much as say anything, he will flare up. If people have surrendered where's the question of anger? One who has surrendered has nothing of his own. That's what it means. So where can he have likes, dislikes, or anger? It is simply impossible.

SEEKER: *After coming to this yoga, my self-image has taken a beating. It is totally shattered.*

SADHGURU: Every human being, either consciously or unconsciously, through the process of what we call life, creates a certain image of himself, a certain personality. This image that you have created within yourselves has nothing to do with reality. It has nothing to do with the Self, with your inner nature. It's a certain image that you have built, most of the time unconsciously. Very few human beings have built a conscious image for themselves. All others have built images according to whatever kind of patterns or external situations they fell into. The external influences – maybe your mother, father, teacher or some great man was looked up to, or with a mixture of all these influences you formed an image of yourself. Everybody has some image of what they are, isn't it? Okay, since you came to this yoga, this image has been taking some beating, but it's not totally broken. It doesn't break so easily. If it's broken completely, if you shatter it totally, you are a Realized being, but it doesn't break because the mind is still active. It just tries to modify the image a little bit, adjust the image to the new situation. You know, if the color doesn't go with the external situation, you repaint yourself a little bit. All kinds of adjustments are made, but there's no fundamental change in the image itself.

'Shattering' means living without the image. 'Shattering' means dropping the image altogether. Changing the image is different. See, when you were in school, you had a certain image of yourself, but when you moved into college your image went through a revolutionary change. Again, maybe from being unmarried to married, the image goes through a big change. Still, the underlying factor, the main aspect of your image, hasn't changed. Even in those cases something of the old has been retained. Maybe a lot of things changed, but still the fundamentals have been retained. The skeleton is still the same. Maybe you even changed the flesh, but the skeleton has remained the same. Wouldn't it be nice if you could change the skeleton and see? Wouldn't it be wonderful?

SEEKER: *How is this skeletal change possible, Sadhguru?*

SADHGURU: When you take this – what you know as yourself – into a different dimension. See, what you know as yourself, you didn't choose consciously; it happened. You picked it up here and there, in bits. It's a rag doll. Now, if you are intelligent enough, if you are aware enough, you can recast your image to a totally new image, whichever way you want it, consciously. It is possible, but you should be willing to leave the rag doll. Can you? Are you willing?

SEEKER: *It sounds too daunting.*

SADHGURU: If you have sufficient intelligence and awareness, it can be done. When you drop it totally, another image won't be needed. You can just pick up things and drop things as needed; they won't stick to you. Now with you, I am not talking about dropping your image. I am just talking about transforming your image. Transformation is always fundamental. I won't tell you how you should be. You decide how you want to be. If you want help, we will help you out, in between. For the skeleton, you decide. Flesh and blood we will fill up slowly.

SEEKER: *Sadhguru, after the Samyama program, I started to feel that I have become more involved in life in a way and it is making me grow at a very fast pace. But at the same time, I feel that before, I had a certain innocence that was allowing me to at least see myself as walking a spiritual path. Now, I feel I am becoming a little more materialistic, selfish, and egoistic. Also, I'm not too sure, but I think I have become too confident and my ego has grown a little bigger and all I wanted to do earlier on was to just disappear. So I ask you, what's happening to me?*

SADHGURU: Marwan, I think I told you that if you're seeking physical and mental well-being, the Isha Yoga program and Bhava Spandana are more than enough. Only if you really want to know – not out of curiosity – when your longing burns you enough that you begin to think, not just in terms of life, but you want to know what are the very fundamentals of your creation, you want to know what this is all about, only if such a longing has come, you must go to Samyama. You have been there; you know it's a different world in itself. It's another world. Someone who hasn't been there won't believe that people can be like that for seven to eight days.

Whatever you call it, hell or heaven, whichever way, it is not of this world. Samyama hasn't made you more egoistic and more of all this that you say. It's just that it has taken away some of your pretensions and you're more bare. A man had a habit of grumbling at the food his wife placed before him at family meals. Then he would say the blessing. One day, after his usual combination complaint-prayer, his little girl asked, "Daddy, does God hear us when we pray?" "Why, of course," he said, "God hears us every time we pray." She thought for a moment and then asked, "Does he hear everything else we say the rest of the time?" "Yes dear, every word," he replied, encouraged that he had inspired his daughter to inquire about spiritual matters. Then she asked, "Then which does God believe, what we say during prayer or at other times?"

What you were hiding in many ways is now simply bare, both to you and the people around you. That's good, because if you deceive yourself about yourself, you're just wasting life, isn't it? If you deceive the world, there is a karma attached to it and it's up to you if you want to do that; but if you deceive yourself, you're lost forever, isn't it? These two things must be understood. This awareness and energy are very deeply connected. If one wants to move into higher states of awareness, the support of the energy is most essential. Without the necessary energy, nobody is going to be aware; awareness is going to be just a dream. People only talk about awareness. You being aware of who's walking next to you or what's happening around you is not it. That everyone has to have; even a dog has it better than you. Awareness means that you're becoming aware of dimensions which aren't in your normal experience of life. Initially, when this awareness comes, your system doesn't know how to handle it; your body doesn't know how to handle it. Your body will go crazy, your mind will go crazy. Your mind doesn't know how to handle it because awareness comes with furious energy, or because of furious energy, awareness comes. So these two things can't be separated. Higher dimensions of awareness mean higher dimensions of energy.

You trying to project yourself as a good man was very important to you at one point. Now suddenly, the deception has fallen off and who you are is simply there. It's good, even if it causes disturbances around you. Being straight with life is more important than being good. If you're not straight with life, then you will get entangled and entangled and more entangled. Those who aren't straight with life, as time passes, sadness overtakes them; they can't help it. Even if everything in their life is working out very well, you will see their faces hanging slowly. They don't even know why. Do you see many faces like this around the world, driving a Rolls-Royce but still their face is hanging, living in a palace but still their face is hanging? Don't you see this all around you? This is simply because of self-deception.

If you don't know how to be straight with life, over a period of time, it will take its toll. Slowly, once youth passes, you will see your face will hang. It's so much more important to be straight with life than to be polite, than to be good, than to be moralistic – to simply be straight with life, and especially with yourself. If you have intelligence, you will understand and come to terms with this. If you don't, you will get knocked around in your life; but that's an external situation. The world around you, you handle it to whatever extent you're capable of, but within yourself, if you don't know how to be straight and address all aspects of who you are properly, then slowly over a period of time, a cloud of unexplained misery will hang around you.

In a short-lived career as a policeman, Shankaran Pillai was assigned to traffic control. Towards the end of the month, in order to meet his quota of speeding vehicles, he stopped a farmer for speeding in his tractor, piled high with hay. Shankaran Pillai began to lecture the farmer about his excessive speed, and began to throw his weight around to make the farmer feel small and uncomfortable. Finally, Shankaran Pillai got around to writing the ticket. As he was doing that, he kept swatting at some flies that were buzzing around his head. "Having some problems with circle flies there, are you?" the farmer asked. Shankaran Pillai stopped writing and said, "Well, yeah, if that's what they are. I had never heard of circle flies." The farmer said, "Well, circle flies are common on farms. See, they are called circle flies because they are almost always found circling around the back end of a mule." Shankaran Pillai says, "Oh," and goes back to writing the ticket. After a minute, he suddenly stops and says, "Hey wait a minute; are you trying to call me a mule's arse?" The farmer fearfully says, "Oh no! Pillai saar (sir)! I have too much respect for law enforcement and police officers to even think about calling you a mule's arse." Shankaran Pillai replies, "Well, that's a good thing," and goes back to writing the ticket. After a long pause, the farmer says, "Hard to fool those flies though!" So instead of carrying a blissful ojas around you, you will carry a cloud of misery around you. Now we can call you evil. You may not have any evil intentions, but you're spreading misery in the world. It's not because you're a criminal that we call you evil, but because you're spreading misery. Every moment of your life you're sowing seeds of misery around you. This is evil, isn't it? Unintentional evil. Most of the evil people in the world are unintentionally evil. They don't really have evil intentions, but slowly their energy becomes that way.

So what's happening to you is fine, because you're becoming aware of things that you weren't aware of for all these days. Some moments, you're not able to handle it; it's okay. See, if you're driving at twenty kilometers an hour, you never go out of control, isn't it? If you go slowly, at ten or twenty kilometers an hour, you won't go out of control. It's only when you're driving at a hundred and fifty kilometers per hour that there's a chance of going out of control, but then you're also covering an enormous distance. In an hour that man makes twenty kilometers; you make a hundred and fifty kilometers. That's an enormous difference, but the possibility of going a little out of control is there. For that, safety measures have always been fixed. These safety measures are like dampers. There are so many people around me who are capable. There are so many around me that, if I didn't have to take care of their safety, we could have dozens of Enlightened beings around us right now. Only because I don't want any one of them to crash, I put dampers along the way. Because of these safety measures, they are a little slow. It doesn't matter. They are driving very fast, but because of the safety rules and the corners they have to slow down. They're not allowed to go at the same speed. This slows down the process, but it's safe.

When you're on the straights, you must go full speed, isn't it? If even on the straights, you're going at twenty kilometers per hour, then it's a waste of life, because you're not going to be here for a million years. There's a certain span of time that you call life, within which something meaningful should happen. Otherwise, one will definitely die in regret, and your life doesn't end with death. If you're hoping that everything will end with death, you're a fool. That's all I can say. Your life doesn't end with death. It takes on so many other forms. It can take on very unpleasant forms. It's these unpleasant forms which we refer to as naraka or hell. Hell is not a place somewhere where all of you will go and suffer, and heaven doesn't mean the other place. If you take on an unpleasant form beyond this body, we say you're in hell. If you take on a pleasant form, then we say you're in heaven. If you go beyond the bondage of all form, then we say it is mukthi or liberation.

A spiritual seeker is not interested in going to heaven or hell. He wants to go beyond this duality of hell and heaven also. So as your energies mature, you may see qualities you never thought were part of you, not because some new quality is coming, simply because something you never dared to face is coming up and you are facing it. It's fine, it's perfectly okay. The only thing is that you shouldn't throw it on all the people around you. You handle it. Okay? You throw your tantrums on people and say, "Now I did Samyama, my karmas are coming out. You have to bear with me." Don't give them your karma, don't throw your circle flies on people around you. You handle them yourself (laughs).

SEEKER: *Master, in my experience on this path, it's not always such a joyride. I feel intense pain too, pain that's around me.*

SADHGURU: Now, that which you call as 'me' or as 'you' are the same. Whatever you do, every action, every thought that you generate touches the world in some way. So whatever you do touches everything. As you become more and more sensitive, as you become more and more aware, as your consciousness expands, this becomes a life experience, not just somebody's teachings. If you're sensitive enough, if you're intense enough, if you're loving enough, whatever happens somewhere will happen to you also. You can actually feel it, maybe in a small way. Though it can happen only if you're open enough at that moment. Otherwise it won't; you will miss it. So your question will be, "Okay, if pain comes to you, why should it come to me?" I am telling you, that will be your growth.

Once, Shankaran Pillai happily agreed to take his wife to visit a holy place, hoping she would renounce some of her worldly desires. So he chose a monastery in Himachal Pradesh and they set off on their pilgrimage. This monastery is perched high on a cliff. The only way to reach it is to sit in a basket and be pulled to the top by the monks up there. Shankaran Pillai, his wife – a big woman – and a monk, huddled together in the basket. The monks at the top were pulling and tugging with all their might. Obviously, the ride up this steep cliff became terrifying. With each tug, Shankaran Pillai was getting exceedingly nervous. Once they reached about half way up, he noticed that the rope was old and frayed. He gave a quick glance towards his wife, then to the rope and again to his wife. Then in a trembling voice he anxiously asked the monk in the basket, "How often do you guys change the rope on this thing, anyway?" The monk thought for a moment and answered brusquely, "Whenever it breaks." So, not everything in life comes as a joyride, Raja. Don't think that you will grow only in pleasure. Most people will grow only with pain, not with pleasure. It's unfortunate, but that's the truth. Generally people only go down with pleasure. They don't go up with pleasure. Please see, the quality of a human being is like this, when life offers more and more pleasures to a man, he doesn't grow. He goes down. In terms of the real quality of a human being, only when suffering comes, when pain comes, does a man stand up as a human being. You can see great human beings surface only when the society is really suffering. When India was under the oppression of British rulers, how many wonderful people stood up? Where are they now? They have just fallen back into their comforts, that's all. All those Gandhis, Patels, Tilaks are still there, but they're dormant. When pain came, they all became alive. They left everything behind and stood up as giants. Where are they now? This is the human misfortune that still there's not enough intelligence in the world that human beings will rise to their peaks when everything is well. They wait for calamities.

SEEKER: *Sadhguru, if the spiritual and the mystical reality are beyond that which is physical, beyond the five senses, is there ever a point where we are cognizant of spiritual experience or growth? How do we know if we're progressing or regressing spiritually?*

SADHGURU: It is only the physical dimension which can grow and diminish. You're constantly going on trying to strengthen your limitations, and at the same time claiming that you want to become spiritual. Stop reinforcing your limitations. Limitations will wear out by themselves. If you just see them as limitations they will fall apart, but you're going on reinforcing your limitations. So don't try to progress or regress. You're talking about dimensions which aren't in your present level of experience. When you're approaching a dimension which isn't in your present level of experience, don't try to create a roadmap. Don't try to make a roadmap of unknown terrain; it will be a great mistake. Just see that you have no map. Right now, you don't have the necessary faculties to know anything which is beyond the physical. If you recognize this, if you understand this, if you accept this absolutely, only then the other dimension opens up.

In certain situations, with overwhelming energy and presence, we have broken the limitations of your five senses and made you experience dimensions beyond, but you're not able to sustain this. The idea of overwhelming you was that once you get a glimpse of something beyond, you will have the necessary intelligence not to attach too much importance to the limitations in which you exist. I want you to understand this clearly. Don't try to do anything about your sense organs. Going beyond your sense organs isn't in your hands. The only thing you can do is to stop attaching importance to your own ways of thinking and feeling, your thought patterns, your emotions, and your opinions. Don't attach any importance to them. Then your limitations will become weaker and weaker and one day collapse.

SEEKER: *I love God very much, but He doesn't seem to be responding.*

SADHGURU: Somu, if you really love God, seeing Him would be the ultimate. Yes? If you love Him, you hold Him as the highest, you hold Him above creation, isn't it? He's the Creator. Seeing Him, being with Him, would be the highest. If you have no trust in Him, then you talk in terms of existence, of no-mind, and all these things. The moment there's no trust, the whole issue becomes terribly complicated. Then you have to split hairs to do things, simply because love is missing. Trust means unconditional love. It's that kind of love where the other side need not respond. You simply love. You must have loved like this when you were in school and college. The other side wasn't responding, but you went on loving. Once it happened, a young boy in college went to his professor and said, "I need your help." The professor said, "Sure, I am here to help you." The boy said, "No, it is not academic, it is something else." So the professor said, "Tell me..." The boy named the college beauty and said, "I am in love with her and I am fifty percent successful. For the other fifty percent, you have to help." The professor asked, "What do you mean, fifty percent successful?" The boy replied, "Well, I am madly in love with her, but she hasn't responded!" In your college-day love, with every step you were expecting that she would at least turn around and look at you. This is not that kind of one-sided love. This has total trust.

When a person has that kind of love that he doesn't expect the other side to even respond, it's okay. If God doesn't respond, it's okay. You have firm faith that he's there. Now look at this and see, we always love those who are not here. With most people it is so; they always love the dead when they're not here any more. When they were living, you couldn't look them in the face, you weren't even on talking terms, but once they're dead you love them. You always love those who are not here, and it's the same thing with God. If he was here with you, if you had to share your food with him, if you had to share your life with him, then you would have had enormous problems with him, but because he's not here now, or at least not in your experience, it's easy to love him. One day, a mother and a little boy went to the cemetery. For the seven-year-old boy, it was his first visit to a cemetery. The mother sat down in one place as she was dedicated to one particular grave, but the boy was curious and went around the cemetery reading the inscriptions on every tombstone. After he was done with his rounds, he came to his mother and asked, "Mom, where do they bury all the horrible people?"

Love is not a joy; it is a deep wonderful pain. It is a very deep, tearing, wonderful pain. Something within you should tear; not just something, everything within you should tear. Only then you know what love is. If it feels pleasant, that's not love, it's just convenience. Maybe you felt a little affection. If you have ever loved, everything inside you tears apart, really tears apart. It's painful, but wonderful. That's how it is. When you start feeling like this about everything and everybody, then going beyond your limitations – physical and mental – naturally happens by itself. It doesn't happen by trying. If you try to go beyond your physical limitations with effort, you only injure yourself; but when it happens like this, it simply happens, physical limitations are no more limitations.

This isn't about training your being. Nobody can ever train their being. It doesn't take any training from anybody. You can't train God. You think it's just like training the dog, Blackie, here. You throw a ball and say, "Go Blackie, go get it, get it Blackie!" It will run and bring back the ball for you. You're trying to train God like this, showing him dog biscuits and telling him, "Come on, get me this, get me that." When you still haven't come to a point in life where a gracefulness, or the Grace of your inner being, has permeated onto the outside, then it's very important that you at least develop some gracefulness on the level of your body and mind. This is not growth. This is like covering a naked man. Without this covering you would be naked and lost. So this is just clothing to protect you until you reach a point where you don't need it. Those who have no hope of being loved by anybody, they are always hoping God will love them. Those people who have no hope of ever being loved by anybody, yes, only God can love them (laughs). Some sage or saint might have talked about loving God, but now that you have a logical mind, a thinking mind, a doubting mind and a questioning mind, don't talk about loving God; it doesn't make any sense. The only reason you have started thinking about God or the Creator is because you have experienced the creation. Before you came, all that you call as creation was there, so you just assumed that somebody must have created it, and you started giving names and forms to that Creator. So your idea of the Creator has come to you only through the creation. Now you hate the creation, you hate the person sitting next to you, and say that you love God; it doesn't mean anything. It won't lead you anywhere, because if you hate the creation, what business do you have with the one who created all this? Only if you have fallen deeply in love with the creation, then you have something to do with the one who created this. It's very significant that Jesus said, "Love thy neighbor." He doesn't mean falling in love with the person next door, he means just loving the one who's next to you right now, this moment, whomever it may be. You don't know what evil could be happening in his mind; it doesn't matter whether he's good or bad, whether you like him or dislike him, just to love him the way he is. If you do this, then you merge with creation. Once you merge with creation, that's the only way to the Creator. Creation is the only way, or the only doorway to the Creator. If you reject creation, you can't know anything about the Creator. So don't worry about loving God. See if you can bring love into your breath, into your step, into every act that you do, not towards anybody or anything; if you can just bring the longing to merge with everything around you, then creation will lead you on to the Creator.

SEEKER: *How will I know when that's happening, when God is actually responding in my life?*

SADHGURU: God never responds.

SEEKER: *How will I know exactly when he stepped into my life?*

SADHGURU: Somu, you will know that God loves you when somebody manages to love you (laughs).

SEEKER: *I sometimes notice that some people seem to keep spirituality separate from life. Why is this? I find it very difficult to understand why this is the case, because awareness is not only when you're meditating. My second question is, if the purpose is 'Self'- Realization, why do we need a Guru?*

SADHGURU: About the first part of the question – if your spirituality is time-bound, five to seven in the morning or six to eight in the morning, or whatever time, you're just trying to be spiritual; there's nothing spiritual about you. What conclusions have you made about being spiritual? If you have made the conclusion that being spiritual means speaking kindly to everybody, you're mistaken. If someone is communicating with different aspects of life in different ways, out of their understanding, out of their sensitivity, out of their own experience – they know how to communicate with a baby, a buffalo, a mountain, they know how to speak to the bus driver – they know it out of this awareness, then it's wonderful and fine. That's how life should be.

If someone, out of their so-called spirituality, is trying to speak with whatever they believe is kindness or goodness, to every aspect of life, they are just moralistic and stupid. Maybe they are good people, but they have no sense of life. There's no inner experience; it's just coming from their goodness and morality. They may make good citizens, but they won't know anything of the beyond. Now, if one is communicating in different ways with different aspects of life because of their unawareness, or because of their prejudices, that's a different aspect altogether. So how one talks to a bus driver may be a way of seeing where that person is, or may not be at all. It's best that you don't judge a person by the way they are speaking to a bus driver or to a man on the street at a certain moment. Now, if one has a pattern of addressing something kindly and another aspect of life rudely, then you know it is coming from ignorance. It has nothing to do with spirituality or anything. First of all let's understand that spirituality is not a moral code. Spirituality means you're beginning to experience that which is beyond the physical. It has got nothing to do with the way you communicate and handle the world around you. The way you do that is just a question of your capability, your intelligence, your exposure, your inclination, and what kind of objectives you have in your life. So how you communicate with the world is in no way an indication of your spiritual process. Swami Nityananda was a yogi, sitting in the forest, absolutely blissful, but if people came anywhere near him, he threw stones at them. He never hit anybody, but he madly threw stones at them. As far as people were concerned, he was a madman throwing stones. It was only much later, when people looked back they were able to see that not once did he hit anybody. He threw stones, always making sure that they didn't hit anybody. He just didn't want people around him. He knew that if people came, they would ask for things, and because of the way he was – his energy was in a certain state – naturally things would happen, miracles would happen. Then people would gather and mess up his whole life. So if people came anywhere near him, he would throw stones at them.

If you go by one's behavior, about what he's doing or what he's saying, then you will definitely come to a wrong conclusion, a wrong judgment. If you had known Sadhguru Shri Brahma, he would even kick people! If somebody came and said something stupid to him, he would just kick them, not out of arrogance, not out of hatred, and not out of anger; that's how he dealt with people. Now he doesn't (laughs). This is not because he has become more Realized or less Realized, it is simply because he has become a little smarter with the world. So how you operate is just a question of your inclination, your intelligence and your exposure, and things like that; it has got nothing to do with your spirituality. If someone is behaving senselessly in his life and always talking about spirituality, you know why. It's a fad; spirituality is a fad for him. Now you saying, "I'm open" – see, what openness you're talking about is in terms of, "I am willing to go anywhere." Willing to go anywhere is good; on one level, it is openness. Now wherever you go, you're willing to go all the way; that's real openness. If you become, "Wherever I go, I am willing to go all the way", that openness would reap more harvest than, "I am willing to go anywhere."

After all this, you demolish your own question: "If spirituality means seeking all the time, why do I need a Guru?" Let's say, all that you're seeking is to go to Kedarnath right now. Somebody is driving; the roads are laid out. If you came alone and there were no proper directions, definitely you would have wished, "I wish there was a map to tell me how to get there." On one level, a Guru is just a map. He's a live map. If you can read the map, you know the way, you can go. A Guru can also be your bus driver. You sit here and doze and he will take you to Kedarnath; but to sit in this bus and doze off, or to sit in this bus joyfully, you need to trust the bus driver. If every moment, with every curve in this road, you go on thinking, "Will this man kill me? Will this man go off the road? What intention does he have for my life?" then you will only go mad sitting here. We're talking about trust, not because a Guru needs your trust, it's just that if there's no trust you will drive yourself mad.

This is not just for sitting on a bus or going on a spiritual journey. To live on this planet, you need trust. Right now, you trust unconsciously. You're sitting on this bus, which is just a bundle of nuts and bolts and pieces of metal. Look at the way you're going through the mountains. Unknowingly, you trust this vehicle so much. Isn't it so? You have placed your life in the hands of this mechanical mess, which is just nuts and bolts, rubbers and wires, this and that. You have placed your life in it, but you trust the bus unconsciously. The same trust, if it arises consciously, would do miracles to you. When we say trust, we're not talking about anything new to life. To be here, to take every breath in and out, you need trust, isn't it? Your trust is unconscious. I am only asking you to bring a little consciousness to your trust. It's not something new. Life is trust, otherwise nobody can exist here.

So if you can draw your own map, if you can drive your own bus, that's wonderful. But on an uncharted path, if you go without a map, it may take lifetimes to find a certain place. It may take lifetimes to cross. If you go with a map you will cross easily. If you go with a good bus driver you will cross very easily; that's the difference. It's not that you can't do it yourself – you can. We don't know how long it will take. That's the question.

With the One Who Knows

With the One Who Knows
Life and death live in me at once
Never held one above the other
When one stands far, life I offer
In closeness, only death I deal
In death of the limited
Will the deathless be
How to tell the fools
Of my taintless evil.
— Sadhguru

After seeking enters a being, sooner or later, one arrives at a point where one desires the guidance and the grace of the One Who Knows, One who has been through this uncharted but inevitable metamorphosis. Blessed are those who seek One, more blessed are those who actually encounter One.

However, relationships repeatedly defiled by imposters and charlatans and one's own inner defilement stand in the way of simply sitting at the Master's feet, just receiving.

Sanctified in the tradition as the Guru-shishya paramparya, being with the One Who Knows is eternal and the most sacred of all relationships. Having been a forlorn seeker himself in a previous lifetime, refusing to bow down before any human form, Sadhguru, in his present lifetime plays the role of the One Who Knows.

Dispelling fears and misgivings of bondage and exploitation, Sadhguru answers questions paramount to the seeker – How do I choose my Guru? Is a Guru really necessary? How best do I make use of the Guru? And then, in case I don't make it in this lifetime, will he see me through in another lifetime?

Secure under the wings of the One Who Knows, the seeker has the luxury and space to explore within, and the entire Existence too, with the kind of reckless abandon that the Creator Himself would envy.

SEEKER: *Like many people around me, I am seeking the ultimate Truth and the right guidance to experience it. Sadhguru, can you tell us how a person finds his Guru?*

SADHGURU: If you are truly a seeker of Truth, Truth cannot hide from you. It is in the lap of Truth that you have happened. Most people who claim to be seekers are only seeking security, solace, or the fulfillment of their desires. Their life is just an expression of their greed and fear. Do you see, many people in the world shamelessly claim to be God-fearing? They are not God loving, they are God-fearing. Unless you have fallen in love with creation, how can you love the one who created it? Like Jesus said, "Love thy neighbor." Everyone can love God, as He does not demand anything from you, but to love the one next to you right now costs life. It is a challenge. It takes much courage to do this. 'Love thy neighbor' is a very good device for breaking your illusion of loving the one who is in the heavens.

A genuine seeker, a person who develops an urge within, will always find his Guru. He may find it in a man, in a woman, or he may find it even in a rock. He will definitely find it somewhere, there is no doubt about it. When any being calls or really yearns, the existence answers. If the thirst within you is strong enough, God always answers.

SEEKER: *Sadhguru, is spiritual transformation possible without the help of a Guru?*

SADHGURU: The reason why there has always been so much importance and stress in this culture on a Guru is that without a Guru there can be no spiritual process. Without him you cannot transform yourself. How can you transform yourself into something that you don't know? You can only work towards what you know, isn't it? How to work towards that which you don't know? To do that, you have to be so aware as to be able to see the natural tendencies of every aspect of energy in the existence, which is moving or is tending to move in a certain direction. You need to understand this and start moving that way. Only a person who has that sense of awareness can walk without a Guru. Others, if they walk without a Guru, they will just flounder and flounder and flounder.

Through the Grace of the Guru, in a moment, with just a clap of his hands, things can happen. Sometimes certain situations or certain energies can also do things to people. In these situations, they are acting like a Guru – maybe not in the physical form, but that is what is happening. Transforming yourself into that which you don't know, or that which you have not tasted, is logically impossible. I am not ruling it out totally. It is possible, but only for very few people. For most people, it is remote. It is not impossible, but it is very remote.

SEEKER: *Is that why so many people seem to love you to the point of madness, since you are the one who can show us the path? But really, Jaggi, personally for me, Realization or no Realization, I just love you very much.*

SADHGURU: I didn't know that. That is news to me...I am the most insensitive man in the world, aren't I? (Laughs). Most of the time, people's longing towards the Master is unconscious. Why such crazy longing is unconscious is because when the energy level deepens, it is neither mental nor emotional. It is just like a plant, not longing for water emotionally or mentally – it is a deep energy longing. If there is a drop of water there, the roots will find their way to it. There is no emotion in it. There is no mind in it. It is a different kind of intelligence. It knows where to go. It knows where its life is. Wherever you place it, it will just find its way. Not even by mistake will it go this way or that way. It will not go any other way because it has a deep longing. This longing is not thought, not emotion, it is just life's longing for itself. That is how it is.

SEEKER: *So, did we have an unconscious longing to find you? I mean, to find a live Guru? You know, unconsciously were we always searching for you and that's why we are here? I'm not sure how to ask this...*

SADHGURU: If you have difficulty in forming the question itself, it must be a very difficult question! (Laughs). Yes, naturally, everything moves in that direction.

SEEKER: *Now that we are accompanying you on this trip to the Himalayas, and some of us even have the privilege of riding on this bus with you, I am wondering, what is it within us that has created the opportunity to have access to you? What is the difference between people who have access to a Guru and people who don't?*

SADHGURU: Now John, you would like to believe that you are the chosen few? Do you know chosen people have always been eternally in trouble? I must tell you a joke. Once, the leader of the Jewish community on planet Earth, Joshua Goldberg, had his annual dinner appointment with God. So he went to dinner, and God arrived and sat down at the table with him. A few breadcrumbs were served for dinner. God said Grace and started eating. Joshua just sat there. God looked at him and said, "Joshua, my son, why don't you eat?" Joshua said, "Father, can I ask you a question?" God answered, "Okay, my son." Joshua asked, "Dear Father, are we really the chosen people?" God replied, "Why, my son, why do you doubt? Yes, you are the chosen people." Joshua asked, "Father, are we really, really, the chosen people?" "Yes, Joshua. Why are you beginning to doubt? You are the chosen people." Then Joshua asked, "Dear Father, are we really, really, really the chosen people?" "Yes, yes, yes, you are the chosen people!" Then Joshua got up from the table, straightened his jacket and said, "Why don't you choose somebody else for a while?"

So why are we here? Okay, if you're just talking about being on this bus, yes, you are the chosen people (laughs). Why does one person get access to certain possibilities? Let us look at it this way: I want you to look at me not as a person, but as a possibility. Why certain people get access to certain possibilities and others don't, that is the question. Now, this is not really true. It is not that only certain people get access to this possibility. Anybody who is truly longing, always has access to this, to this energy, which you right now refer to as me. Everybody may not have access to the person; that is obvious. It is always so.

Maybe I have to tell you this at this point; I have initiated more people I have not met than people I have met; that is the reality. When someone really longs, I initiate them, wherever they may be, when the longing is deep enough to receive me. When someone's heart cries out to know, I am always there. So as far as the possibility is concerned, this possibility has happened to a lot more people who have never seen my face, but if you're talking about the person, that is not of great significance. Maybe it is a pleasure, or, if you're too close around me, like Doug, it could be a torture putting up with me and my demands – like holding this microphone on this bumpy bus ride, finding my sunglasses or locating my favorite Frisbee (laughs). If you're sitting two seats away from me, it can be a pleasure. If you're right next to me, it can be a torture.

Being with a Master is never comfortable, because He will break all your limitations, all your ideologies. So knowing the person or having access to the person can be on many levels. Having access to the possibility is only because of the longing that one may have. There are many people who have close access to the person, but don't know anything about the possibility yet. Knowing the person is of no great significance. Probably it has been put forth by many people in many different ways. Gautama put this forth very beautifully. When somebody asked about Ananda Tirtha, who was constantly with Gautama throughout his life and remained unenlightened until the end; when people asked, "This man is with you all the time. Why has nothing happened to him?" In answer, Gautama asks, "Can a spoon taste the soup?" So that says it all. You need sensitivity, to be life sensitive, not ego sensitive.

SEEKER: *Sadhguru, a lot of Enlightened beings have a few people who are close to them. Is it because they are able to relate to these people better, or is it because of some past life connections?*

SADHGURU: If a person is Enlightened, he can relate to anybody. There is really no problem about relating with whomever he is with at that moment. He can absolutely relate to any person, be totally with anyone. It is very possible for him. Even if the other person is not willing, he can still relate to him and his limitations as well, and still be okay with him; but he might choose, at certain times, to be with certain people. One reason is, he has a specific objective. He has a plan as to what he wants to do. For that he needs certain people.

For example, Ramakrishna Paramahamsa was deeply attached, or at least it looked like he was deeply attached, to Naren, who was later known as Vivekananda. People around Ramakrishna resented this. Many other people who were always around him, hankered to be with him. Vivekananda was a truant disciple to begin with, overly logical and arrogant. The others were so much more dedicated than he was, but still Ramakrishna sought Vivekananda. Every other day Vivekananda would get angry with Ramakrishna and walk off saying, "I will go back to my college, I have got work," and Ramakrishna would go searching for him in the town. This man had never really been in town, but he would go with tears in his eyes, search for him, and then beg him to come back. All the other disciples of Ramakrishna would be deeply offended, "Where is the need for our Guru to run behind some hothead, begging him to come? All of us are here, he can teach us. Why does he go after this fool?" Not only his disciples, but also his wife Sharada was deeply offended. She would ask, "Why Naren all the time? So many people are here, waiting for you. Why do you go after this Naren?" But Ramakrishna knew, without Naren things would not happen. His message would not be taken to the masses. He knew, today these people could be on, tomorrow, they could drop off.

Once this comes up in the society, all sorts of rumors will go on. "Oh, maybe it is like this. Maybe he is his real son, his biological son. Maybe it was hidden from us. Maybe he is homosexual. Maybe he is seeking this young boy in some other way." These kinds of things happened around Ramakrishna, but the reason why he was seeking Vivekananda like that was, he saw him as the ideal carrier for his message. He knew, if Vivekananda was not sufficiently prepared by the time he leaves, then his whole work, whatever he had to offer to the world, would die with him; he knew that. So he acted almost like Vivekananda's slave. Many people thought it was totally undignified for him to behave like that with Vivekananda, but he went about like this because he had a clear objective, and he had no problem as to how to do it. He just did what worked, that is all.

Another aspect of it is that there could have been energy bonds, not emotional bonds. It is not a question of being able to relate better. There could have been a certain energy bond, which people could not understand. That is, this Enlightened being may not have been able to operate as a physical person without the support of somebody else, maybe one, two, or even ten people. He may have been just using them to keep his physical body going, in many ways. Otherwise, he would have been incapable of sustaining his physical body by himself. There could have been energy bonds. Or it is just that people think that somebody else is closer, simply because for everything that has to happen, this person generally depends on one person, because he sees this person seems to have much more sense and a deeper understanding of everything that is said and done.

This was very beautifully demonstrated by Ashtavakra, an Enlightened being. Ashtavakra was the Master for Janaka Maharaj, who was a king. Janaka was a Realized being himself, who continued to be a king because Ashtavakra told him, "You must continue to be a king because people deserve an Enlightened king." Whenever Janaka found a break from his administrative and royal duties, he always came to Ashtavakra, who was in a hermitage in the forest, and spent time there, as any other disciple. He sat there with the other disciples. All the other disciples were monks. They were bhramhacharis, fully dedicated to Ashtavakra. Their Master's word was everything for them. Their life was for him to do anything he wanted with them. Janaka was a king; he was married with many wives, and as a king he had many social involvements. He had everything, and more, than any normal king.

So there was resentment with the other disciples who were monks. First of all, someone had taken this step of being a monk or a bhramhachari out of his own choice, because he sees it as a suitable path to walk upon. He sees that by going into a family situation, his spirituality or his spiritual urge could completely evaporate. Just to see that his spiritual thirst is not evaporated, he is willing to forgo certain things in his life and pursue his path in totality. He need not have any resentment towards someone who has all this and still pursues spirituality, but unfortunately he does, because somewhere, there is resentment that they are enjoying all the luxuries that life has to offer and spirituality as well. They are having the best of both worlds, so there is resentment.

Ashtavakra treated Janaka with utmost graciousness, so that too was bothering them. Though they have accepted him as their Guru, somewhere, the logical mind asks these questions: "Is it only because he is a rich man, a king, that he is being treated better than us?" This question was always there, and now, there are so many emotions that are involved in this, which is a daily affair for every Guru. This was not just for Janaka, but for Janaka it was dramatic because he was a king. I am sorry to say that this is not so just for Ashtavakra, but for every Guru, this is an issue in his life. For Ashtavakra, it was such a dramatic situation, because he was handling a king and monks together. The difference and the distinction between the two was too vast and too stark.

One day, they were all sitting in a sathsang, and one of the disciples asked this question: "Why is it that you're always treating Janaka special and we are not being treated the same way?" Ashtavakra just smiled and said, "I will answer this, but not now." They felt even more hurt, because they thought he was avoiding this question because Janaka was there. Ashtavakra waited and at a certain time he engineered a situation where somebody came running and said, "The monks' clothes! The monkeys are taking them away!" These clothes were nothing except loincloths and maybe just a piece of cloth to wrap around their shoulders when it got cold. These clothes were hung outside to dry. When Ashtavakra was still speaking in the sathsang, the moment they heard the news, all the monks got up and ran to save their clothes. Then they came back and sat down. Ashtavakra just continued to speak and after some time, one of the king's messengers came and blurted out, without even asking the Guru's permission whether he can speak or not, he just blurted out that the king's palace was burning. Janaka just looked at him and asked him to get out of that place. He said, "How dare you enter this place without the Master's permission? Get out!" Then Ashtavakra waited for a moment and said, "His palace is burning, and he got offended that his man interrupted my speech, but you people, just your stupid clothes, which are not worth anything to anybody, the kind of clothes that would be thrown away – for that, without even looking at me you ran after them. That is the difference! And that is why the difference."

Janaka's way of being was such that, though he was an Enlightened being and a king as well, a rare combination, sitting at his Master's feet was the highest Grace in his life. He was always aspiring for this opportunity and still sat there, which most people would not do. So such a man being treated special was very natural. You don't carry rocks in your hand the way you carry a flower. You carry a flower with a different sense of gentleness and give a different priority to it, isn't it? When you want to offer something to God, you don't offer a rock. I am not saying a rock is any less; it is just that a flower is more evolved. Accordingly it gets treated. This goes for people also. This does not mean you don't care for a rock. You care for it, and you do more work with it because it needs more work. That is different, but definitely the way you handle it is different. If you don't have this distinction, then you will be a fool with life. In the name of equality, you will destroy all the beauty of life.

SEEKER: *Sadhguru, can a relationship between the Master and disciple in previous births be carried on for lifetimes?*

SADHGURU: Yes, definitely. Generally, this is the only relationship which can be carried for lifetimes. The work continues. There have been husbands, wives and lovers who have come together again for lifetimes because their love was so strong, but that is very rare. Generally, it is the Master-disciple relationship which gets carried for lifetimes. All the other relationships come together for convenience. Once it is over, it just breaks apart. To know this, first of all you need to come to an understanding as to what a relationship is, why there are human relationships. Now, you have formed various types of relationships in your life, some for your emotional needs, physical needs, financial needs, social needs, psychological needs, or a few just for comfort; in many ways you have formed relationships. Whatever kind of relationship you have formed, fundamentally it is concerned and based only with the body. When the relationship is based in the body, once the body drops, the relationship just evaporates. That is the end of it. Only if a relationship transcends physical limitations – when I say physical, I am referring to the mental structure and emotional structure also as physical – only when you in some way transcend the physical limitations, there is a possibility of this relationship extending beyond lifetimes or across lifetimes.

So generally, it is only the Master-disciple relationship which extends this way, though there could be a few examples of other relationships going beyond physical limitations. This is because the Master-disciple relationship continues always. Even if the disciple has no idea of the Master's being, the Master's business is only with the disciple's being. This relationship is always energy-based. It is not emotion-based, it is not mind-based, nor is it body-based. It is only energy-based. An energy-based relationship does not even realize whether the bodies have changed or not over lifetimes. It continues until the energy reaches dissolution. It just continues. For the energy there is no rebirth. It is only the body which is reborn. The energy just continues as one flow and accordingly carries the relationship. So definitely, this is one relationship which is carried on because it is purely an energy-based relationship.

SEEKER: *Sadhguru, are there people here with you now that were connected to you in your past life?*

SADHGURU: Yes. Many people who were connected to me in some way over three hundred and seventy years ago, not only those who supported us, but even those who persecuted us, who tormented us, are somehow mostly in Coimbatore today. All of them are not our meditators, but they are with us. It is like that. That is the way life functions.

Why all these people land up in one place is – why is the breeze blowing in this direction and not the other way? Do you know why? See, the whole momentum of the wind in the world is just this: the sea is a place where the humidity is high, so the pressure and the density are also high. When the land gets heated up, the density is low. Wherever the density is low, there the wind rushes. Then it rains, and then that becomes high density. Then the wind moves backward, as the wind movement is always towards low density. Wherever there is emptiness, everything rushes there. So when the karmic bag is empty here (pointing to himself), all those other bags of karma which have been one way or the other connected to that for so many lifetimes tend to slowly move towards that direction, knowingly or unknowingly. Mostly unknowingly, they slowly move in that direction, because for all of them there is a possibility now. When one bag empties, everybody has the opportunity to become empty.

Sometimes it also happens that a nearly empty bag comes in search of past karmic connections to empty itself. That could be an opportunity for both beings to dissolve that aspect of the karma, but if one is not alert to their inner situations, these opportunities could be completely missed. Someone here among you knows this firsthand. Let us ask Bharathi how she missed one such situation.

BHARATHI: A few years ago, before the Dhyanalinga consecration, Sadhguru specifically told me that my father of my Raigarh birth, who was in his final stage of spiritual evolution, would come and visit me. He described this person, his attire, and his demeanor, and said such a person would visit me in thirty days. Many times, I had seen such a person in certain states of meditative clarity. Sadhguru went on to say that he was within one hundred to two hundred kilometers away in the southerly direction, that he would find me within thirty days, and when he comes I should ask him in and serve him a meal. By doing this, I would be able to dissolve some of my unfinished karma which had been hanging on for a long time. About two weeks later, towards mid-morning, the security person at the gate sent word that there was a man asking to see me. When I asked what he wanted, I got a message that he just wanted to see me. Engrossed in my routine, I said that I was not willing to meet any strangers. After some time, I came to know that the man was still waiting at the gate, insisting on seeing me. In irritation and curiosity I stepped out of the house and saw this person standing with a certain dignity, obviously not expecting anything from me. He looked at me with an unusual sense of tenderness, which I ignored. I said, "I don't know who you are and I want nothing to do with you," and turned my back on him. Later, suddenly, in a moment of clarity, it dawned on me: this was the man of my vision and also of Sadhguru's description. I immediately contacted Sadhguru who was traveling, and the first thing he said was, "He came and went. He has emptied himself." Then I knew how, in my unawareness, I missed such an opportunity.

SADHGURU: Whatever the past karma, it is like this: let us say, until the age of thirty you earn ten million rupees. Now you can either squander it or make it grow. In the past, you might have created some riches within you. In this life you may either add to it or squander it, but definitely some quality of that will be there in your life, though in unconsciousness it may go to waste. So because of your spiritual practices, sadhana, those riches may manifest now in terms of material comfort, like a good house, the right kind of atmosphere, or maybe good people around you. In spite of all this, you may not make use of it and just become complacent. That is the whole cycle. Why I repeatedly say that the whole game is like the *Snake and Ladder* game is: you climb the ladder and there you're happy. The very comfort that comes out of it, that comes out of good karma, may make you complacent and that is it, down through the snake you go. Then once suffering comes, you start looking and grow. You may squander it and go down again. This is the way of the fool, wasting his energy; but someone who has sufficient intelligence in him should even take each breath as a step towards growth. It is very much possible. Like how she shared, the reminder comes. Even after reminding a person hundreds of times, if he still does not wake up, if he is still lying down in his comforts, what can we do? He will be lost. He has to suffer once again, and then maybe seek growth.

This whole spiritual process is not happening to even one percent of the population. For all others, when things are going well they are laughing, and when things go bad they are crying. There are very few people in the world who, whichever way it is, are okay and balanced. For them nothing is a great benediction, nothing is a problem. Everything is just another life situation through which they can become free. The rest of the people are all the type who will go the way the situation pushes them. They are like cattle. You have evolved into a human body, but otherwise there is no real difference. Between the way animals live and generally the way people live, is there any great difference qualitatively? Maybe quantitatively there is a lot of difference. There is more variety to your activity; you drive a car, you watch television. All that nonsense you do, but qualitatively, where is the difference?

If the difference has to come, it can only come with awareness; there is no other way. This awareness need not be just dry. When it is filled with love, this awareness just multiplies. Generally, mental alertness is mistaken for awareness, but awareness is a far deeper dimension than just mental alertness. When awareness arises within you, love and compassion will be the natural follow-up. When you're very loving, you are very aware; can you see that? Now, if you're not able to relate to things around you, to people around you, it is not because there is something wrong with you. You're either a little misplaced, or out of your own foolishness you got misplaced in this life.

Once you become aware, you have to make the little arrangements that are needed to put yourself in the right place. If you know you're a coconut, then you should have fallen here at the foothills, not on the mountaintop. It is of no use; you can't grow there. You have to roll down somehow. If you have to roll down, maybe you have to lose something. If the coconut has to reach the foothills, maybe a man has to pick it up and bring it down. Maybe he will peel it and take off the skin. You don't know what you will lose. Something will be lost. The man who carries it is bound to take off something. Life is like that. For whatever you do, you have to pay a price. Let me tell you a joke. A man sat in a train traveling from Bristol to London, with a baby in his arms. Halfway through the trip, another man with two big suitcases got on the train and sat down next to him. The first man said, "Those two suitcases look just like mine; are you a salesman too?" "No," the other man replied, "I'm on the way to the airport. I'm flying to Greece." Then he asked, "So what are you selling, anyway?" "Condoms," the first man replied. Shocked, the other man said, "Condoms? And you're taking your son with you while you sell condoms?" "Oh, this is not my son; it is a complaint from Bristol."

Without a price, you get nothing. You better know this. Whether you pay the price here or there, you can't escape it, you will always pay. That's the law of karma. There is a price for everything. What kind of physical situations you land up in have a very strong karmic basis. The very fact that you are here today proves that your physical situation has been conducive enough to allow you to be here. There are many who desire to be here, but for many reasons it has not happened for them. They are yet to earn it.

SEEKER: *Master, you have ignited a flame in me, and I am burning up now. Tell me how to take it to the world. I want the whole world to know you. I want the world to know this…*

SADHGURU: The journey has begun. When you first came to Isha, many of you simply came either out of curiosity, or maybe seeking some physical or psychological benefits. After some time, even after you finished the program, being around was still good entertainment. It was a place to come to meet people. But after a while, some of you were helplessly pulled towards yoga. Whether you wanted to come or not, somehow you were here. Until now, I would say most of you, more or less, have remained spectators – maybe involved a little, but still spectators. Are you willing to change and make this shift from being a spectator to being a real participant in this yoga?

Moving from being a spectator into actually becoming a part of the action are two very different things. When you are a spectator, if things go well for your team, you jump up with joy and clap. When things go bad, you look the other way. Now when you become a part of the action itself, both your involvement and your experience will change in a dramatic way. There is no real risk for a spectator. He may enjoy the game or he may feel a little depressed because the game didn't go well, but when you are a part of the action itself, everything is at stake in so many ways. It is like this: if there is a race going on, to sit and watch as a spectator is one thing. Mind you, a spectator is also involved, but the person who is actually racing is on a different level of involvement: he's the one who really takes the risk of racing. Now that you have decided to take the step of moving from spectator-hood into the real play, into the very core of the action, you had better know what the nature of this action is, and what it demands from you.

Now that many of you here have taken the step of being involved, let us see what is needed out of a person who's taking a step like this. Right now, whatever you call as 'yourself' is simply a certain formation of the mind you have collected. It is a certain type of information in your mind. When you say, "I'm a good person," "I'm a bad person," "I am haughty," "I am meek," or whatever you may say, all those things are simply certain formations of the mind, or in other words, it is just past accumulation. You simply live through your past. If the past is taken away, most people are just lost. Everything depends on the past. It is the previous moment which rules everything. This moment is not important. As long as the personality is important, it simply means the previous moment is important. This present moment is not important, because the personality belongs to the past.

In this moment you really have no personality, do understand this. The personality that you carry is a dead thing. When you're carrying a dead body over your shoulders, you can't walk very far. With a dead body, which way can you head? Only to the burial ground, isn't it? If you carry a dead body for too long, you will have to bear with terrible smells. Your personality, the stronger it is, the more odoriferous it is. You can go far in life only when you can leave your past. This is like a snake shedding its skin. Do you know how a snake sheds its skin? One moment it is a part of its body, the next moment it sheds its skin and just goes on without turning back. If every moment one is like a snake leaving the skin behind, only then there is growth. When a person is living moment to moment like this and doesn't carry the burden of the past with him, he is a truly sinless person. He does not carry anything with him. Being sinless doesn't mean that he did not do anything with his life. That would be being a dead person. He did everything that a person could possibly do to know life, but his actions never left any residue, nor did he build a personality out of the actions he performed.

Have you heard of the Saint Suka? He wrote the Shrimath Bhagavatham. He was Saint Vyasa's son. Suka was a pure being, a truly sinless being. He had a certain flavor about him which could change at any time. This quality is like that of a flavor, which is not really a flavor. It is flavorlessness, but it is not bland either; it has its own quality. There was a particular incident which happened in his life. One day he was walking by himself in the forest, naked. As he was walking by, there was a lake where a few nymphs, jala kanyas, were bathing. As they were by themselves in the forest, all the women were bathing together and playing in the water, naked. Suka came upon the lake, looked at them, and just walked by. While looking at them he just kept walking. The women were not ashamed, nor did they try to hide themselves, they just continued their play. Suka walked off.

While looking for Suka, his father Vyasa came after him. He was over seventy years of age, an old man, and a great saint. Vyasa came and saw Suka passing by this lake where the nymphs were having a bath. He also came into the clearing near the lake while following Suka. When the women saw him, they immediately rushed for their clothes. Suka was a young man in the prime of his youth and naked. The ladies were not ashamed. They were also naked and they were not upset about it. Vyasa was an old man, completely dressed. When he came, they rushed for their clothes! So he went to them and asked, "What is this? I am an old person, and I am dressed properly, whereas my son is young and naked at that. When he came near you, you were not disturbed, but when I came, you're acting like this. Why?" They said, "He has no sense of sex about him. We did not feel anything. He carries no sexual identification. He's just like a child; but you, though seventy years old and finished with the physical aspect of sex, it is still very much there with you."

Only that person who does not carry the previous moment to this moment, only that person is free from everything, and that quality will be felt everywhere. Within a few moments of meeting you, people will trust you to the extent that they would not even trust their parents, or husbands, or wives, simply because you don't carry the burden of the past with you. If you carry the past with you, then you will also smell like anybody else. The whole world stinks with personalities. Everybody has his own strong smell or personality. These are the various stenches in the world, and they keep clashing all the time. When one does not carry this odor, one can cross over this existence. One not only passes through this world effortlessly, one will pass through the very process of life and death effortlessly. This person crosses the ocean of samsara without any effort. What looks like a great effort for somebody else will be happening for this person without any effort. Everything just simply happens. All your anger, hatred, jealousy, fear, everything is based in the past. The moment you carry the past and future, you become a donkey. You become a real ass, because the burden is such. Carrying that burden, there is no way anybody can live his life intelligently.

Much love and compassion is needed to carry this message. You may pretend, but when you are burdened, compassion can't come through. When you're so light that nothing matters, only then you can truly be compassionate. Love and compassion flow out of a person only when there is no sense of burden. Now, what you're normally calling as 'love' has become a great burden. It's not love; it is simply various needs, your own needs and your greed covered up with a pretense called love, which is not love at all. To fulfill many things you cover it up with a raiment called love. You can taste love and compassion in your life only when you are in this moment, fresh, absolutely without any burden. If you are carrying your personality with you, there is no way this is possible. There may have been some moments in your life when you felt true compassion towards something or somebody. In those moments, all your personality, who you are, what you are, everything would have melted. Nothing would have been there. You are simply there in that moment.

SEEKER: *Why is there so much stress on love and compassion on this path, Master?*

SADHGURU: Of all emotions, compassion is the highest that man can experience. When someone lives in compassion, not just love, only then he is a real seeker, because very easily love becomes attachment and a bias. Love can become a great prejudice against you, somebody else, or anything.

In the Indian culture you never told your parents, your wife, your husband or your children, "I love you." This was not a part of this culture because the moment you say it, it's almost like it's not there. You're only trying to assert it. Love is not an assertion. Love is a supplication. An asserting mind can never be a loving mind. On the day of the big men's-only booze party, a gentle, quiet, and unassuming fellow who had missed a few of these kinds of parties was goaded by his chauvinistic friends to be more assertive with his wife. "You don't have to always do the things your wife asks you to do. Go home tonight and show her you're the boss." The man, after hearing these same words many times over, was finally set on fire with enthusiasm and couldn't wait to try the friends' advice. He rushed home, slammed the door, shook his fist in his wife's face, and growled, "From now on you're taking orders from me. I want my supper right now and after you put it on the table, go upstairs and lay out my best clothes. Tonight I'm going out with the boys and you're going to stay home where you belong. And another thing, do you know who is going to comb my hair, iron my pants, polish my shoes, and tie my tie?" "I certainly do," said the wife very calmly, "the undertaker."

Patanjali, to differentiate between asserting and loving, called this 'the original mind'. What is this original mind? The mind that you carry right now is a collection, an accumulation. It is garbage that you have piled up over a period of time. If you can leave it behind and walk away, then you are in your original mind. Others may call this 'no mind', this original mind. This is something that 'was', something that 'will be', always. When you are in your original mind – there might have been rare moments in your life when you tasted your original mind – true love or compassion just well up within you. Only if you can leave your garbage and walk away this moment, only then is this possible. Only then the seeker who carries my message becomes a Master, otherwise he just stagnates. Just carrying my message is itself an accumulation, some nonsense that you gathered somewhere. Maybe it is useful for a few people, but may never lead to any great transformation.

The few that carry my message to the outside world are teachers. A teacher is an eternal student. The moment he stops being a student, he is not a teacher anymore. That is the way it is. The day he thinks, "I am a teacher," he is finished. It is over. This is a constant process of learning. Once you are in this moment, there is no past. Everything is new; everything is seen fresh. If at any moment you think you know, and you teach, that means you're carrying the past burden. Maybe right now this is convenient, but the same convenience will become a tremendous torture after some time. It will. I have seen people systematically destroy themselves, step by step. Not carrying the past burden can be very easily done for the person who can simply be here.

The process of training people to carry my message is not to go out and do some nonsense to somebody else. That is not the point. This whole process is a way of growth. It is an effective tool for your growth. Teaching is for you to grow and during the process somebody else might be benefited. In the African lore there is a saying: "When the lion feeds, many animals eat." That's all it is. It's not a service that you're doing. It is just that you chose that kind of a path, that when you walk, many others benefit. When something is left unfulfilled within you, when a complete illumination has not happened within your own being, there is nothing one can really teach. There is nothing that can be transmitted. It is just that you're a driver, and you take the passengers along with you. Maybe you have the opportunity of handling the wheel for a while. That does not make you big in any way. It is just that you're also a passenger, but happen to be the one who is holding the wheel. If a person has to develop, he has to grow into humility and love. He has to evolve into a certain gracefulness; a gracefulness not of the body, not of the clothes, not of the exterior, but a certain gracefulness which can't be expressed in words. If a person has to grow into this, it can only come when moment-to-moment life becomes caring, the kind of caring which hurts. This can happen only out of deep love and compassion.

SEEKER: *Sadhguru, tradition always teaches us to be reverential towards God. How is this understood in relation to the way Mirabai or Akka Mahadevi or many other such saints have taken God as their lover?*

SADHGURU: Where there is no love, how can there be reverence? When love reaches its peak, it naturally becomes reverence. People who are talking about reverence without love, know neither this nor that. All they know is fear. So probably you're referring to God-fearing people. These sages and saints, especially the seers that you mentioned, like Akka Mahadevi, Mirabai, or Anusuya and so many of them in the past, have taken to this form of worship because it was more suitable for them. They could emote much more easily than they could intellectualize things. They just used their emotions to reach their ultimate nature. Using emotion and reaching the ultimate nature is what is called as bhakthi yoga. It's a different form of worship.

Every culture has various forms of worship. Some people worship God as the Master, themselves as slaves. Sometimes they even take God as their servant, or as a partner in everything that they do. Yet others worship Him as a friend, as a lover, as their own child, the Bala Krishna. Generally, you become the feminine and you hold Him as the ultimate purusha – the masculine. So how you worship is not at all the point. How you communicate is not the point. The whole point is just how deeply you relate. These are the different attitudes; but whatever the attitude, the love affair is such that you're not expecting anything from the other side. Not even a response. You crave for it, but if He doesn't respond, you're not going to be angry, you're not going to be disappointed or anything. Your life is just about craving, and making something else tremendously more important than you. Whether it is existent or not, even that doesn't matter. That is the fundamental thing.

For the whole path of bhakthi, the important thing is, something else is far more important than you. So Akka, Mirabai and the others like them, their bhakthi was in that form, and they took this mode of worship. They took to worshipping God or mainly Shiva as their husband, because in India, when a woman reaches a certain age, marriage is almost like a must and it always happens. These women, these bhakthas, wanted to eliminate that dimension of being married once again to a man, because they have chosen the Lord Himself as their husband. They did not care for any other relationship in their lives.

The purpose of the path of devotion is just dissolution. In fact, the very word devotion comes from the word dissolve. The only objective of a devotee is to dissolve into his or her object of devotion. So how they relate to their object of devotion does not really matter. Whichever way they can relate best, that is how they do it. The reason you asked this question, in terms of reverence juxtaposed with love – being a lover or a husband – is because the word 'love', or being a lover, is always understood as physical. That is why this question. How can you be physical with somebody and still be reverential? This has been the tragedy of humanity that lovers have not known how to be reverential towards each other. When I say 'reverential', in fact the very objective of love is to dissolve into somebody else. The English expression of falling in love is really appropriate and very beautiful, in the sense that they always talked about 'falling' in love. Nobody ever talked about standing up in love, or climbing in love, or flying in love, but falling in love, because always, when what you consider as 'me' falls, a deep experience of love can happen within you.

If you look at love as an emotion, you can see that love is more like a vehicle to bring oneness. The very object of love is to become one. It is the longing to become one with the other which we are referring to as love. So when it is taken to its peak, becoming reverential to that which you consider worthwhile, to become one, is very natural. For whatever sake you are willing to dissolve yourself, it has to be reverential. Otherwise, how can you feel it is worthwhile to dissolve? If you think it is something that you can use, or something that you can just relate to, and benefit from, there can be no love because the object of love is always to dissolve. Whatever you consider as worth dissolving into, dissolving yourself into, is bound to be revered; there is no other way to be.

SEEKER: *Sadhguru, you have said at times, in a few sathsangs, that the problem with women in spirituality is that they go after the Buddha rather than the Buddha-hood, or in other words, after the Master rather than his teachings. How do you substantiate this?*

SADHGURU: (Laughs) I didn't say this, Gautama said it.

SEEKER: *You also said this.*

SADHGURU: I just repeated Gautama's words. I only reminded you about that, probably in some sathsang. When his disciple, Sangamitra, insisted that women should be allowed on the path of Dhamma that Gautama was offering to the world – when women were not yet a part of it – Gautama said, "My path will stay vibrantly alive for two thousand five hundred years, but if I allow women onto it, it will last only for five hundred years." When Sangamitra insisted and asked, "Why is it so?" Gautama said, "If a woman comes and sits with me, for her, more than my Buddha-hood, I will become more attractive because of her emotions and the very duality of man and woman." It is in this context that he said that women prefer to go after the Buddha rather than the Buddha-hood. Of course, a Buddha is the embodiment of the Buddha-hood, but she would miss the point. In other words he meant that she would be attracted to the man who embodies this quality more than the quality itself, because there is a natural attraction within her towards the opposite.

So it was said in that context, but it need not always be true. At a certain point in her life, a woman will look beyond that and seek. History and the present situation also prove that. Definitely, there is a tendency for a woman to get more attracted to the embodiment of the quality than to the quality itself, because generally for a woman, her fundamental way of seeking would be through emotions, and emotions always need an embodiment. Without embodiment, emotions can't flow. It is because of the path of bhakthi that we have embodied every quality in this culture as different gods. They are just different qualities in nature, but we have identified them or embodied them with different forms, because the people who were seeking were doing so through their emotions; and without embodiment, they would not be able to seek. It is in that context that Gautama said what he said.

SEEKER: *Sadhguru, to make it more personal, how has it been in your life? And what was your experience in handling such people?*

SADHGURU: Even when Mirabai or Akka Mahadevi sought, they still saw Krishna or Shiva as a person, as a man. The embodiment was important for them. Now, coming to the present situation here at Isha, from day one, a lot of care has been taken to present this as a science, not as an embodied quality in a certain person – as a possible quality in every human being. The methods are very systematic and scientific. So in many ways, we are not giving room for emotion in the beginning of one's spiritual journey in Isha. For example, when people come to the Bhava Spandana program, there is a huge emotional upsurge within them – using emotion as energy to reach a peak experience. In that space, it is very much possible that they can be attached to the person who is offering this, but a living Master always sees to it that the emotion is eventually channeled towards the thirst for the Ultimate rather than the one who is offering it.

For example, in the higher programs like Samyama, all emotions are cut down and just pure awareness is brought about. With me, all methods are being handled very scientifically, not giving too much importance to emotion. As long as I am embodied, the emotional dimension of the path of Isha will be kept very low, but once I am beyond this body, we will definitely encourage people to seek through emotion. For many people it has always been so, that emotion is the quickest vehicle to deliver one to the other side. Bhakthi has always been the quickest way to realize. At the same time, if bhakthi is not tempered with the necessary awareness and alertness — if the necessary foundation of practices to create this energy and awareness in a person are not put in — it is very easy to hallucinate. Bhakthi can also be a tremendous tool to access dimensions which would otherwise take a very long time for a person to attain to. Doing yoga kriyas, activating your energies to reach certain states, will take elaborate practices and preparation, but with bhakthi, on just the mere strength of emotion one can move from one dimension to the other in a moment.

We definitely don't want to destroy the emotional aspect in a person, because emotion can be a tremendous tool if it is properly used with the right sense of awareness. My level of involvement with people, my physical presence with people, as the emotional dimension increases in them, I am just receding to a smaller group of people who understand what it is all about. With larger groups, with a larger mass of people, there is always a tendency to use emotion as a way to reach. It is a natural urge in a human being to use emotions to reach the highest, because somewhere they have known only emotion as the deepest experience within themselves. Their thought or their energy has never been so intense, but they have known intense emotions, which are bringing them to the deepest space within themselves. So there is always a natural tendency to use emotions as a way to get there. Where there is emotion, we always keep a certain physical distance where, in their understanding I am a little beyond their reach, so that they don't get too emotionally attached to the individual.

SEEKER: *I think I am getting somewhere, but the moment I sit in front of you, Sadhguru, I feel I am simply deceiving myself. I'm right back to square one.*

SADHGURU: It is good to know that you realize the deception is on. Once, while visiting a modern art museum, a lady turned to an attendant standing nearby. "This," she said,

"I suppose, is one of those hideous representations you call modern art?" "No, madam," replied the assistant, "that one is called the mirror." So Deepika, don't think. Start looking. Don't use your stupid mind. It's the same nonsense. You can't think any other way than you have been trained to up until now. Don't think. Just look. The whole idea is to drop your stupid thinking. All this high and low, right and wrong, is only in your mind. When you simply look at everything, everything seems to be okay. If you stand here and just look – the grass, the trees, the hill, the big mountain, the small mountain, are all just part of the scenery. Does the cloud look better than the mountain? Or does the sky look better than the mountain? Everything is just a part of one unit. If you stand here and think, "This is a mountain, that is a cloud," then everything seems separate. The moment you project like this, all your nonsense, lifetimes of karma confront you. If you are simply here, looking at everything as it is, you become a different kind of being altogether. You will mellow down to something totally different. Now, you said you're back to square one. Tell me, what is square one? You started projecting. The moment you project, you're back to square one, where else can you be? There is nowhere else you can be, because that is the only place your mind can be. When you are in your mind, you don't travel anywhere. You only hallucinate. The first stanza of the Guru Pooja is just that:

Apavithra Pavithrova,
Sarvavastan Gatopiva,
Yasmareth Poondari Kaksham,
Sabahyabhyantara Suchihe.

'Anyone – whether holy or unholy, whatsoever state he has reached – who meditates upon the lotus eyed lord, becomes sanctified both internally and externally.' This means you are not involved in your own self-emancipation. You're not trying to improve yourself. You're not trying to purify yourself. You just contemplate on what you hold as the highest right now.

Whatever is your highest, you just contemplate upon that. Your inner and outer purity will happen naturally. If you try to emancipate yourself, to improve yourself or to purify yourself, the more and more you do it, the more of a mess you will be. You simply contemplate on what you hold as the highest. Maybe God, maybe the Guru, or whatever you hold as the highest. Or just contemplate on the sky; it is enough. Simply be with it, don't project God or anything on it. It is simply smaran. Smaran means remembering or contemplating on the highest. Now, everything changes; inner and outer purity naturally happen. Why temples are not working for people is because they are projecting about God. If they shift from projecting about God to smaran, there will be a tremendous transformation in them. People cannot remember God. If you have to remember, you should have seen Him somewhere or in something. Maybe in a child's face, your wife's face, your lover's face, maybe in a flower, in the clouds, somewhere you could have seen at least a glimpse of God; only then can you remember them. Others can only think. Smaran means it has happened. In this smaran everything is purified. Now you don't have to work on how to correct this or that, how to make this okay. Don't worry about all that nonsense. You just remember the highest aspect of life that you have seen. Just go on remembering that. That's your God right now. Everything can change out of that.

SEEKER: *How do I use every opportunity, even every hardship that comes my way, as a stepping-stone for my growth, Sadhguru?*

SADHGURU: How to use everything and everybody for your growth? First of all, you grow in gratitude, not in benevolence. I don't want you to become benevolent. I want you to become full of gratitude. Benevolent people, after some time, become uncaring people. Gautama gives one sutra where he says, "It is hard to understand that by giving away your own food to somebody else and starving, you become stronger, not weaker." It is hard to understand this. How can you give away your food and be stronger? Giving away things which are plentiful to you is not it. Giving away what one needs most, one's very sustenance itself, is what leads you closer to the Divine. A monk is hungry most of the time. He only begs for his food once a day and eats. Today somebody may give a little. Another day he might get much less. Whatever he gets, the practice was that he begged only at one house per day and there would be times where he would get nothing. Over a period of time, they relaxed this 'one house' rule and extended it to three houses because people became more and more cautious with their giving. So monks are constantly hungry, and Gautama is saying that if you give away your own food, you become stronger, not weaker. This is hard to understand, but it's true. It is really true.

There is a very wonderful true-life story, which happened during World War II in the ill-famed German concentration camp, Auschwitz. Every day numbers were called out, and people were led to the extermination area, because the camp became full. Numbers were called at random, or the weak and the old who couldn't work were chosen. If your number was called today, you were going to your death. You were going to be shot and buried en masse. Now there was a man whose number was called and he was terrified. He didn't want to die. There was a Christian missionary, young and healthy, next to him, whose number was not called. Seeing the man's fear he said, "Don't fear. I will take your place." The man felt ashamed, but at the same time could not refuse the offer. He wanted to live. The missionary was shot. It so happened that the very next day the Germans lost the war and our man was freed. For many years he lived with this sense of defeat and shame and later narrated this incident in his life. He saw that there was simply no point, because his life itself was somebody else's charity. It was because of another man's greatness that he was living. Otherwise, he would have been shot that day – it was his number.

The missionary, who didn't know him – he was not a friend, a father, a son or anything – just to ease his fear and suffering, he took the call. Now that man will know life - that man who went, not the man who stayed back. Only the other will know what life is. Only he can experience something, a certain strength, a certain power within himself, that somebody who is trying to protect himself will never experience. This does not mean you have to go sacrifice yourself or some such nonsense. The man who went to his death was not thinking in terms of sacrifice. He just did it; that is all. It was not that he was waiting to sacrifice himself for somebody else. At that moment, he saw what was needed and just did it without a second thought. That's fantastic; but if you're trying to sacrifice yourself because you're going to get strength, or you're going to go to heaven, that is not it. That is really not it.

If you can run your life without the offer of heaven, you are on the path; but if by taking the offer and by cutting a deal you can still run in the right direction, go ahead and do it. If such a situation comes in your life, if such a level of maturity comes to you that you don't need any deals and you can still do it, it is good. If you have grown out of this limitation that something has to be offered for you to do something, where no increments are needed and you still are willing to work overtime, then you have a different kind of strength. The man who does only as much as is needed will only get that much. He will always remain a beggar in his life. He will never know what strength really is, he will never know what Divinity is; he will never know what Godliness is, simply because Divinity does everything purposelessly. Just see! Everything is done purposelessly.

SEEKER: *Sadhguru, I hope something fruitful comes out of this whole sadhana. I also fear I might not be living up to your expectations. At times I ask myself, "Why this sadhana and what is its nature?"*

SADHGURU: So there is a hope. There is a hope that something will happen, that is why you do all this. Where there is hope, there is always fear attached to it about whether it is going to happen or not. When you are hoping for something, when you're looking forward to something happening, the fear or the frustration is waiting just behind. Right now, there is a big hope in a lot of people's minds that something will happen out of this sadhana. Somebody thinks he will see Shiva, someone else thinks his Kundalini will burst into his Sahasrar. All these are hopes. Another way of looking at hope is as an expectation. If a person has no hope he is truly blessed, because that person has no fear of failure. Fear of missing out on something is totally not there in a person who doesn't hope. How can a person not hope? The whole sadhana is that you have to do everything intensely. Life has always been like this: if you have to do something, you either need to be enticed or be pushed forcefully. Life has always been such that you think in terms of what you will get if you do something, or maybe the circumstances in your life or the people around you push you to do things. If somebody or something pushes you, it is always misery. If hope is pushing you, there is an expectation of joy, an expectation of fulfillment, which keeps you going; but as long as hope is there, there is always the fear that it will be shattered. The whole nature of sadhana is such that it is a process of growth, but sadhana can also be a barrier. When Patanjali finished with karma kanda and moved into what is known as kaivalya pada – 'kaivalya' means ultimate liberation – he said that you could have a glimpse of the Divine in many ways. This could happen in so many ways, either by using drugs, incessantly chanting some mantra, practicing severe austerities, or by deep samadhis.

Now, to come to drugs...Patanjali was a scientist. He was not the usual religious kind of man. He was not afraid of anything. He looked at everything. A religious man would generally not talk about drugs. Patanjali said a drug is also a possibility to divinity, but the lowest possibility. What happens with a drug? If you take a chemical like LSD or marijuana, what happens is, the nature of the chemical is such that somewhere it breaks the mind. Ultimately your mind, body, everything is just chemistry. Whatever sadhana you're doing now also is just to change the chemistry of the system. Drugs are usually described as mind-blowing. You put this drug into your system and suddenly the mind cracks up. You're able to look at the existence through this crack, without the mind, just for a moment, and it is fantastic. Everything is just fantastic. Then you get hooked on the drug. The next time the dosage will increase. There is no growth. There is no transformation. It just becomes a trip. After a while, there are most probably no more trips. The drug becomes just a helpless dependence for you.

You can't deny that at least some people who are on the path of drugs have big experiences, but you will see that the man doesn't grow, there is no transformation in the way he is. He remains the same. In fact, he never attains to Grace, he sort of retards. He never attains to any kind of fragrance. He just has big experiences to talk about, otherwise he slowly retards. Only the dosage increases. The dosage becomes larger, but the man himself shrinks. Even before any recording of history happened, people have used drugs on the spiritual path. The puranas, mythological texts, say that Shiva himself was the first to use drugs. So it starts from there. Understand that Shiva can contain it, not you.

Once, Adi Shankara was traveling with his disciples. He stopped at a place and drank a lot of country liquor and then resumed walking. A few disciples thought that by seeing their Guru drinking alcohol, it meant they could also drink. At the very next place where the liquor was available, they drank and were wobbling behind Shankara because they were unable to hold it. When they entered the next village, Shankara walked directly toward the blacksmith's and took a vessel full of molten iron and took a drink from it. Now, the disciples who imitated him in drinking the country liquor got the point. Even here, there are a few people who are imitating me and doing things that are beyond their perception. They are only asking for trouble. So drugs are the lowest possibility, but still a possibility. On the yogic path drugs are a taboo, not because of moral correctness, but because of the limitation that they are. We have other ways to blow your mind.

The next one is the mantra. Just repetition of a mantra changes the chemistry of the system, because ultimately everything is just vibration and sound; the whole existence is just that. If you use the right sound properly, with the right amount of intensity and perseverance, it will change the chemistry of your system. You can use any word, and if used incessantly with the right sense of awareness, it can cease your mind and give you a glimpse of reality. Mantras are vibrations which can transform your energies and prepare you for a higher possibility. Without the necessary awareness, they can act like any drug, deadening the mind and causing hallucinatory states. Mantras are always good preparatory states. From time immemorial, Enlightened beings have known mantras to be a very limited process, because the danger of getting addicted to the mantra is always there. There is a beautiful story in Zen. In a certain village, there was a monastery. One morning the people heard the recitation of the sutras and they knew the Master had left. When there is no live Guru, mantras become an essential support. If the right kind of atmosphere, preparation, and awareness is created, a mantra can explode you into a different level of consciousness.

A large number of people are into mantras. They are too busy chanting Gita, Vedas, Upanishads or other spiritual scriptures... If you remove the mantras, if you take away the chanting, so many people will become unemployed. In terms of transformation, there is none. They can give you a glimpse of the Divine, definitely, if you go into it deep enough. Today, every ignorant fool is into mantras, not from any awareness of what it is, but just from their belief system. So much Gita chanting and Veda chanting is going on that, if taken away, it could cause a huge unemployment problem.

Now, for performing austerities on the spiritual path, what it means to perform an austerity is just this: learning to say no to everything that is natural within you. Now, if you're hungry, you say to yourself, "No, I need to do my pranayama." You want to eat something nice, you say, "No, I will eat only dry bread." You feel sleepy right now, you say, "No, I will meditate." This is denying, making an attempt to go beyond your likes and dislikes – going on saying 'no' to the mind. This is definitely far superior to drugs and mantras, because it will lead to a certain transformation within you. As you continue to say 'no' to your mind, the mind becomes more and more subdued, it becomes lesser and lesser. It loses its edge. The mind loses the control over you, as you go on saying 'no'. Whatever the mind says, you say no. That is the practice. When you become a total 'no, no' to your mind, you will become a big 'yes' to life. That is the level of austerities that can be done. This can lead to some amount of transformation, and may also lead a person to the highest level of consciousness if he really goes into it, if he is strong enough to go through it. Definitely a person can attain to a certain level of Grace, but a person who gets too much into this path of austerity tends to become dry. A sort of lifeless dryness enters him. He will not be the kind of person who can just look at the mountain and enjoy it. He will deny it, saying, "It is beautiful, so I will not look at it." He will attain to a certain dryness, but don't be deceived by this dryness. Dry souls are always very wise souls, but if it's not tempered with certain other qualities, this dryness tends to become a dead kind of dryness, which you will see in many yogis. They have become dry. They don't have compassion in them. They have denied passion consciously, but have lost even their compassion.

The next thing that Patanjali mentions is that you can also attain to divinity through samadhi. Now when he says samadhi, he is talking about penetration. Samadhi means to slice through whatever is the barrier. Samadhi is the state of equanimity. A mind that is neither like or dislike, craving or aversion, wanting or not wanting, love or hate. A mind that is beyond these dualities has a heightened level of penetration which can give you a steady vision of the beyond. Now these samadhis are of many different varieties. Whichever process you choose, whichever sadhana you choose, when it is based upon your hope that one day you will see something, it has its limitations. When your sadhana is based on hope and fear, you won't attain to anything. Anyway, you will miss it. This reminds me of a story about a stupid servant. One day the Master asked him to go and get flour and salt, and gave strict instructions that he should not mix these two things together. So he took a bag and reached the shop where they were selling flour and filled it. Then he asked for salt. He did not know where to put the salt, but remembered his Master telling him not to mix the two. So he flipped the bag and filled it up. By doing so, the flour fell out. So he carried the salt to his Master. The Master asked him, "Okay, this is salt. Where is the flour?" The servant just turned the bag over and the salt fell out. Hope and fear are just like this. When you start doing something with hope, whether it happens or not, both ways you are the loser. Do your sadhana joyfully, not with the hope of making it or the fear of not making it. Just do it joyfully.

SEEKER: *You have always been saying that sadhana should be done intensely and without hope; now Sadhguru, you're adding 'joyfully' to the list?*

SADHGURU: Yes, Somu, there are even many more on the list! Now, coming back to the sadhana, make it an offering. You're hoping and hoping and hoping that you'll get something. The fulfillment always falls short of what you hoped for. The dream and what happens in reality never match. The dream is always more colorful, more vivid. It is minus all problems, minus the price that you have to pay for it. You can just dream without paying the price, but when it gets actualized, it comes with a price. Now how to do the sadhana intensely but without hope, that is the question. How can a person work intensely, but without any hope? When can a person do something very intensely without any hope about it? Only through love can one do it, only when you really, really love. Generally, what you call as love is simply some kind of hope. When you truly love, whatever you do with your love is insufficient. Even if you offer yourself, it is insufficient. It is quite hopeless, but very intense.

If anything has to be done intensely, but at the same time without hope, love is the only way. There is no other way; it has to be very intense. There should be trust also and there can be no trust unless there is love. When you don't love somebody, there is no way you can trust him. You may make a calculation like, "I trust my business partner." It's not trust. It is just a calculation. It's an adjustment that you make; otherwise you cannot function. There can be no trust. Tomorrow, if you see him packing up your office and putting it in a suitcase, immediately you'll think all kinds of things. You will not say, "Okay, let him take it away, after all he's my partner." No, all kinds of suspicions will come. The same goes for your wife, your husband, your child, or even your mother; it doesn't matter who it is. If he or she does something very unusual, you will become suspicious immediately. One day, on a whim, and feeling like really doing something loving and nice for his wife, a man decided to surprise her with a dozen beautiful red roses. The minute he opened the door, his wife started screaming at him. "This is the worst day that I have ever had. The kids have been terrible, they got into a food fight, the washing machine broke and flooded the basement, I burnt the dinner, the dog chewed my best pair of shoes, and now you have the nerve to come home drunk!"

So you might have lived with them, you might have been born out of them, and you might have shared so much, you might have shared life with each other, but tomorrow morning if they do something unusual, doubts will come, isn't it? One minute you may be falling at their feet and you may be saying, "You are everything," but if something unusual is done, immediately there will be doubt. That is not trust. There can be no trust where there is no love. Now, this word, 'love' – today it is almost obscene the way it is being used. Saying, "I love you," is like saying, "Open sesame." It is the magic mantra that will open doors for you.

When I say 'trust', I am not asking for your loyalty. There has always been a tremendous amount of stress in the tradition on the Guru-shishya relationship; the Master-disciple relationship has been stressed upon in so many ways. This stress, when used by the wrong person, becomes a means of exploitation. This stress could be laid by a certain person because he wants to secure things for himself. This stress could be laid by a person out of his own insecurity, because he needs the support, he wants the loyalty. If somebody is asking for loyalty, there is nothing spiritual about that place or that person, because a spiritual person doesn't need loyalty. I am not in need of your loyalty. You can do what you want. Tomorrow, if you want, you can curse me. If that is how you feel, you can do it. I will not curse you back, because we have never looked forward to your loyalty. How long will you be with me? What are you going to do here? What are you going to do for us? We have never looked at it on those terms.

SEEKER: *Sadhguru, I seem to have failed in all my personal relationships. I don't know where I stand with God either. I love you very much and I hope I reach liberation and not end up getting caught up with you too.*

SADHGURU: Love is needed. I don't need it, but if you're not loving, you will not grow. To love, to simply be loving, takes a tremendous amount of maturity. You always need an object to love. So initially, what kind of object to choose? You choose that kind of object where the possibility of getting stuck is the least. If you love this pole, you may get stuck with the pole – at least the pole will not get stuck with you – but if you say, "I love my wife and children," it is not only that you may get stuck, the other person involved also can get stuck to you. Tomorrow, even if you want to disentangle yourself, the other person will not be willing to let you go. Now, you may love a stone, a pole, or anything. If you can really give yourself like that to even inanimate things, it is wonderful; but generally that is too far off for most people.

It happened in the Himalayan region, there was a band of sanyasis doing sadhana on the banks of the river Ganga. On a certain day, one of the sanyasis noticed a furry rug floating down the river. Immediately he thought, "With this rug I can be so much more comfortable during the winter." He, being an able swimmer, jumped into the river and went after the rug. He got his hands on the rug and then started screaming for help. The other sanyasis on the riverbank thought he was being carried away by the current and said, "You fool! Let go of the rug and come back." The sanyasi shouted back, "I can't let go of this, it is holding on to me. This is not a rug, it is a mountain bear." So you better know what you're going after. If you fall in love with a person who has enormous needs of his own, then you will see, you have got yourself into a bear trap. This is the reason why the Guru-shishya paramparya, or Master-disciple relationship, has been celebrated in this culture, as the Guru is one who has no needs of his own and thus there is no bear-trap.

People say, "I love God." I am telling you, you don't love God; you just hope that God will do something for you. It's not that this will not work, but it is too far away. You say you love God and if you can really love Him, it is beautiful; but it is not the truth. It is a hope, an expectation, and a fear. Instead of deceiving yourself like that, if you can simply say, "Okay, I am scared, that is why I am coming to you," it is better. Be straight. It doesn't matter if you don't know how to be spiritual. At least learn how to be straight. It is very, very important. If you don't learn how to be straight with yourself with every feeling, with every thought that occurs within you, you will become self-deceptive. Don't give it beautiful shapes or nice forms. If it is ugly, see it that way, bluntly see life the way it is; this is very, very important. Unless you see this, the question of growth is impossible. Just forget it. Don't think of growth, because that possibility will not arise until you are a hundred percent straight with yourself. There is no possibility of growth for that person who sees his fear as love, who sees his hope as love, or who sees his greed as love.

People have not come together simply because they are loving. They have come together only out of their greed. They need something. Maybe it's physical, psychological, emotional or economic; it doesn't matter which way. Something needs to be fulfilled, so two people come together. You think only if you stay together you can fulfill these things. So the drama continues. Suppose you stop fulfilling all the needs of the other person; then everything breaks down, doesn't it? So you have not come together because of love, but only out of greed. Let us be straight about this, otherwise you can forget about spirituality. You will never even taste love in your life if you're not straight. If you want to experience love, you should be sincere. Without being sincere there is no question of being loving. It's not possible. Sincerity doesn't mean sticking to some code that somebody else has fixed for you; that's not the point. Within yourself, you need to be sincere.

SEEKER: *Sadhguru, I sense a deep stillness in you, as if time itself has stopped, but there is an underlying current of great urgency also. What is this contradiction?*

SADHGURU: Yes, that's how it is. This urgency can be both a great boon and a curse. In this urgency people will grow very quickly. At the same time, because of this same urgency, many people will drop off. They can't take this urgency. They can't take the speed. It seems almost like sheer madness. Many people who have been extremely close to me have fallen off, simply because they just could not take this urgency. They read somewhere that a Master is never urgent, but they find this one is too urgent and think it's crazy.

SEEKER: *But Jaggi, do we have to work as if there is no tomorrow?*

SADHGURU: As if there is no tomorrow? Yes, there is no tomorrow. That's what you need to understand. You said it right; there is really no tomorrow. For a person who is walking the spiritual path, there is no tomorrow. Today is the day. When tomorrow comes, we will see about it. Whatever needs to be done, it has to be done now; this is the moment. That is why this sense of urgency. There is this old photo of Ramana with his disciples sitting around him that I would like to show you one day. You should see the disciples, the intensity with which they are sitting there, whereas Ramana is completely relaxed. His disciples, they are all sitting like tigers – urgent. If that urgency is not there, nothing can be done. Ramana seems to be relaxed, but his presence had such urgency that it set all his disciples on fire. Without that intensity and urgency, his presence could not have Enlightened crows and cows, too. That's something incredible.

SEEKER: *Sometimes I get lax and slip into a laid-back attitude and end up being disappointed with myself, others, and sometimes with you as well. How do I strike a balance and maintain this urgency?*

SADHGURU: You have different emotions and different kinds of tricks to get yourselves into some protective cocoon or to get somebody else to build that cocoon for you, don't you? Just don't continue the same tricks here. This has been going on all your life, you playing these tricks endlessly. Now, once you step onto a path like this, it's time to stop this. Only then there are no more expectations, no more disappointments with life. The way it is, is the way it is. At every step you get disappointed with people, because they are not fulfilling your expectations. They're not supporting your ego; that's all it is. Once a young couple got married and left for their honeymoon. When they got back the bride immediately called her mother. The mother asked, "So how was your honeymoon?" "Oh, Momma," she replied, "the honeymoon was so wonderful, so romantic." But suddenly, she burst into sobs. "Momma, as soon as we returned, David started using the most horrible language. Things I've never heard before. I mean all these awful four-letter words. You've got to come and take me home; please, Momma!" "Sarah, Sarah, get a hold of yourself. Calm down. Tell me, what could be so awful? What four letter words?" "Please don't make me tell you, Momma," said the daughter, "I'm just too embarrassed and they are too awful. Come get me, please." "Darling, baby, you must tell me what has upset you so. Tell your mother those horrible four-letter words." Still sobbing, the new bride said, "Oh Momma, words like DUST, IRON, WASH, and COOK."

This is one reason you're disappointed with life, because you have your own ideas of what life should be, and also how others should live. Otherwise, how can you get disappointed with somebody? Just because somebody is not the way you expect him to be or is refusing to be exploited by you, that's all. If you want to put it very bluntly, somebody refuses to be exploited by you or is not stupid enough to be exploited by you, so you get disappointed. Once you are on this path, we will make sure that you will not only be disappointed, but frustrated as well. We will make sure that you will reach the deepest level of frustration. You have to stop your tricks. These tricks are only towards you building protective structures around yourself. How long do you want to go on doing this? You demolish one structure and build another one. The old house is out of style so all that you do is build a new house. Isn't it so?

SEEKER: *I have left everything behind me and come here. Why shouldn't I look at this ashram as my home, Sadhguru?*

SADHGURU: This is not your home. It's just a transit point. Do you understand? You just stop here for a while, that's all. Don't make it a new home. Be unsettled. Don't try to settle down. Your whole problem is, you try to settle down with everything that is given to you and the moment it is unsettled, you're disturbed and frustrated. The whole purpose of walking this path is to remain unsettled, not to settle down into a new situation. If you pluck yourself from one settled situation and land up in another, what's the point? Moving into an ashram, moving onto a spiritual path, is not to settle down into another cocoon. It's about learning to live without cocoons. It is about being vulnerable, continuously, by choice. It is like you take off your armor and bare your chest, only by choice. Let whatever may happen, happen, not because somebody peels it off, but by your choice. When you refuse to peel it off, maybe somebody or something or even your Guru will try to slowly peel it off once in a while, but somebody peeling it off always hurts. It is better to peel it off yourself.

SEEKER: *Sadhguru, since I have been on this path, I have become sort of still and quiet. I question myself as to whether this is actually stillness or stagnation. What is the difference?*

SADHGURU: Stagnation is a certain disease. It is anti-life. Stillness is a tremendous amount of life not manifesting itself in any way. It is just there – potent. That is God. God is stillness, not stagnation. The mind is stagnation. Sadhana is a force which moves you from stagnation to stillness, but between stagnation and stillness, when they are together, there seems to be very little difference, because your logical mind only understands in terms of moving and not moving. Not moving is stagnation, but stillness is also not moving. This non-movement, you may call it stillness or stagnation because it's purely subjective. If you look at it objectively, stillness and stagnation are about the same. Physically they could be seen as about the same, but qualitatively they are worlds apart. A person who is meditating and a person who is sleeping may look about the same. One is sitting and sleeping, another is lying down and sleeping, that is all. For a person who doesn't know the difference, that's all he sees.

Have you seen with how much sarcasm people look at meditation – those so-called dynamic people of the world? They think it's for people who don't even know how to sleep. Externally there may be no difference between stillness and stagnation. Internally there is a tremendous difference. From stagnation to stillness, from ignorance to Enlightenment, that's the difference. In a way, it is the same thing; only the quality has to change, that's all. But how can you know the qualitative difference when you're drowned in ignorance? This is why the movement of sadhana has to go in full circle. Depending on how stupid a person is, that is how long the sadhana has to be. Physically and mentally, push yourself to the limit and see what is there. If you stop for every little discomfort, you will never know what it is. Just push yourself to the limit. Physically, mentally, emotionally, in every way push yourself to the last point. Either you must go mad or you must get Enlightened, that's all there is; and we will not allow you to go mad, don't worry.

SEEKER: *But for how long, Sadhguru, how long? The path seems so long and gets so difficult, and it doesn't make things easy for me, especially when I see someone freaking out with joy, for no reason, as soon as they close their eyes for meditation or whenever they are around you.*

SADHGURU: Your problem is like this: there was this family who had two boys who were twins, and the only thing they had in common was their looks. If one felt it was too hot, the other felt it was too cold. If one said he liked the cake, the other said he hated it. They were opposites in every way. One was an eternal optimist, and the other a doom and gloom pessimist. Just to see what would happen, on the twins' birthday, the father loaded the pessimist brother's room with every imaginable gift – toys and games, and for the boy who always sees the brighter side of life, with horse manure. That night, the father went to check on the doom guy's room and found him sitting amidst his new gifts sobbing away bitterly. "Why," the father said in anguish, "after all this?" The boy replied, "Because my friends are going to be jealous, I will have to read all these instructions before I can do anything with this stuff, I will constantly need batteries, and my toys will eventually be stolen or broken." Passing by the optimist twin's room, the father found him dancing for joy on the pile of manure. "What are you so happy about?" the father asked. The boy replied, "There's got to be a pony in here somewhere!"

What to do with someone like you who will throw away everything I give you? Whatever this existence gives you, you crib and bitch about it. What to do with people like you? Marilynn and Laurie, are you listening? If you drive yourself in different directions, what to do? A little discomfort and you give up. Sometimes when you sit there with your eyes closed, the mind goes here and there. It becomes uncomfortable, and you let yourself fall back into your old nonsense. That is not the way. Get into the sadhana full force, go like crazy, then let us see what's going on. Whether you are going to flip this way or that, let's see. That's all it takes. When Gautama went and sat under the bodhi tree, he decided, "Until I get Enlightened, I won't get up from this place. Either I will die here or I will get Enlightened." That's all. The man sat and, within a moment, he was Enlightened. That is all it takes. He didn't have to sit for twenty-five years to do it. When a man has come to that kind of sankalpa that, "This is it. This is the only thing that matters right now." How long will it take? How long can it take to see what is already here? Not even a wink of an eye. Then why is it taking so long? It is simply because it's not intense enough.

That is why I keep asking you, "What is your priority? What is it? You have to increase it." Every time I ask that question, you have to push it up one more notch. To the point of discomfort you have pushed, but don't let up; push it up one more point and yet another point. It has to be pushed to the ultimate, to the optimum. Only then can the mind dissolve by itself. You don't have to do any other sadhana. This is the only sadhana needed. All other activity in the form of sadhana is just to get this one thing done. Make it in such a way that your sankalpa is unshakeable.

Why someone is asked to go and live in the Himalayas for twelve years is not because if they live in the Himalayas the rocks could give them Enlightenment. It is because he is even willing to waste his life for twelve years, with all kinds of hardship, just to seek Truth. If that kind of sankalpa has come, that man is very close. In a way, it is like literally wasting your life. When the whole world is eating well, drinking well and enjoying themselves, you are sitting there in the cold and chanting, "Shiva, Shiva, Shiva," knowing nothing might happen. If you live there for long enough, you may come to know. Shiva probably will not come and bail you out. When you're hungry, you're plain hungry. When you're cold, you're just cold. You know it may turn out to be hopeless being there. In spite of that you stay, because the most important thing in your life is something else. When that sankalpa comes, it does not take twelve years. In one moment, it can happen. Nobody needs to wait for twelve years. This can be the moment. It is because you don't use this moment that you have to wait for the next one. This is always the moment. Are you going to tighten it up, or every time discomfort comes, will you think, "Oh, this is not for me." It is definitely not for you if this is so. I am not saying the path is difficult; it's just that you make it difficult. The path is not difficult. It is very simple. If you are simple, it's very simple. If you are all wound up, the path is very, very winding. That's all it is.

This moment, when you're very simple and at ease, life is very simple, isn't it? When you're wound up, just see how complicated it is. Don't become all wound up. There is enough nerve-racking past in you, which is already in knots. Don't create new knots now. The old knots are already causing a lot of pain, causing a deep pit inside, which is eating you up in many ways. Some of you have become aware of this, and some are yet to become aware of it, but it is there in every human being. There is one empty pit within you which just eats you from inside. That is enough, isn't it? Don't create more now. What you have created in the past is enough. Many lifetimes of opportunities have been wasted, but this one need not go to waste too. Those of you who feel the urgency, please go on unrelentingly. To those of you who think, "Anyway, another ten thousand years are there, no problem," I am saying, "Why only ten thousand? There is a whole eternity ahead of you. There is no hurry. After all, what is wrong with life?" When I say it, it may look like a curse, but it is not a curse. I am saying, in this situation, when the energies are high like this, if you don't make use of this situation and me, if you don't see this, well then…

SEEKER: *Master, how does a seeker use you best on the spiritual path to liberation?*

SADHGURU: How to put the Guru to the best use? See, if I give you a little toy, say a toy car – you know how to make it work, you know how to use it. Even if I give you a regular car, you know how to drive it and enjoy that also, but if I give you a spaceship, you would not know the head or tail of it, isn't it so? Probably, even if I give you an airplane – when you see those hundreds of knobs and meters – you won't know what to do with it. If I give you a spaceship, definitely you won't know what to do with it. So a Guru is a vehicle who wants to take you beyond your present dimension of existence. Let us call the Guru a spaceship. You wouldn't know how to use it. You just wouldn't know how to handle a spaceship. A car, maybe you could drive around, but a vehicle which could take you to other dimensions, you don't know how to handle it. So don't try to use it, you just learn to be with it.

If you just learn to stay within the space of the spaceship, wherever it goes, it takes you there, isn't it? So just learn to sit in his space, don't try to use him. Trying to use him would be a big mistake. That is a great mistake that millions of seekers have always made for ages, trying to use the Guru. Like I was telling you the other day, that boy, that young man that I met on the way back from Kedar, was very simple. He had been with his Guru for eight years. The Guru did not give him any sadhana. "I am just serving him and waiting. When he gives sadhana, I will do it. Right now I am just there. Whatever he says, I do. I cook, clean, sweep and just wait," said the man. He will definitely know it; there is no question about it. A man who can just be this way is an intelligent man, not an idiot. If you had seen those other four people with him, they were very bright, intelligent people. They were not goat-like people, but willing to simply wait for eight years, without even an initiation into a simple process. Just learn to sit in the spaceship without getting off at every excuse. You might not go anywhere; just learn to be in his space. What has to happen will happen.

SEEKER: *Sadhguru, what is your day-to-day awareness in regard to your disciples? Are you aware of our every thought and emotion, or only general situations? Can we call upon you in times of need or distress?*

SADHGURU: If I say what I should say now, you will start doing freaky things to seek attention. Your question is, "Are you really there for us or not?" You're just putting it in a very polite way. Fundamentally you're asking, "Are you really there for us or not?"

SEEKER: *Yes, fundamentally that is it, but you have said prayers can lead to hallucinations, so I'm wondering if I can call on you in prayer during times of distress.*

SADHGURU: I never said that being prayerful leads to hallucinations. What I would have said is about prayer as it is being done today. If you're really prayerful, the basic condition is to have no expectations, isn't it? If you request something, then you will expect it. If you pray, how can you expect? You are just praying, but today prayer has just become a wish list. It has taken on a completely different meaning; otherwise, being prayerful is a wonderful way to be, because it's a quality, like meditation. Prayerfulness is a certain quality in which you make something or somebody else in your life so big, and make yourself very small. Not yet into nothing, not into Shoonya, but at least you have made yourself small. Now, if you're so small, how can you tell that which is so big what to do? This doesn't make sense, isn't it? In that sense, prayer is meaningless, senseless; but if you're able to sit here and see something as enormous, and yourself as small, it's a wonderful device. That is the reason why we took you to the Himalayas, so that you would feel like an ant. Suddenly, you look at the Himalayas and you feel like a little ant crawling up there. It doesn't mean anything, whoever the hell you are.

About calling me...if you are in spiritual distress you don't even have to call, I am always there. Now, am I aware of your problems, your this and that, and your day-to-day whatever? If I wish to be I am, but not otherwise. Most of the time, I am not, because your nonsense doesn't mean anything and is of no value. Today you think something, tomorrow you think something else; it just does not mean anything. It is like I set two lines, an upper limit and a lower limit for everyone. Within these two lines, whatever games they play, I don't bother them. If they go below them, yes, and if they go above them, immediately yes. If they are playing within that playing field, it's okay, it is up to them. I don't want to meddle with them and the little things that they do. If they sink below that, immediately there will be help. If people rise above that also, immediately there will be help. If they are playing around in the middle, I just let them handle it. They have been given brains, isn't it? The Creator gave you brains and you have got to use them. Going low can take you below the physical, which can be very damaging; also for people who go above the physical there will be help. Within the physical, just play the game as you know it. There is no need for me to look at it.

SEEKER: *When you say, "go below the physical", what exactly do you mean, Sadhguru?*

SADHGURU: These things can lead to a lot of fear and confusion among people – these types of questions. Anyway, now you asked for it! Going below the physical could mean that physically you are ebbing; the body's life is coming to an end. It is not always so; most of the time it's not so. Suddenly, today I call someone that I have not spoken with for ten years. Neither that person has come into contact with me, nor have I come into contact with him in all these years. I just call and chat with him for a few minutes. This man might die in the next three or four days. It is not that I am causing it; death is anyway coming. He has forgotten what is alive within him, so we are just making a call to remind him. Just one little reminder – it need not necessarily always be through a telephone. It can also be through any other device. With some people I use a telephone, but every time I call, don't think you have only three or four days left! (Laughs). I am not Yama or something. For those of you who don't know, Yama is the god of death in India. I'm not Yama.

As for going above the physical, suppose they are going to cross certain limits, I may get in touch with them, just to remind them to be stable. Usually, I will not talk about it at all. Most of the time I never do, because just talking about it will spoil the whole thing. Their mind will become overactive and it just takes them off in a completely different direction. Going low could also involve negative energy influences. For example, say you got angry or you became sad. Usually, you will come out of it. You must make an enormous effort to stay there, otherwise nobody can stay there. If they are going below the line, they will be reached because they could derail themselves from the track of prarabdha karma. If they go above the upper line, there also they will be reached, either to guide them or to slow them down, because in that state they may not be able to retain their body. Between the two parallels, it is their business to handle that part of their life. If I take up all that, there is no end to it.

There are some people who might be going totally off the track, forgetting the reason why they are here. I call them and very gently coax them to come back around, but whatever I say, they might not budge. They just continue to go on with their nonsense. Then I have to tell them not only about their actions, but also about what's going on in their mind. So I just ask them, "Yesterday at ten o'clock, what were you doing?" They come up with something and then I say, "This is what you were thinking and this is what you were up to at ten o'clock in the morning." When they realize there is nothing they can hide from me, they break up. Until then, they will not come around. It's not that yesterday I was watching them. It is all there, written to be seen when they sit in front of me. So this is not normally done at all, but only rarely, if somebody is going to extremes. Otherwise, I don't want to look into everybody's nonsense. There is nothing much worthwhile in looking into people's minds. What is in there? Nothing.

SEEKER: *Sadhguru, when you get into the deepest crevices of my mind and everything that I call 'myself', I feel cornered, like my privacy is always being invaded. This weighs heavily upon me.*

SADHGURU: The whole thing is just that everybody is looking for a loophole. When they don't find a loophole, either they have to see the point or reject the whole thing; that is all there is. Why is it weighing heavily upon you? This is simply because there is no loophole for you to escape. Who can be cornered? When can you corner a man? Physically, when can a man be cornered? Suppose this place is wide open, can you corner him? When can you corner him? Only when there is some boundary, when the man is closed in; only then can you corner him. When the man is not so, how can you corner him? You're feeling cornered because you're closed. There is a boundary beyond which you don't allow anybody. So now, when your Guru enters there out of his responsibility and tries to push you where you need to go, you feel cornered. You have set a boundary beyond which you don't allow anybody to enter. My whole effort is to break that boundary. Maybe you give this a good name such as privacy, or space, or whatever, but do see that it is a boundary and a corner. So what's your privacy? When you use a word, you must know why you're using it or at least the meaning of it. What is your privacy, tell me. What is private for you? Anything that you hold as personal and are not willing to talk about.

SEEKER: *At times my feelings get trampled and I just want to be left alone and seek some privacy.*

SADHGURU: Being by yourself is different; being alone is different. When are you alone? When can you be really alone? Within yourself, you can only be lonely. When can a man be really alone? Only when everything that is around him becomes a part of him and when nothing else exists. That is ultimate Realization or aloneness. The aloneness you are talking about is just loneliness, just separation, just exclusion. Separation is not aloneness. When everything has merged within you, you are alone, because nothing else exists. It is when you finally realize, "I am alone here because there is nobody else but me." Only then there is aloneness.

So what is this privacy you're talking about? Whenever you feel uncomfortable, you want to be left alone. Why is this so? I don't want any philosophies; just come to the specifics. You have some, 'Sometimes I would like to be left alone' moments. Why? Now you say that your feelings are being trampled; why are you feeling that way? There is nothing that happens without a reason. Right now you feel like being left alone from everything and everybody. Let us look at this. Nobody is intruding. They don't even know how to intrude. The moment you set up a barrier, they just leave you alone and go, isn't it? Only one person is intruding into everything. Even when you set up your barrier, he will find a way in, and if you set another barrier, he will find yet another way in. Every time you set up a barrier, if your Guru had left you like that, would you be here today? I didn't give you a choice, did I? (Laughs).

Many of you are still in that state where, if you were simply told something, even if it's the best thing for you, you would get a little irritated because you still have your own personality, your own will, your own privacy and whatnot. So when I talk to you, I talk as if I am asking, but actually I am really telling you. Even if somebody tells you what is best for you, you will resist because they are telling you, so I make it appear as if I am asking. All this is unnecessary. If your surrendering is total, this is unnecessary. For a rare few, I just say, "You have no choice, you come." I never ask them, "What will you do? Will you give up your job? Will you do this?" No. For some people, I just tell them, "You leave everything and come." They never felt there was any choice; they felt they have chosen. They were only told because if given a choice, they might have done something irrelevant with their life. When there is a need for privacy, there is offense. If somebody oversteps that privacy, you will be offended. So the need for privacy means a possibility of being offended. If there is no need for privacy, then there is no possibility of getting offended, because then anything can be said or done. The only thing is, you need trust to hand yourself over so completely.

SEEKER: *Sadhguru, why aren't I one of the chosen few you tell what to do with their life?*

SADHGURU: In so many ways I have indicated to you what is best and what could be done, but after a few days you have come back and said, "This is not for me." What to do with people like you? For most people, I don't interfere beyond a point, and don't think this is because of your individuality. Forget about this 'you'. There is no 'you' right now. As long as your being is not established, there is no 'you'. There is only a mess inside which is your mind, feelings and emotions. All the nonsense that you carry, don't consider all of that as 'you'.

That's where the whole problem is: whatever you think or feel, this is not 'you', this is only a mess that you have gathered from outside. Now when I am talking to you, I know I am not talking to you as a being. There are moments when you are with me as a being and at that time there is absolutely no problem. In those moments, nothing needs to be said, everything happens the way it has to happen, but when you come with your mess, you have to be talked to, because it is a tangle. This tangle has to be handled carefully, very carefully. If I make one wrong move, I know this tangle will run away. The being may crave, but the tangle has its own pride, the tangle has its own problems and it will run away. The being inside may be dying to be here, but the tangle – you know, the ego – has its own problems and it will run away; isn't it so? The inner being may have been crying for lifetimes, crying to just be here. This is so with most of you here around me, but sometimes the mind and the ego together will do something, which will take you away. So when we handle your mind, your feelings and your emotions, we have to tread carefully and handle it the right way. There have been moments when there is no more 'your being' and 'my being'. In those moments, there is no problem, because my being and your being are not different anyway. When you exist on that level of experience, there is no problem. This is what can be referred to as universality. In those moments anything can be done and there is no question of privacy.

SEEKER: *But Jaggi, everyone does need some amount of privacy.*
SADHGURU: Yes, everybody needs some physical privacy, but when we look at universality, what does it mean to you? Universality means there is no 'everything' and 'everybody'. There is only 'you', or another way to look at it is, this 'you' is not there; these are the two ways of looking at it. Now the path of responsibility is: there is only you. The path of surrender is that 'you' are not there. If only 'you' are there, the whole existence is 'you', so there is no question of privacy. If 'you' are not there, again the question of privacy does not arise. Only if you exist, if the physical body exists, it needs some privacy; that is different. If you as a person need privacy, that is very different, but even in the physical sense, there is a distorted sense of privacy about your body. You can show so much of your body, but a little more than that and it

becomes a problem. This is not privacy. You have instilled these boundaries which say, "This much is public, the rest is private." To protect this boundary, you will give up your life, isn't it? There are moments when people have given up their lives, just to protect this sense of privacy.

For example, when you fall in love with somebody, you no longer feel a need for privacy. You're willing to shed even your clothes. Privacy is no longer needed because you're in love, because somewhere there is a feeling of oneness. Now, suppose in this moment you are able to see your universality; will you need privacy from the world? Again, this is just an example. A yogi who walks naked on the street, he has no problem. I am clothed not because I need privacy, but because you will not be able to digest it, because you need privacy. Wearing clothes or not wearing clothes is not about me; it is just that the situation requires it. Even the type of clothes worn is whatever the situation demands, isn't it so? There is no real choice of wearing them or not. Even to look at me, your sense of privacy will disturb you. The moment love enters into your life, the need for privacy disappears. Only because love is lacking, privacy has become a big issue in your life. In moments of love, the need for privacy is not there. In fact, privacy is a barrier and you destroy everything that is precious in the name of privacy. The need for privacy is the need for separation. It is a boundary that you have put there. You call it privacy, you call it your space, whatever nonsense you want; it is a boundary. It is as clear as that.

SEEKER: *Sadhguru, I am unable to contain this play of energies which are happening within me. At what point in this do you come in as the Guru?*

SADHGURU: If you want to seek that which is eternal, that which is all pervading, that which is all inclusive, the normal energy that you have is not sufficient. If you want to seek God, the energy that you have just to walk around, to do something, to earn some money, is not sufficient. You need a lot more. Even if you're giving yourself one hundred percent, that kind of energy is simply not sufficient. That's why all the sadhana is done, to raise one's energy. When you are seeking the unlimited, however much energy you have seems to be insufficient. Now, by channeling all this energy towards one goal, towards the one and only goal in life, there is some possibility that you may progress towards that goal. Whether you attain the goal immediately or not is not the point; you begin to progress. The goal becomes approachable. One fundamental requirement for anybody who wishes to grow on the spiritual path is to have an un-deviated flow of energy towards one and only one goal in life: to attain to the highest and not settle for anything less than that.

If there is a person who is capable of channeling himself without any break he is blessed, but rarely do people come like that. Most people lead their lives only in jerks; a few moments of running, then they stop, or maybe even take a few steps backwards, then start running again, or maybe even run backwards. Like this, life is wasted for most people. There are a rare few, once they get started, there is no stopping for them; they just go on. For those others who are 'start-and-stop' people, they need somebody to keep them moving all the time. That 'somebody's' job is to use the carrot and stick with some equanimity as the need arises. Sometimes carrots don't work, then we use the stick. Sometimes sticks don't work, then the carrot. It's like that. I think that Ramakrishna had described a Guru in his own way. He described three types of Gurus or religious teachers who were like three different classes of doctors. There is one type of medical man who, when called upon, looks at the patient, feels his pulse, then prescribes the necessary medicine and asks him to take it. If he declines to do so, the doctor goes away without troubling himself further with the matter. This is the lowest class of doctor. In the same way, there are some religious teachers who don't care much whether their teachings are valued and acted upon or not. Doctors of the second type not only ask the patients to take their medicine, but they go a little further. They expostulate with them if they show any reluctance in taking the medicine. In the same way, the Christian religious teachers, who leave no stone unturned in order to make other people walk the way of righteousness and Truth by means of gentle persuasion, can be said to belong to this class.

The third and the highest kind of doctors would proceed to use force with the patients in case their explanations fail. Such an advisor would go to the extent of putting his knee on the chest of the patient and forcing the medicine down his throat. Similarly, there are some religious teachers who would use force on their disciples, if necessary, with a view of making them walk in the way of the Lord. These belong to the highest class. Now, in every aspect of life – it's not only in terms of doctors and spiritual teachers – in every aspect of life, these three types of people are there. When Ramakrishna considers the last one to be the highest, he takes the risk of becoming unpopular. He takes the risk of being labeled cruel or being considered not at all spiritual.

Let us see why these kinds of teachers exist or why they are needed. It's because by your own nature you might not reach. Look at the frog: wherever he sees a mosquito, there he goes. Maybe he started off in this direction, going after something, but if he sees a mosquito on his side, he goes to that side, another one on the other side, he goes to it. If you go like this, you will not get anywhere. At the most you will fill your belly, that's all. If filling the belly is the only purpose of life, then wherever there is food, there you will go sniffing. Have you seen the dogs, how they go sniffing? Wherever there is food, wherever there is pleasure, there they go. Once you're on the spiritual path, once you have seen the goal of your life, this sniffing around should stop because there are many things that smell good along the way. Wherever something smells good, if you turn in that direction, you are not going to get anywhere in this world or the next. Even the man who wants to simply fulfill his material requirements works with undivided interest in what he is doing, isn't it? Even a man who wants to make money, a man who pursues his pleasure, even he goes with a hundred percent involvement towards what he wants. If that is so, when you're seeking the highest, you know how you should be. Whatever I say will fall short of how you should be. So many things may come up on the way, but you should be strong enough, brave enough, and adamant enough to go after what you want, otherwise things will not happen.

SEEKER: *So Sadhguru, what exactly should I do to make this happen for me?*

SADHGURU: Spirituality is not for pussycats, do you understand? You can't do anything else in your life, but think you can be spiritual; this is not so. If you can take up and do anything in this world, then there is a possibility that you may be fit for spirituality, not otherwise. If you have the strength and the courage to just take up anything in the world and do it well, then maybe you can be spiritual. This is not for people who can't do anything else. Right now, this is the impression that the whole country has, probably the whole world has; that useless, good-for-nothing people are spiritual people, because the so-called spiritual people have become like that. People who are incapable of doing anything or people who can't bear the ups and downs of life, all they have to do is to wear the ochre clothes and sit in front of the temple; their life is made. That's not spirituality; that's just begging in uniform. If you have to conquer your consciousness, if you have to reach the peak of your consciousness, a beggar can never reach there.

There are two kinds of beggars. Gautama, the Buddha, and

people of that order are the highest kind of beggars. All others are plain beggars. I would say the beggar on the street and the king sitting on the throne are both beggars. They are continuously asking for something from the outside. The beggar on the street might be asking for money, food or shelter. The king might be asking for happiness, or conquering another kingdom or some such nonsense. Do you see, everybody is begging for something? Gautama begged only for his food, for the rest he was self-sufficient. All others, the only thing they don't beg for is food. It is for everything else that they beg. Their whole life is begging. Only food they earn, but a spiritual person has earned everything else from within, only for food he begs. Whichever way you think is better, be that way. Whichever way you think is a more powerful way to live, live that way.

To be spiritual means to be an emperor within yourself. This is the only way to be. Is there any other way to be? Consciously, would anybody choose to be anything where he has to seek something from someone or something else? Maybe out of his helplessness he seeks, but consciously would anybody choose to do this? Wouldn't every human being want to be that way, where he is hundred percent within himself? It doesn't mean you have to become totally self-sufficient. Always there is interdependence, but within yourself everything is there; you don't have to seek outside. Even somebody's company is not needed for you. If another person needs it, you will give it, but by yourself, you don't need anybody's company. This means you're no more a beggar within. Only for external things, maybe you will have to go to the world outside. This is ultimate freedom.

Once it is like this, this person leads a different way of life. Once there is no hankering, once there is no need within him, only then he knows what love is; only then he knows what joy is; only then he knows what it means to really share. People who have missed this joy of sharing only know exchange.

People generally know only the barter system. "You give me this; I will give you that!" This is not sharing. Most relationships are not about sharing; they are only about bartering – your money, your body, your emotions. Now, sharing is, "You don't have to give me anything because I don't need anything from you, but anyway, I will share this with you." Setting up a whole life of barter may be convenient, but it is the way of the weak. This weakness is the first thing that has to go if you want to meet Shiva. If you want to meet Him, you had better be on His terms. He is not going to come and meet a mere beggar. You either need to learn to meet them on their terms or dissolve; these are the only two ways. Gnana and bhakthi mean just this. Bhakthi means you make yourself a zero, then you meet Him. Gnana means you meet Him on His terms; you become infinite. Otherwise, there is no chance of a meeting.

Love, or bhakthi, looks like a much easier path. It is, but there are more pitfalls on that path than in gnana. With gnana you know where you are going, you know if you fall. In bhakthi, you don't know. Even if you have fallen into a pit you will not know; that is the way it is. Even if you're trapped by your own illusions, you will not know. In gnana, it is not like this. Every step that you take, you know. Every step of growth, you know; every step backwards, you also know. I can't say it is a hard path, but it's the path of the courageous, not of the weaklings. The weaklings can never make it, but everybody has the possibility of making it. Everybody has the capacity to do it if they rise above their limitations. It is just about whether they are willing to do it or not, that is all.

The way we think is the way we become. Whatever you hold as the highest, naturally all your energies get drawn towards that. You know there are different kinds of people, different associations in society. In a group of drunkards, the highest thing is to be able to drink a certain amount. They are always talking about who can drink more. So naturally their whole life is about that. Pleasure seekers are thinking who can have more pleasure. So naturally their whole life is about that. People who are after money are thinking about more money, so naturally their energies are towards that. Similarly, a person who wants to walk the spiritual path has to make it that way in his mind, that this is the highest, that, "This is the first and the last thing that I want in my life." So naturally all his energies are oriented towards it. Only then the moment-to-moment struggle is gone and you don't have to struggle to correct yourself.

SEEKER: *Sadhguru, I know what you're saying, but at times I have this inner struggle that I am still missing out on many things in life by walking this path. How can I cope with this?*

SADHGURU: When this one thing is not fixed within you, then every moment is a struggle, because every moment has a doubt; "What shall I do? Maybe I am missing out, maybe I am missing life, maybe this or that may not happen to me," all kinds of things. There are so many things that we don't know about, that other people may be doing. They may be eating, enjoying and doing many other things. Nathalie, have you ever eaten cockroach pickle? No, isn't it? You missed it? But for someone who has eaten it a few times and it is not available anymore, only he misses it. It is just the way we make it in our mind. Nobody is missing anything. It is just that you make it that way within yourself. "Oh I did not eat this. I didn't go snow skiing or disco dancing!" This is simply because you have made these things important in your mind. If you fix the goal of your life, you will not miss anything. All these vasanas are there within everybody. The past karmas have influences over you, they push you this way and that way. All your passions, all your desires, you can't fight with them. Don't ever try to fight with your passions and desires. Fighting with them is like fighting the demon, Mahishasura. If one drop of his blood falls, a thousand Mahishasuras will rise up. Your desires and passions are just like that. If you try and fight with them, if you chop them, they will spill blood, and with every drop, a hundred or a thousand will come up. There is no point fighting them. Just educate your passions, educate your desires to flow in the right direction, that is all. You can never fight them. Fighting them will be futile; it will be a waste of life.

SEEKER: *Then what can we do with our desires?*

SADHGURU: Just desire the highest in life. All your passions, direct them to the highest. Even if you get angry, direct it only toward Shiva. Even with your passion, that's the way to do it. Every bit of energy that you have, you expend it by making it into desire, passion, fear, anger, and many other things. Maybe these emotions are not in your hands for now, but channeling them in one direction is in your hands. Maybe when you are angry you cannot be loving; you can't suddenly turn your anger into love, but the anger itself can be directed. Anger is tremendous energy, isn't it? Lust is tremendous energy also. Direct it in the right way; that is all. Every ounce of energy that you have, every passion, emotion, thought, if they are focused in one direction, the results can be very, very quick. Things will happen. Once you know there is something higher and you want to be there, there should be no other question about it. Only people around you should have questions about it, not you. There should be simply no questions about it.

Now for you, again and again, this spirituality, this Enlightenment, this God-Realization looks so far away. It appears to be close this moment, the next moment it appears to be light years away. Then a certain complacency will come. They have always told you, "A bird in hand is worth two in the bush." What is there now is better than something somewhere else. What you need to understand is, it is not somewhere; it is all here and now. Only because 'you' are not, it looks like that for you. Shiva is not somewhere, he is here and now. It is you who is not. That is the only problem. It is not difficult, but definitely it's not easy. It is extremely simple. Moving from here, from wherever you are right now, to the infinite is very simple, because it is right here. Do know, simple need not necessarily be easy. It is subtle and delicate. Unless you put your whole life energy into it, it will not open up.

With half-hearted appeals, God never comes. With half-hearted appeals, Realization never happens. It has to be everything, only then it can happen in one moment. It need not take twelve years. Probably a fool takes twelve years to become intense enough; that is different. If you make yourself intense enough, it is just one moment. After that, life is just blessed. You simply live on, whichever way you want, whatever way you choose; but without creating that one moment, going on doing all kinds of nonsense, not finding yourself, if you say, "I have found the world," what is the use? You are not even present doing all of those things, but you think you have found the world. What is the use?

SEEKER: *Sadhguru, this initiation into sanyas that is happening today, why is this? What does it signify?*

SADHGURU: A time has come when we need to establish this order. Whatever we have done all these years is not that we have not already laid the foundation for this; we have, long ago. Yet, still we kept a certain choice open depending upon so many factors that may happen. Now, this order of bhramhacharya has progressed to a certain level of maturity. Maybe it is yet to bear lots of fruit, but it has definitely reached a certain level of maturity. Somebody who does not recognize the mango tree without fruit may think it is a wild tree, maybe a barren tree. Only someone who recognizes the mango tree knows that with a little nourishment, sweetness will ripen.

This is a huge step in establishing Isha as a permanent

spiritual process for the world. This is a huge step of gratitude towards my Guru. For a man like Him, though a few individuals attained around Him, and of course there is the Dhyanalinga, but someone like Him not leaving a living order of spiritual process behind Him has always been something that has bothered me. He never stayed in one place, so He did not leave any kind of spiritual order behind Him. Even though He was a man whose experience, understanding and wisdom was far beyond what most people can dream of, He did not leave any kind of spiritual order. Once the Dhyanalinga consecration was complete and after life started flowing again through my once-almost-finished-body, I've been thinking that we should set up a truly powerful spiritual order which would befit Him and which should go on with His Grace.

He Himself is a man who lived without a name. He never had a name in His life. Because He remained in samadhi for a long period of time somewhere close to the town of Palani, people just called Him Palani Swami. But He never had a name. Here, all our bhramhacharis and sanyasis have such wonderful names. These names come from the traditions where truly proud and shining, brilliant spiritual orders have come from. These people lived in such a way that gods would be envious of them. They lived so powerfully, with such dignity. We want this order of sanyasis in Isha to definitely stand up and live that way.

Especially in today's world, where many spiritual orders have fallen into bad times, I think it is an enormous responsibility. It is an enormous responsibility and also a tremendous privilege that such a responsibility has been bestowed upon us. See, all these people here are not perfect human beings... Oh, I'm making it so gloomy and serious. Let me tell you a story.

Once, there was a spiritual Master who had a servant to help him with his daily chores. This servant used to carry two pots of water hung on a bamboo on his shoulders everyday to the Master's house. He would go up and down many times. When he was carrying this water, one of the pots that he was using was slightly cracked and it was always leaking water. The other pot, which was perfect, was always mocking the cracked pot – there are many crackpots here (laughs) – so the perfect pot was mocking everyday, "See how I'm serving the Master? See how you are; you're cracked. Half the water is gone by the time you reach the house."

One day, after a long period of seclusion, the Master came out into the garden and walked along the pathway. He noticed, only on one side of the pathway, all along, there were lots of flowers in bloom. The Master looked at these wonderful flowers and said, "Whoever is the cause of making these flowers bloom on my pathway, let him attain," He blessed. And the cracked pot attained! So there is hope for the cracked ones also. Now, don't make it your right to be cracked!

Why this sanyas, what it means is... if we can un-burn the pots, cracked or otherwise, into the basic material of clay, we can make so many things out of it. Instead of making a pot, we can make a deity out of it – a Divine vehicle. If you can bring people down to just life, just life energy, with no personality, then this life energy can be used in so many ways. Such incredible ways that you wouldn't imagine life is possible like this. That is why this order of monkhood or sanyas. People's expectations of Isha bhramhacharis are very, very big. This is not a burden. It's a tremendous privilege when thousands of people look up to us and expect something wonderful to happen out of us. It is an enormous privilege. When people expect only lowly things from you, you will naturally fall into that. So, when people expect the highest things from you, knowingly or unknowingly you have to shift your gears to the highest point.

It's a tremendous privilege. It's an opportunity for us to rise beyond our limitations. Please make that happen, both for your sake and everybody's sake. It is very, very important. It is much more important than you will understand right now.

So, today we take this step.

The Only Bondage

*You did escape the trap
of elemental hive.*

*But it is your own doing
that is the ultimate trap*

*Till you go beyond your own crap
there is no way to break this trap.*

— Sadhguru

As kings and dynasties were replaced with democracies, and tyrants with popular uprisings, the twentieth century saw the quest for freedom in mankind, as a whole, reach new heights. In spite of human rights being enshrined in constitution after constitution, of nations across the globe, man remains hopelessly enslaved to his karma – the only and the ultimate bondage.

Unknown to the deluded being is the wicked reign of karma, seeping into the being – into every cell, predetermining how a cell, an organ or an individual behaves, controlling every breath, thought and emotion. Untold despair befalls the seeker as he realizes one day that his most prized 'freedom' is but a complex function of the karmic influences from the past.

The Only Bondage

Smitten by ignorance and unawareness, man's entanglement in this unseen web of the all-pervading karma deepens with each futile struggle to break free.

Shattering this illusion of 'freedom', so fanatically pursued in our times, Sadhguru reveals the laws of karma and offers antidotes from his inexhaustible repository of spiritual practices. Shifting the focus from action to volition, from fear and beliefs to awareness, Sadhguru de-mystifies the most widely used term in the Indian spiritual jargon, initiating the liberation of the seeker.

SEEKER: *Sadhguru, how do I go beyond action or karma yoga? Personally, I have no urge to do anything. I feel like drifting towards a state of non-doing.*

SADHGURU: When a person has made ultimate reality the goal in his life, action becomes meaningless. Once action is meaningless, any kind of self-image is of no great significance; but right now, in the state you are in, there is still a need for action. You have not yet reached a point where you have transcended action. You are unable to be without action. So perform the kind of action you think is best right now and do what is needed for the situation. For my people, or my disciples, when I am around, I am not thinking in terms of devising a little better karma for them. This idea of better karma is only when the Guru is either a dud or dead. Do you understand? Better karma can only mean your Guru is either a total dud who is useless and a fake, or he's dead and gone.

SEEKER: *You are the brightest, the most sharp-witted and the most genuine person I have ever met, Sadhguru.*

SADHGURU: Brightest and sharpest, yes. About being genuine, how do you know that this one is not a dud? On the plane that you exist, you can never know. Doubts do come sometimes, don't they? Yes, I know they come, unless you have developed such a deep trust that it does not matter whether your Guru is real or a fake – whichever way, your trust in him is such that you will anyway be with him. Until you evolve into such a state, doubts will come. And even if he is a dud, there's no way you can know. All your standards of judgment simply will not hold true. How do you judge whether the person is a genuine Guru or a fake? Either you jell with him or you don't. That's all there is. You cannot really make a judgment about it. That's why so many of the tribe thrive. I am asking you, how will you know?

SEEKER: *There are certain qualities in a Guru which pull an individual beyond his logic and that's why I am here with you, Sadhguru.*

SADHGURU: What are the qualities that can attract you? What can you look for? See, you are just impressed and maybe even attracted to him as a person. Maybe you like the way he looks or speaks, or even maybe the work that is being done. Your attractions cannot go beyond these things. To recognize a Guru and become his disciple, one needs a different kind of quality. When Adolf Hitler decided to start his own party, he had only a handful of friends with him. He sat in a basement with these people and spoke to them in such forceful ways that fired their imagination to great heights; he made them believe that he was going to take over the world shortly. He was just an unemployed youth, a nobody, but he was such a forceful speaker. To them, he was God who was going to rule. He was the future of this planet. This is how he built his self-image. Hitler's self-image was so powerful, he believed that he would rule the world. His self-image was so powerful that it almost came true. If you create any image without a break in it, if there is a continuous mental focus towards it, it will happen, no matter what.

There is another way to create without asking for anything, without ever thinking about anything, where things just happen. Before we arrive at that, a little bit of fired-up

The Only Bondage

movement is needed. People who have never been on fire will not know the coolness of water. People who have just lived their life in a half-hearted manner, sedately, can never know the other way. Becoming a fanatic at least for a while can be useful for your energies to reach a boiling point and get moving. Then, to transform them into something else is very easy. That's the whole purpose of karma or action. Why a sadhaka chooses action is just for this reason. We are going to perform action anyway. Now we have the choice whether we want to perform Hitler's or Mahatma Gandhi's type of action. Whichever way we feel is best right now, we'll do that. That's all there is to it. Anyway we have to perform action, so let us do it whole-heartedly, and let us choose the form of action that we want to do. Do you know the self-image that you want? Do you want to rule the world or do you want to serve the world? Ultimately, that is the choice. Normally, everybody wants to rule the world. It is just that, because a man is half-hearted, he is only able to rule his wife. He doesn't get to rule the world, so all he's able to do is rule his children, wife or something like that, but what he really wants is to rule the world. The fool doesn't have the capacity or the intensity to do it; otherwise, he would be a potential Hitler. The man who physically abuses his child or wife because they don't conform to his ideas – suppose that tomorrow he is made the king of the world, he will use a sword instead of a stick. That's all. It is just that he's incapable and doesn't have the intensity to rule the world; otherwise, he is already the ruler.

Now the choice is just this – either to rule or to serve. Whichever kind of image you think is most harmonious, the closest to Divinity and closest to Realization, that kind of action you choose. Every moment, do it with tremendous intensity, without giving it a single moment's break. Then a day will come when action is not needed anymore. A man who does not know action – real action, intense action – can never move into inaction. If you try to, inaction will just become lethargy. Only if you have known intense action can you know inaction. People who are always resting in their life must be experts about rest, isn't it? But that is not the truth. Only a man who works intensely can know what rest is. So this non-doing business, if you really want to know it, first you must discover what doing is. You have not done that yet. In every waking moment of my life, unceasingly I pursue this work of offering myself, physically and mentally. Unceasingly I pursue it twenty-four hours of the day, every waking moment and even in my sleep, with tremendous intensity. It is only out of that, that all of this has happened in my life. It has become so powerful simply because it does not mean anything to me, but for twenty-four hours, I am at it. Now this has a different kind of power. That is the whole meaning of sacrifice. It is only out of that, that something else happens – both inside and outside – which can never be put into words.

There have been many sages in the world, Realized beings who, even today, are spreading their energy, but by themselves, they are not able to do anything. Only a few are unceasingly at it, day in and day out and only out of this, something can be created. This is how Vivekanandas are created. They are not born. This is how Mahatma Gandhis are created. This is how every powerful individual in this world is created. This is the science of creating a truly powerful being. This is not power to rule. This is not a power that can be taken away at any moment. Nobody can take it away, because wherever you are put, that is what you do. If you want to rule, you have to sit on the seat. If somebody pulls you off the seat, you will be miserable. This is not like that. Wherever you are put, you just do your work. It does not matter what the situation is, what the result of your action is, because that's what you do anyway. If they put you in hell, that is what you do. If they put you in heaven, still, that is what you do. This releases you from action. First of all, this releases you from the fruit of action. Once you are released from the fruit of action, the action will happen by itself. You don't have to stop working to be released from action. Simply, it will dissolve, melt and disappear. Once the expectation of the fruit of action is completely removed from your life, the action occurs by itself. You don't have to do anything about it.

In one of the Zen monasteries, there is an old Master who is over eighty years old. Every day, he works his heart out in the gardens. In Zen monasteries, gardening is one of the most important parts of the sadhana. Day in and day out, people spend time in the garden. This Master has been doing this for years. Many times his disciples have tried to dissuade him. They say, "You stop working, we are all here, we will do it," but he will not listen. He just goes on doing what he can. His capacity to work physically might have come down, but the intensity has not come down. He works with the same intensity. So one day the disciples took away his tools and hid them somewhere, as he will work only with these tools. That day, he did not eat. The next day, there were no tools, so he did not eat. The third day also, no tools; he did not eat. By then they got scared, "Oh! Because we hid the tools, he is angry. He is not eating." Once again, they replaced the tools where they were usually placed. On the fourth day, he worked and ate. Then in the evening, he gave his teaching: "No work, no food," and he went back and died. That was the last day. The four days of fasting were too much for him; but the last day he worked, he ate, then he left his body, and he just gave this teaching: "No work, no food." For this kind of a man, action is like this. Wherever he is put, that is how he will be. Hell, heaven or earth, you put him in any of these different worlds and he will be the same. Once you are like this, you are released from the external situation. By just closing your eyes, you will not become released. The moment you open them, everything will come back and catch up with you. If you run away and sit on the mountain, you will not become free. This is the way to work it out. It has to be worked out.

SEEKER: *Sadhguru, does this mean that we should perform good actions that will free us from the bad karma we have accumulated?*

SADHGURU: Karmas are classified in terms of gunas. What is a guna? It is a quality. Quality is not exactly the word. The Hindus generally talk about three types of gunas. The Buddhists classify them into seven types. Karma can be classified as good karma and bad karma. What I am saying is, whether it is good karma or bad karma, it is still bondage. For people who are only interested in leading a comfortable life, this classification is important. They are always thinking how to perform good karma so that they will be born with wealth, well-being and comfort in their next life. Only a person who is living with duality, for that person there is good and bad karma.

For a person who is thinking in terms of transcending life and death, good karma is as useless as bad. To him, karma is just karma; any classification does not matter. All karma is bad for a spiritual person. Good or bad, it's bad for him. For a person who wants to transcend duality, become one with existence, for that person there is no good and bad. All karma is a barrier, a burden for him. He wants to drop all burdens. It's not like, "If you give me gold, I'm willing to carry even one hundred kilos, but if you give me one hundred kilos of garbage, I will not carry it." That's not the attitude. For a seeker it is, "I want to drop the load." Whether it's gold or garbage, both are heavy, but the other fools think carrying gold is great. Do you understand the difference, Nicholas? A man, who has become wise enough, sees that whether he carries gold or garbage, it is anyway burdensome. The other man is thinking gold will be better than garbage because right now he's carrying garbage.

SEEKER: *Master, is karma also affected by thoughts and not just deeds?*

SADHGURU: See, the moment you say this is a good thought and that's a bad thought, this is a good deed and that is a bad deed – if somebody is doing the bad deed then he's a bad person, isn't it? "Yeah! I am a good man; you are a bad man." It's obvious! Good and bad were mainly invented by people who are selling tickets to heaven. Once a preacher of the old school was describing the events of judgment day, and of course, he used biblical phraseology whenever he could, "Oh! My friends," he intoned, "imagine the suffering of the sinners as they find themselves cast in the outer darkness, removed from the presence of the Lord and given to eternal flames. My friends, at such a time they will be weeping, wailing and gnashing their teeth." At this point one of the eldest of the congregation interrupted, "But reverend, what if one of these hopeless sinners has no teeth?" The preacher crashed his fist on the pulpit, "My friends, the Lord is not put out by details, and rest assured, teeth will be provided." These are the kind of people who invented good and bad.

Every action has a consequence. When I say, 'action', it is not just of the body. It does not pertain to body alone. Action can be of thought, emotion or energy. An action which brings a negative consequence into your life, you generally try to term it as a bad action. It is not a question of bad action, it's just that different actions produce different kinds of consequences. As a human being, your business is just this – every one of us has the intelligence to do this – if you are aware enough you can see that for every single action there is a consequence. If you can joyfully accept the consequence, do anything that you wish to do, but if you do something today and when the consequence comes, you cry, then please curtail your actions, thoughts, emotions, or whatever. Do not start something that you cannot handle. This is not about good and bad; this is just about living your life sensibly. Now you don't pick up a rock that you cannot carry – it is as simple as that. You pick up something that you can handle. So every action is just that. If you bring it into your awareness, you don't have to worry about what is good and bad; you will just do what is needed for you – nothing more, nothing less.

SEEKER: *Sadhguru, if I had accumulated a lot of bad karma in unawareness, past life, will it make me suffer now, in this life? Should I try to perform good karmas to make up for that?*

SADHGURU: Yes, if you are only trying to enhance the quality of your life, good karmas are useful. Good karma does not mean good action, it means action that comes from good volition. That's why there is so much talk about love everywhere. In love, you will perform good karma. When you perform good karma, the quality of your life will be enhanced, that's all. If your love becomes just intensity, beyond any sense, then it can become a process of liberation. Otherwise, love is just allowing you to do good karma.

You are always judging people as good or bad by looking at their actions. I am telling you, the so-called 'good' people never get into action. They are treacherous; they never act, because they are so cunning. They know that the moment they act, one way or the other, they are going to be found out. These 'good' people are the really treacherous people. Maybe they don't do anything physically, but this does not absolve one from the karmic processes. If you restrain yourself or your actions out of your goodness or sense, that is different, but if your fear of the consequence is all that restrains you, then the karma is very different. The 'good' people are the true criminals in the world. They never do anything, so they never get caught. They are the people who perform the worst kind of karma, maybe not in actions, but in their thoughts. For every small thing, they're willing to kill the whole world within themselves. They are like that. These are people filled with jealousy, with hatred within themselves, but they don't do anything wrong outwardly because the flesh is weak, or they don't have the courage to take action, or they are just plain cunning. That's the only thing that has stopped them.

Now there is a really wonderful person who has got a nice big house, a great wife, a very good life, but something will come up, just to remind him. Life has its ways. Once, a businessman boarded a flight and found himself sitting next to an elegant woman wearing the largest, most stunning diamond ring he had ever seen. Awestruck, he exclaimed, "Wow! That's a beautiful ring you have there!" The woman replied, "Yes, this is the Schroeder diamond. It is beautiful, but it comes with a terrible curse." "What curse?" asked the businessman. "Mr. Schroeder," answered the woman. So something will come up. If everything is right, one thing will crop up and go on bothering you, needling you. It's always like that. Otherwise, you will forget life and try to become God. You forget your limitations, so something will come up. That's your karma. The karma, though a process of bondage, is finding expression for you as a reminder of your emancipation. If you are unaware, you get entangled with it. If you are aware, it becomes the way to your liberation.

For a person who knows his limitations, even if something comes up in life, he's not really affected; it doesn't really touch him. Let us say somebody lost their child. These are simple people. If their child dies, at that moment they feel something; the next moment they leave it. There are other kinds of people whose child died ten years ago and even today, they are in turmoil. Just the thought of it and they find themselves in great turmoil. Yes, that is karma.

It does not matter what happens in life, we can blunt the edge of karma. Maybe you cannot immediately remove everything, unless you walk the spiritual path. Even a person who is not walking the spiritual path, if he's sensible, can blunt the edges of his karma and make it ineffective to a large extent. Only certain things will really take effect; other things can be minimized. Only when a person consciously walks the spiritual path, that person can definitely leave all that. If you have the urge, if you really have the character to do that, by the end of this Isha Yoga program, you can simply leave your 'load of bananas' and go. It is very much possible. The opportunity is here. Whether anybody makes it happen or not, the possibility is always wide open.

SEEKER: *Sadhguru, at times I am not sure if I am doing the right thing by being here at Isha. There is much disappointment at home. Am I piling up more karma by causing this pain to my family, Master?*

SADHGURU: They brought you up with many expectations, which caused disappointment to them. The nature of karma is not in the action that you perform. Karma means action, but this gathering of past karmas is not because of the actions you have performed. It is the volition, the intention, the kind of mind that you carry. That's your karma. What is disappointment? Now Kumar asked this question. Let us take your situation as an example. Your wife has some expectation of you that you should be in a particular way, but you're not like that. Now you are unable to break that expectation, or you have not had the courage to break it, or you still have not had a chance to break it. Maybe there is an urge to break it, but you are keeping quiet because of society's norms. It's almost like you have broken the karma.

There is a story which the wonderful sage, Ramakrishna, used to tell. There were two friends who used to go visiting a prostitute every Saturday evening. On one such evening, while they were walking towards the prostitute's house, there was someone giving a discourse on the Gita. One friend decided not to visit the prostitute, saying he would prefer to hear the lecture on the Gita. The other man left him there. Now the man sitting in the lecture hall, his thoughts were full of the other man. He began thinking that the other man was having the time of his life while he was caught in this place. He thought the other man was more intelligent in choosing the prostitute's place rather than a Gita discourse. Now the man who had gone to the prostitute's house, his mind was full of the other man. He began to think that his friend had chosen the path to liberation by preferring the Gita discourse to the prostitute's place, while he got caught in this. The man who had gone for the Gita discourse and was thinking about what was happening in the prostitute's house pays by piling up bad karma. He suffers, not the other man. You don't pay because you have gone to the prostitute; you pay because you are cunning about it. You still want to go there, but you think by going to the discourse you'll be one step closer to heaven. This cunningness will take you to hell. That man with the prostitute knows it's worthless, and seeks something else; his is good karma. So it's not about action.

Right now, why you think in terms of 'right' and 'wrong' is simply because of the social moral code. It's not your innate nature which is telling you that this is right and wrong. It is just that society has fixed some rules and they have always told you, right from your childhood, that if you break them you are a bad boy. So whenever you break these, you feel like a bad boy. If you feel like one, you become one. If you are used to gambling, maybe gambling in front of your mother or your wife, in your home, or even to utter the word is sacrilege, but once you join your gang, there gambling is just fine, isn't it? Among the gamblers, the one who does not gamble is not fit to live. It's like this everywhere. If all of you are thieves, you are all fine, isn't it? Among thieves, do they feel it is bad to rob somebody? When you fail, they think you are a no-good thief. That is a bad karma, isn't it? The question, this karmic thing, is just the way you feel about it. It's not about what you are doing. It is just the way you are holding it in your mind. Why we are talking about acceptance,

acceptance, acceptance, is, if you are absolute acceptance, whatever life demands, you do. If you have to fight a battle, you go and fight; there is no karma. The karma is not made in physical action; it is made only by volition. It's just that some fool has formed some rules and you expect every human being to live by them. It's impossible, but society needs such rules to maintain the social ego.

SEEKER: *So what is social ego, Sadhguru?*

SADHGURU: Society has its own ego, isn't it? For every small thing, the whole society gets upset. It need not be wrong. Suppose it's summer in the United States. Everybody is hardly wearing anything or maybe they are in miniskirts. Let's say you're fully clothed. People will get upset: "What is she doing? Why is she all covered up?" Here in India, if you dress like that, they'll all get upset. So this is one kind of ego; that is another kind of ego. It's the social ego which is getting upset, and your karma is becoming part of the collective karma. I want you to really understand this with a certain depth. Your idea of good and bad has been taught to you. You have imbibed it from the social atmosphere in which you have lived. See, for example, a bandit tribe, like the Pindaris, who from a young age were trained to rob and kill, they even had gods who taught them skills and brought them success in their banditry. When the British army was let loose on them, they were shot and killed indiscriminately. They were completely bewildered, as in their perception they had not done anything wrong. The Pindari ego was just to be a good bandit. The same happened for the Native American Indians also. Among some Native American tribes, unless you had killed a man in your life, you were not much of a man. They collected the scalp of the man and wore it around their neck. So what is right and wrong, what is good and bad, is all about how the social ego functions.

SEEKER: *Sadhguru, if a child dies, whose karma is it? They say we should not cry; what about that? Is this a part of the karmic process? Does some past karma dissolve for the parents?*

SADHGURU: Definitely you don't have to cry. Whether karma dissolves or not, there is no need to cry. If you cry out of love, if tears flow out of compassion, it's good, but if you are going to cry because the physical body collapses, you need to understand, it has to collapse. Right from day one, you know this body is not eternal. Nobody is foolish enough to think it is, but people are thinking on those terms. In the West, have you heard that they are preserving bodies for the future? In England, they have started this process, with all this scientific equipment; the dead bodies are being preserved for the future. They are making blood circulate through machines, and the body is kept intact. It doesn't deteriorate. You have to pay a lot of money to keep your body like that. Now the thing is, some day all souls are going to come back, and when you come, you can come back to your own body. This is nonsense. It's really a stupid thing, an immature thing to do, simply because somewhere, Western philosophy misread the whole situation.

Jesus did not even talk about the continuation of life; he probably just wanted people to make use of this life. "You grow now, when I am here," he said. He never talked about the next life. He said, "This is it. Now, this is the chance. You have to do it now. It is now or never." That's how he spoke. Every teaching he gave was a 'now-or-never' teaching. The philosophy just stops there, with this life. So that is why the Western mind has become so tremendously active. The Pingala has become so active because life is going to stop here. When you die, it's going to be over. Nobody has talked about what is next. There is a tremendous kind of hurry in the West, in every field, simply because for them, life ends here. A certain kind of thought comes that if you're going to die tomorrow, you want to do everything today; that's the attitude. Here, in India, we know there are many lives. What's the problem? If not this time, there is always the next one.

One day, Shankaran Pillai returned from visiting a doctor about his liver problem brought on by his heavy drinking. He mournfully told his wife that he had only twelve hours to live. After wiping away her tears, he asked her to prepare him a nice dinner. Sometime later in bed, he started to make romantic overtures and his wife, with a heavy heart, dutifully responded. Three hours later, Shankaran Pillai gently woke her up and said, "I only have seven more hours to live. I was thinking that maybe, you know…" She agreed. Still later, Shankaran Pillai, bursting into tears, Realized he had only five hours of life left. He nudged his wife and said, "Please, just once more before I die." She agreed and afterward sighed heavily, rolled over and quickly fell fast asleep. Shankaran Pillai continued to hear the clock ticking away in his head until he was down to three more hours. Again he nudged his wife to wake her, and sobbing away, turned to her and said, "I only have three more hours left, could we?" His wife sat up abruptly and turned to him and said, "Listen, I have to get up in the morning AND YOU DON'T!"

This question about, "If a child dies, is it dissolution of the parents' karma?" No, the death itself may be your karma, because for you, generally a child is a valuable possession. So losing your child is not a good experience. If your child dies, you are not going to clap, jump around, and say, "That is great; he went back to God or existence!" No, you are going to be all wound up. So it's not dissolution. It may be just that it has to happen like that for you. It's your karma. You cannot say it is dissolution. Nothing is dissolved. You are going to suffer from it. The child is gone but your suffering continues, isn't it? The karma is not in your child. The karma is only in your attitude and in your suffering.

SEEKER: *Is karma passed on from generation to generation, Sadhguru?*

The Only Bondage

SADHGURU: Is your karma handed over to the next generation? What, Balu, are you asking whether your karmas are being handed over to your children? Hereditary karmas? See, wherever you are, or whomever you are with at any moment, whatever that man's karma, it also affects you one way or the other. Let us say, your friend is a thief. You never did anything, but when the police come and catch him, they will catch both of you. Maybe you won't get one-year imprisonment the way he does, but you will at least spend one day behind bars. This is his karma which has rubbed off on you, but it's your karma that you were with him at that moment. Similarly, the parents' karma affects the children. Whatever nonsense you do definitely affects the child. Transferring? No. If you're thinking of handing it over to your son and going, it will not work that way. It is just an influence. It's just like this: if you're next to a flower, you will get the fragrance of it, but you cannot become the flower. If you want to become a flower, you have to become the flower out of your own nature. Even if my daughter has to seek the peak of her consciousness, she has to seek it out of her own nature. Maybe being here, in this energy field, is good karma for her. She has this opportunity, even if she is not meditating, but it's not essential that she has to turn spiritual. We don't know; that is left to her. That, nobody can decide. You don't know who she is anyway, what her attributes are, what her karmic basis is. I don't want to go into that.

SEEKER: *You don't want to go into that, but now that you have started it...*

SADHGURU: I shouldn't have started it. I started simply because you have to know. Don't look at anybody based on what they are right now. There is so much behind every person. It could be good and it could be bad, it could be positive and it could be negative, but there is so much behind every person here. If you are sensitive and subtle enough, just by looking at a person, you will be able to see his whole lifetimes of karmas, here and now. That will be your understanding of people and who they are.

Meditation may be a quick way which takes you to that level of subtleness, but for a lot of people it is not possible, because their karma, their body or their mind, something will not allow them to meditate. One purpose of doing the practices and yoga kriyas is that you become sensitive. If you just touch a person for one moment, you should know his one hundred lifetimes, and what his karma is. You may not know all the details, which city he was born in, where he lived, what he had for dinner today…that is not the point. You know the general trend of his karmas. This is not imagining or hallucinating. It must be crystal clear, just like seeing with your eyes. That is how it should be. Now the way you act, the way in which you handle people, will be with a different kind of maturity. Just by looking at them, not by looking at their present image, you will know exactly what that person needs at this moment. Even he may not know what he needs at this moment, because he only knows what he is at this moment. He does not know what he was in another lifetime, but you know what he was then; so you can handle things with a totally different kind of maturity which will not come through thought. If that sensitivity has to come, one has to work towards it; there is no other way.

SEEKER: *Master, you have told us many times that if we have bitter experiences in our life, it is because of our past doings. What type of activities should we do today to avoid future bitterness?*

SADHGURU: Subbarao, the bitterness of any experience is not in what has happened. The bitterness of any experience is in terms of how you have received it. What is very bitter for one person could be a blessing for another person. Once, a grief stricken man threw himself on a grave and cried bitterly, hitting his head against it. "My life! Oh! How senseless it is! How worthless this carcass of mine is because you're gone. If only you had lived! If only fate had not been so cruel as to take you from this world! How different everything would have been!" A clergyman, nearby, overheard him and said, "I assume this person lying beneath this mound of earth was someone of great importance to you." "Importance? Yes, indeed," wept the man, wailing even louder, "It was my wife's first husband!" The bitterness is not in what is happening. It is in how you're allowing yourself to experience it, how you are receiving it. Similarly, whatever the past activity or karma is, is also not in terms of action, but in terms of the volition with which it is done.

What is happening with you all, if you are a little open to me or to the teaching, is just that the volition is taken away, so you just do what is needed. That is what awareness means; there is no volition. Where there is no volition, there is no karma. You are simply doing what is needed; that is what acceptance means. That is what unbounded responsibility means, that you don't have any volition about anything. In every given situation, simply whatever you see as needed, as per your awareness, as per your capability, you just do it. You build karma only with volition; whether it is good or bad, it does not matter. The strength of your volition is what builds karma.

People ask me, again and again, the same question, "What's your mission?" When I tell them, "I have no mission; I'm just fooling around," they think I'm being frivolous. They don't understand this is the deepest statement that I can make about living in the world, because there is no particular volition – just doing what is needed, that's all. In this, there is no karma. Whatever you go through, there is no karma. Whatever you are doing is just happening, as it is needed. So karma is only in terms of your need to do something. When you have no need to do anything, and you simply do what is needed, there is no karmic attachment to it. It is neither good nor bad.

SEEKER: *Until I reach that state of awareness where I have a choice about what I think and do, am I not accumulating more karma unconsciously? How is this choice made, Sadhguru?*

SADHGURU: Swami, you are just asking me, "Until I have become aware, until that point, where is my choice?" Is that the question?

SEEKER: *How is the choice made?*

SADHGURU: Everybody is making choices; even their compulsions are their choices. Choices made in unawareness are compulsions. Let us say you get angry right now. It is your choice, actually, to be angry. Somewhere, you believe that's the way to handle the situation, but the choice is made in such unawareness that it is a compulsion; it's happening compulsively on a different level. So you're living by choice, but choices are made without awareness – unconscious choices. It so happened, once Shankaran Pillai walked up to a bar with an ostrich behind him. After he sat down, the bartender came over and asked for the order. Shankaran Pillai said, "I'll have a beer," and turned to the ostrich, "What will you have?" "I'll have a beer too," said the ostrich. The bartender poured the beer and said, "That'll be one hundred and fifty six rupees, fifty paisa." Shankaran Pillai reached into his pocket and pulled out the exact change. The next day, he and the ostrich came in again, and he asked for a beer. The ostrich said, "I'll have the same." Once again, he reached into his pocket and paid with the exact change. This became a routine, until late one evening, the two entered again. "The usual?" asked the bartender. "Well no, this time I'll have a large scotch," Shankaran Pillai said. "Same for me," said the ostrich. "That'll be two hundred and seventy nine rupees," said the bartender. Once again, the exact change came out of his pocket. The bartender could not hold back his curiosity any longer. "Excuse me, Sir. How do you manage to come up with the exact change from your pocket every time?" "Well," Shankaran Pillai said, "several years ago, I was cleaning the attic and I found an old lamp. When I rubbed it, a genie appeared and granted me two wishes. My first wish was that if I ever have to pay for anything, I just have to put my hand in my pocket and the right amount of money will always be there." "That's brilliant," said the bartender. "Most people would wish for a million dollars or something, but you will always be as rich as you want for as long as you live!" "That's right, whether for a liter of milk or a Rolls Royce, the exact amount of money is always there," said Shankaran Pillai. Then the bartender asked, "One other thing, sir. What's with the ostrich?" He replied, "My second wish was for a chick with long legs."

Now the whole thing is to shift into making conscious choices. Even a simple act – like when you wake up in the morning, the unconscious choice is that you don't want to wake up. When the sun rises, you want to pull the sheet up a little higher over your face. Do you see this? This is the unconscious choice. Your physical body wants to remain in bed for some more time, and some more time, and some more time. For so many reasons, it doesn't want to get up. There are so many aspects of life, so many limitations in your experience of life, that in many ways, unconsciously, you're not really looking forward to the day. Let's say tomorrow you have planned to go on a picnic. Do you see, before the sun rises you will wake up on that day? Consciously you have decided the previous day; you are excited. You are looking forward to tomorrow. It is a joyful experience. You will see, you will wake up before the sun comes up. Otherwise, unconsciously, you try to pull the sheet higher up over your face because this light is not something you are looking forward to, because with light comes today's stock prices; with light comes today's problems; with light comes the whole world into your life. So you're trying unconsciously to screen yourself from that; but now we make a conscious choice. Even after you wake up, the unconscious choice is that you want to drink a cup of coffee; the body feels comfortable with that. But now you can make a conscious choice, "No, I will have a cold water bath and do my yoga asanas."

Why ascetic paths were set is simply because of this: you start doing things that are naturally not comfortable for you. Once you start doing such activity that is uncomfortable for you, you do it, but you don't like it. If you have to do something that you do not like, you can only do it consciously; there is no other way to do it. Yes? Things that you like, you can do compulsively; but things that you don't like, you can only do consciously. That is why the ascetic path. You start doing everything consciously. There is no other way to be. Now, slowly, you are practicing how to be conscious in various situations in your life. When you are hungry, the natural urge is to grab food and eat. Now you make a conscious choice, "I am very hungry, but I am not eating." To stay away from food, there is no other choice except being conscious about it, but to go and eat, you don't need consciousness; you can simply go and grab it when you are hungry. These simple things are set up in life so that you start doing things more consciously. For example, we have only two meals in our day-to-day life, or sometimes only one meal. By the time this meal comes, naturally you are very hungry, but you don't immediately eat. You wait for everybody to sit down. You wait for something to go onto everybody's plate, then you utter an invocation, and then you slowly eat. This needs consciousness. Just to give that break when you are hungry – just to wait for those three or four minutes – it takes an enormous amount of awareness for a person. To grab and eat would be very simple, but you will become more and more unconscious.

The Only Bondage

This consciousness is brought into your life. Early morning, you want to drink coffee, but you sit and do your yoga kriyas. You can't do it any other way but by being conscious about it. Drinking coffee, you can do in unawareness. I'm not saying you cannot do that in awareness, but you can easily do it in unawareness. Now, you can't do your kriyas in unawareness. You have to be aware. So like this, you're cultivating awareness into different aspects of life. Maybe initially your awareness is only for half an hour a day, but gradually you are bringing awareness into various aspects of life like this. The idea of cultivating awareness is so that it slowly seeps into your life. In one way that is a reality; you are cultivating awareness. One thing it does is, it enhances the quality of your life, but that's not everything. The main aspect is that if you can maintain awareness in various kinds of situations in life, only then will you even become capable of being aware at that moment when you have to part with the body. Otherwise, that never arises in your life.

Leaving the body is the moment of moving from one dimension to another dimension or, in a way, getting released from a certain level of bondage. That moment is also an opportunity for one's ultimate liberation. When life has run its full course, when one is free of prarabdha and about to shed the body, the next allotment of prarabdha is yet to happen. So this situation or space gives an opportunity for one to completely dissolve if the necessary awareness is maintained. This brief period of life where the current prarabdha is over but the next allotment is yet to happen, your situation is virtually like that of a liberated being. If you can bring the necessary awareness, it becomes a possibility for ultimate release.

SEEKER: *Excuse me for interrupting, Sadhguru, but does this mean that whatever we are doing in this life is trying to rid ourselves of our prarabdha karma? We don't have other karmas to work out?*

SADHGURU: There are certain other karmas which will not take effect now. If you do something today, it will always wait for the next phase of your life. It will not take effect in this life. Now the spiritual process is about dropping the whole stock, or the sanchita karma. It is not about dealing with the prarabdha. All the moral teachings and trying to live a good life is limited towards dispensing your prarabdha alone, which means invariably the sanchita will come out with the next allotment of prarabdha, which leads to rebirth.

Here, we are cultivating awareness in the most difficult situations – be aware, be aware. If somebody abuses you, to abuse him back, you don't need any awareness, but to remain quiet you need enormous awareness, isn't it? So just doing things that you don't like brings an enormous amount of awareness. Like I was telling you the other day in the ashram, first thing in the morning, we eat a neem ball. "Bitterness – why start life with bitterness? Why can't we eat a sweet?" There are health and other benefits to it, but that's different. One important aspect is, neem is not something that you can like. It's bitter, but you start the day with this, because you cannot eat the neem ball in unawareness. You have to eat it with great consciousness; there is no other way. You can eat a sweet in total unawareness. Like this, certain aspects are brought into your life so that it brings awareness into different dimensions of your experience – one is on the physical level, another at the level of the breath, another at the level of the energy, another at the level of your emotions.

If you use them – the physical body, the thought process, the emotions and the energy – you will see on all these four levels you'll begin to become more and more aware, which is definitely happening; there is no question about it. So this awareness is cultivated. As this happens, slowly awareness sets things apart. As you become more and more aware of the body, you will see that you and the body are separate. As you become more and more aware of the mind, you will see that you and the mind are separate. As you become more and more aware of emotion, you and that emotion are separate. As you become more and more aware of your physical life energy, you and that physical life energy are also separate. So what is 'you' becomes a formless thing. It may not still be a living reality that you truly are formless. Formless also means boundless. Form means bound. It may not be an actual reality that you are formless, but slowly the form is becoming weaker; that's for sure. With the practice and with the devices that are given, depending upon how intensely and how diligently you are applying these devices in your life – using these devices – accordingly, to that extent you will see, your form is becoming weaker. Your form is just a falsehood of individuality that you have created. It's just a limitation. A form means a limitation, isn't it? A form is a limit; formless is limitless. So the spiritual process means you are always seeking the limitless. That means to somehow break the form; but you cannot seek the limitless because you don't know what it is. You know the limited, so you start chipping away at the limited. If you break away everything that is limited, the unlimited is bound to happen. Unlimited is not something that you create. Breaking off the limited is all that you can do. So that's the whole process.

SEEKER: *Sadhguru, is there a difference between having a desire to do something and actually acting on that desire?*

SADHGURU: Does action spring from desire? I don't see how you can separate this. Desire itself is an action. The desire itself is a certain action. This also springs from your awareness. If desires are happening unconsciously, that means your action is happening unconsciously. Action need not necessarily mean physical action. There is mental action, there is emotional action and there is energy action. If all these are happening unconsciously, you tend to believe, "This is my nature." When people get angry, you ask them, "Why?" They say, "This is my nature," because it is so compulsive. That's why they are saying it, isn't it? For anything that is compulsive within you, you declare, "This is my nature." That means you got yourself deeply identified with that action. Once you are so deeply identified with that action, there is no question of you being aware, or of anything happening in awareness or consciousness. Desire is not different. Desire is also one kind of action. It is not that action is springing from the desire; the desire is the beginning of the action.

The word 'karma' literally means 'action', but the action is not what you do with your hands. The quality of your action is not in what you do. Right now, I pick up this stone. This is an action. It has no quality of its own, but in my mind, I have the intention of taking it and throwing it at you. I have still not thrown it, but already the karma is done. I did not even pick it up. I have a feeling that I want to take this and throw it in your face. The karma is already done. Now if I take it and throw it and accidentally it hits your face, then it is a different kind of karma, a karma of negligence, not a karma of anger or something else. Now the stone is here, I just want to take it and throw it in your face. I have not even thrown it yet, but I look at your face and I look at the stone and I want it to hit your face. That karma is already done.

SEEKER: *I'm in trouble, Sadhguru!*

SADHGURU: Yes, Somu, you are very much in trouble, unless you work it out (laughs). Now let us say that I actually took this stone, I was just playing with it and it landed on your head and injured you, that karma is not so serious. It's the karma of negligence. That karma is different from the karma of wanting to hit you. It also revealed that your head is empty, but that is your karma (laughs).

SEEKER: *Master, what about the karma of wanting to hurt the person and actually hurting him? If I throw the stone in his face, is there any difference between that and wanting to throw the stone?*

SADHGURU: Now once you perform the action, there is a consequence. Do you understand? The consequence is not a punishment; it is always a way of working out the karma. The consequence is a way life is trying to work out the karma that you are constantly creating. If you do only mental karma, there is no external consequence, so the suffering is always deeper.

SEEKER: *Does being angry with somebody in my life and being angry with you at times – I mean, I do get angry – is it any different, Sadhguru?*

SADHGURU: Being angry with me is a very bad karma; get this straight! (Laughs).

SEEKER: *And why so?*

SADHGURU: See, the question of being angry with somebody does not arise. You are not angry with anybody, you are just angry. Your anger has nothing to do with somebody else. It's about you. Whether you are angry at a rock, God, your Guru, or whatever – anger is simply anger. It has got nothing to do with anybody or anything. You need to understand this first: your anger has nothing to do with anybody except yourself, only yourself. Only because you believe your anger has something to do with somebody, it keeps happening over and over again. If you see that it is only about you and you alone, it would not have lasted this long.

So being angry and upset about something, whether I say it or somebody else says it, comes from a strong sense of like and dislike. This strong sense of like and dislike comes from a very deep identification with a certain way of thinking, a certain way of feeling, a certain way of life – which you think is the best way to live, which you think is the best way to think and feel. If somebody is not in line with that, you get angry at those things. As your likes and dislikes become stronger, as your identifications become stronger with one thing or another, all that you are doing is excluding existence. If I say, "I like this very much," in a big way I am excluding the rest of existence at that moment. So the stronger it becomes, the deeper the exclusion becomes. The very process of liberation is to include, not to exclude. In exclusion, you become trapped. In inclusion, you become liberated. When everything – not just everything – when the whole existence is included in you, only then you are liberated. In exclusion, you become separate. There are methods of exclusion that lead to ultimate inclusion; that is different. That is the nethi, nethi, nethi process that we are doing – I am not this, I am not this – excluding yourself from everything. Probably the word exclusion, in that sense, would be mistaken and misunderstood. It is more about dis-identifying yourself, starting with your clothes, body, house, family, every cell of your body, your ideas, thoughts, education, culture, everything, and saying, "I am not this, I am not this, I am not this." Once you are dis-identified with everything that is not you, you become all inclusive once again. So anger is just a small indicator of where you are going. Anger itself is not the karma; the exclusion is the big karma. It is because of the exclusion that the anger overflows, because you have not included somebody or something as part of yourself. Anger is just an indicator. Anger is not the karma. Exclusion is a huge karma.

SEEKER: *This is frightening, Sadhguru! Even my very thought can create karma? Living itself becomes difficult, because the mind is such that it can create many, many thoughts – many, many unnecessary emotions within me.*

SADHGURU: Yes? It need not be scary, because every moment you have the option. Right now, if you look at this person and the very way she is sitting, one part of your mind says, "She is not okay. I don't like her." You can give an enormous amount of importance to that thought or you can just not give any importance to it. That choice you always have. The thought itself, you may not have a choice about because it is coming from a certain culture you were brought up in; but giving importance to that thought or not, getting identified with that thought or not, that choice is always in your hands, every moment. If you don't exercise that choice, then yes, every thought can become a huge karma, every thought can become a trap, every thought can become a process of self-destruction.

SEEKER: *Do Enlightened beings create karma? For instance, when Jesus got angry, did he create karma, Sadhguru?*

SADHGURU: When a man like Jesus goes about – you know this one particular scene where he entered the synagogue, the temple, and threw out all the people who were doing business there? He literally, physically, threw them out. He went in and threw out so many people. His fury was such that nobody could stop him. He was just furious, so it was krodha, isn't it? It was anger; he knew that he could play with anger for a while and the next moment he could dissolve the whole thing. He involved himself in intense activity outside and then he said, "Now it is time for me to go into the mountains." He would go into the mountains, stay there, dissolve everything and then come back. Intense activity needs that break, but you know for that physical action what consequence it brought him. Otherwise, if he did not attend to it, he would have been in trouble. When the time comes, he would be in trouble. Nobody is spared, do you understand? Nobody is spared. The law is law. When you go by the law, that is the way – it is there. When you don't go by the law, you pay the price. If you understand the law, this moment you can open the door and get away. If you don't understand the law, even if you roam for millions of lifetimes, no way.

Once an intellectual understanding comes, the next thing is to step into the experiential aspect. Intellectual understanding is not a must. One can step into the experiential and an understanding flowers from within. That's also true. Intellectual understanding is needed simply because people don't have an urge towards anything that they don't understand. They're not willing to go. They are not willing to take a step, so we tell them, "It is like this. It is like that. If you do this, ultimately that will come." It has to be offered, otherwise, if it's just trust and love, intellectual understanding is not needed. You simply go for your own dissolution. If it has to be given to somebody, yes, you need understanding.

SEEKER: *Sadhguru, in the cycle of rebirth, does the child select the parents?*

SADHGURU: Selection, yes. Selection does not mean the child chooses consciously. That's not the point. It is just like this, if we throw all of you into this hall, suddenly, the first day when you enter, everybody settles down in his own place, isn't it? There is a reason for this. That reason is your karma. Your karma may be back pain, then you will settle down near the wall. Your karma may be to always hide and look. You want to be there in the class, but you don't want to be pointed out. So you will find a big person and sit behind him. It may be unconscious, but that's how you do it. Your karma may be that you always want to be in the front row, so you just come and sit there. It does not matter where you sit, but your karma makes you settle down in some place.

Similarly, your karma makes you settle down in some particular womb, with those kinds of tendencies and with those kinds of attributes. Somewhere, there are millions of beings waiting for this. One half is there, it has to find the other half. It just finds a suitable plug and somehow gets notched up. It's not that this person is named for that person. This is not the way it works. It's just like the way many things settle down in certain ways, beings also settle down according to their attributes and tendencies. That's all it is.

The Only Bondage

SEEKER: *Sadhguru, is there such a thing as destiny?*

SADHGURU: Once it happened that the pope went to the United States, and he had many engagements. He landed up in Cincinnati, Ohio. A chauffeur-driven stretch limo – you know the stretch limo? In the U.S., they stretch a limousine to its limits. The chauffeur was driving. The pope got a little excited because he had never driven a car like this. He told the chauffeur, "I would like to drive." How could the chauffeur say no to the pope? He said, "Okay." So the pope took the wheel and the chauffeur took the back seat. The pope started enjoying the car and pressing the gas more, and more, and more. He was hitting ninety or one hundred miles per hour. He did not realize the speed he was going at, and the Ohio police are terrible. If you go two miles over the speed limit they will catch you. He was zooming and he had the flashing light behind him. So he pulled to the side. The cop got out, and carefully, with his hand on his gun, slowly approached the car. It was the pope himself driving! He looked in the back seat and somebody was sitting there. Then he said, "Wait." He went back to his car, took the radio out and called the police chief. He said to the chief, "I've got a huge fish." "Oh come on. Who is it? Is it Ted Kennedy in trouble again?" "No, somebody much bigger than that." "Is it Chelsea Clinton, driving drunk?" "Oh no, somebody much, much bigger." "Is it the President himself?" "No, somebody far bigger than that!" "Come on, who else could be bigger than the President of the United States? What have you got on your hands?" He said, "I don't know who it is but he's got the pope as his chauffeur!"

So you don't know who is driving your car. Destiny is something that you have been creating unconsciously. You can also create it consciously. You can rewrite your destiny. What we have been trying to do with you in the last few days is just that. If you can touch that core in you, if you can for one moment see, "Everything is my responsibility," and shift your whole focus to yourself, you can rewrite your own destiny. All the time your focus is scattered, because what you consider as 'myself' is your house, your car, your wife, your child, your pet, your education, your position, your power and your other nonsense. If I strip you of all these things, you will feel like a nobody; yes or no? So what you call 'myself' is spread around you right now.

When I say 'you', it is you, not this carpet, not this wall, not your child, not something else. When I say 'you', it's just you. If it shifts to this, you can rewrite your destiny whichever way you want. Right now, what is 'you' is spread out; you are a scattered being. You're not an established being; you are a scattered being. You still have to gather all this mess, put it inside. Then it becomes you. You still have not become you; you are a crowd, isn't it? The crowd's destiny is always predestined. Once you become an individual – individual means, it comes from 'indivisible'– it cannot be divided anymore; it is this. It cannot be here and there. Once you become a true individual, your destiny is yours. I want you to understand this. Why in the spiritual process people who are in a hurry for spiritual growth are not getting into marriage, children and relationships, is because the moment you have a wife or a husband, you cannot help it, 'me' gets identified with 'this one'. Otherwise, they will not let you live, isn't it? Once you have children, you get identified with them. Now, your 'me' includes them also. Once you get identified with them, one by one, you get identified with too many things. Now you get scattered.

Once, it happened that Indra, the king of all gods, decided to come to earth for pleasure. You know, the gods come to earth for pleasure, but people want to go to heaven. He landed on planet Earth, then had to choose some form, some body. So he chose the body of a pig, the form of a pig, because generally, in terms of physical pleasure, the pig is best. He became a pig, found himself a beautiful female pig, and they

The Only Bondage

started living. Then dozens of piglets came. He got deeply involved with them. He got attached to his wife and children. Many months passed. All the gods in heaven waited and waited. They thought it was a short pleasure trip, but he did not come back. Then they came down to see what was happening and saw this whole pig business going on. They tried telling him, "You are Indra! What are you doing here as a pig? Come with us." He said, "Nothing doing," so deeply involved and attached he was to everything around him. Then they had a meeting in heaven. "What to do, how to get our king back?" Then somebody said, "He is so deeply attached to his children. Let us kill one of his children. He will realize and come back." They came and killed one piglet, one of those beautiful piglets. When one goes, you cling harder to the remaining ones. That's the way it is happening. Suppose you have five children and you suddenly lose one, you will cling harder to the remaining four. If you lose one more, you cling to the remaining three even harder, isn't it? They killed one, then they killed the next one, and the next one, and he clung to the remaining ones harder and harder. Like this, they killed all his children. Then he and his wife got busy producing more children. Then they thought, "Oh! His real attachment is to his wife. If we kill her then he will come back." So they killed the wife. With his beautiful wife dead, he was in great distress. Then after a few days, his pig friends and relatives suggested that he take another wife. They always do, isn't it? Again the whole pig business started. The gods were at a loss. Then Narada, the celestial sage, came and said, "Why did you go about killing all these innocent beings? His attachment is to his body. If you cut his body, he will come." They went and cut his body into two halves. He came out, and asked, "What the hell am I doing here?" Then he went back to heaven.

That is how deep the bondage with the body is. It is the source of all attachments. You don't have to go on searching for non-attachment somewhere else. You don't have to go about distancing this and that in your life, but once you get scattered, your destiny becomes predestined. Whichever way your karma is, it just goes that way. If you become an individual, the significance of sanyasa or bhramhacharya is just this: shifting your whole focus to you. When I say 'you', it is just you, not even your body or your mind. If you are unable to be like that, you just choose one more identity. When you say 'you', make it you and your Guru. You attach yourself to the Guru without any hesitation, because you have no entanglements from the other side. You can get as entangled as you want with him; he is not going to get entangled. The moment you are ripe, you can drop it. With other relationships, it is never so. If you get entangled, even if you want to become free, the other will not let you go. Either you can rewrite your own destiny or, if such awareness does not come, we can very easily rewrite destiny if you can just give yourself to me. So don't worry about the predestined thing. You just create a longing to grow, to dissolve, to know. What has to happen will happen. Why are you worried about all those things?

SEEKER: *Master, you say that if I have to become an individual I have to be focused on myself?*

SADHGURU: Once you become an individual, your destiny becomes yours. If your destiny is in your hands, will you choose bondage or freedom? What would you choose? Freedom, because the very longing of life, the deepest longing of every life is to become free, to become free from the very process that we refer to as life or death, to become free from that itself. So once your destiny is happening in awareness, the next step will just happen by itself, because life within you has the intelligence to choose freedom, not bondage. Only because your destiny is being created in unawareness, you go about weaving bondage around yourself.

The Only Bondage

SEEKER: *According to the karma that we have when we die, can this human body become a snake or even a tiny amoeba? Our evolution, can it go down as well as up, Sadhguru?*

SADHGURU: You cannot say that it is going down, because to fulfill certain aspects of life, sometimes one who has been a human may take on an animal form. Let us say right now, for example, you have certain desires which are not fulfilled. Your desire was to collect a billion rupees. You neither have the brains to earn it nor the courage or capability to go and rob a bank and get your billion. You're not made like that. So what is your desire? It is to collect. If you get ten rupees, you will save five. You will starve yourself. You will go through all kinds of difficulty. Save, save, save and save. You want to collect one billion rupees. So with this process of collecting, most probably, by the time you die, your target will not be reached. Let's say you have saved only half a billion. Now there is a big urge within you to collect the remaining amount, but you die before that with the same lust of wanting to collect. Your karma does not know what you want to collect, whether it's money or stones. What nonsense it wants to collect, it doesn't matter. It only knows it has to collect. It does not have discriminatory power. It's almost like your genes. It is a subtler gene, not a physical gene. It only knows that you like to collect. So the next time, this gene may decide to collect. Which will be the right form for you to collect? Maybe you will become an ant, or maybe you will become a bee. We don't know.

These are just examples that I am using. If a particular quality is very dominant in you, to fulfill that quality, what kind of body, what kind of physical situation would be best for you, it will seek that. It need not necessarily be an animal form. It may choose that kind of human form in that kind of a situation and in that kind of surroundings where it can be fulfilled. It could be in any way.

SEEKER: *Sadhguru, is spirituality the exclusive domain of the human life form or is it open to other life forms?*

SADHGURU: Do other forms of life, the other creatures on this planet, know something spiritual or could we regress to that state again? It's not a question of regression or progression; it is just that life is always finding its way by its tendencies. Traditionally, we call them as your vasanas. Do you know what vasanas are? Vasana literally means 'smell'. Whichever way the smell is, that is the kind of thing that it attracts. Whatever kind of stuff you hold, that is the kind of smell you emanate. Whatever kind of smell you emanate, that's the kind of thing you will attract to yourself. Suppose that tree is in full bloom. With flower and fragrance, it attracts bees. If there is some filth outside, it attracts flies. According to the vasana, that is what comes to it, isn't it? So according to your vasana, what kind of fragrance you are leaving, accordingly, those kinds of things come to you. This is not a prize; this is not a punishment; this is not progression; this is not regression. This is just nature, functioning according to qualities. It is not in terms of punishment and prize, just as per its qualities.

Let us say, for example, you are obsessed with food. I'm not saying that you are; I am just giving an example. Let us say you are too obsessed with food, and even at the moment of death you are thinking about food. Now your vasana was that. Somehow, this eating, you could not eat to a point of satisfying yourself. Somewhere it is still longing to eat. This karma in you is very strong. Now it may choose, let us say, the body of a pig because it can go on eating throughout the day. That kind of body can eat throughout the day. You taking on a pig's body is not a punishment; it is just that nature is trying to work out a certain quality. What could not be worked out in a human body is finding a suitable body to work out that kind of tendency in you. This is not a punishment, this is not regression, this is not God trying to fix you and make you a pig. That's not the point. It is just that a certain quality is trying to find its liberation. Food was so important, so it is picking up that kind of body with which food can be handled in that way. Let us not give you more examples (laughs); one is enough. So there is such a possibility, but it is rare because nature has its own buffer for you.

If you live a complete life – when I say 'complete' – there is something called prarabdha, or allotted karma. Your existence here is ruled by your karmic structure. If you have no karma, you cannot be here for a moment. I don't know if you have noticed such things. Let us say an old person, somebody who is of a certain age, cannot sleep properly or sleeps for just half an hour. Suddenly, once he crosses a certain age, you find he sleeps extremely deep. If he sleeps, he sleeps like a log. Such deep sleep comes to him because his prarabdha is getting over. Once the prarabdha is exhausted, it is not that all his karma is over, but the allotted karma, one installment, is drawing to an end. Suddenly, there is a new sense of freedom in him, a new sense of peace in him. If this comes, unless something else is created, he's coming to the end of his life. It is very clear. Oh! I should not be telling you all these things. Then if anybody sleeps deeply, you will think, "Oh! He is going to die tomorrow." So, Radhika, your mother-in-law is old and sleeps deeply; don't go looking at her with glee (laughs). Once the prarabdha is over, a certain state of balance, a certain state of equanimity comes to him. The turmoil has come down in that person, because the inner quota of karma is over. One installment is over. So the chance of somebody falling back into another kind of body other than that of a human being, or a less evolved body, is quite remote, but it can happen. It will not happen to you, those of you who are with me, because of certain things. It will not happen; I assure you that.

As for the other creatures, do they have any spiritual possibility? For the other creatures, nature is giving them a free spiritual ride. They just keep evolving by themselves. They need not know anything; it's a free ride. But certain creatures are aware. One day, Shankaran Pillai's front gate sported a sign saying: "TALKING DOG FOR SALE." A man rings the bell, and Shankaran Pillai tells him, "The dog is in the backyard." The man goes into the backyard and sees a mutt sitting there. "You talk?" he asks. "Yup," the mutt replies. "So what's your story?" The mutt looks up and says, "Well, I discovered this gift pretty young and I wanted to help the government, so I told the R.A.W. Secret Service about my gift, and in no time, they had me jetting from country to country, sitting in rooms with spies and world leaders, because no one figured a dog would be eavesdropping. I was one of the most valuable spies for eight years. This jet setting really tired me out, and I knew I was not getting any younger, and I wanted to settle down. So I signed up for a job at the airport to do some undercover security work. Mostly wandering near suspicious characters and listening in. I uncovered some incredible dealings there and was awarded a bunch of medals." The mutt sighs heavily and then says, "I had a wife, a mess of puppies, and now, I'm just retired." The man is amazed. He goes back in and asks Shankaran Pillai what he wants for the dog. He says, "Two hundred rupees." The man says, "I will buy him! Just tell me one thing, this dog is amazing, why on earth are you selling him for two hundred rupees?" Shankaran Pillai replies, "He's such a liar!"

Now if a very powerful situation is created, certain creatures become aware of something more than their physical body. The three animals that are very capable of doing this are a cow, a snake and a crow. You know they told you, if your father dies or your grandfather dies you must feed the cow, the snake or the crow. This is because these are three creatures that are capable of a little awareness if a powerful situation is created, not otherwise.

The Only Bondage

SEEKER: *Sadhguru, then how could Ramana Maharshi have Enlightened animals like a cow and a crow? How could he release them from their karma?*

SADHGURU: What, Kumar, do you think it would have been easier if you had come as a cow or a crow? Do you see the difficulty here of making you grow? Where is the question of enlightening an animal? You are asking how Ramana Maharshi could have Enlightened or created an opportunity for dissolution, or mukthi, to an animal. See, nobody can ever enlighten an animal unless the animal has come as a reincarnation of a human being. It is only possible when these beings have already seen the human form. For some reason, now they have come with the animal form. Only then such a thing is possible, by taking him back and regressing him to his human nature within that animal body and helping him out of that situation. But you can never make an animal realize, because the basic quality itself is absent; that consciousness is absent in an animal. What is there in a human being is not there in the animal. Only by regressing them into that human quality can it be done. He can be released from there, not from here, because that is the only way it can be; it cannot be any other way.

Right now, let us say you are in some other form, not in human form. So in this form, in this level of consciousness, there is no way you can attain to anything spiritual. You cannot be released from this level; but if there was a previous birth which was that of a human, then yes, I regress you back to that life and from there, I release you. Experientially, I take you back to your human life while you are still physically in the animal form. Only then it is possible, not otherwise. Let us say certain minor karmas become major in your life, like food, for example. Maybe you are a yogi in this life and you did so many things, but food became a big problem within you; you denied yourself food, food, food all the time. So somewhere, the clinging to food was not gone. Now this yogi, if he comes once again in a human form, all the hassles of a human being are there – growing up as a human being, there are so many things that he can get caught up with. Now, only food is a barrier for him. Everything else, he has mostly cleared. So he does not want to – it may not be a conscious choice – that being does not want to come in the human form and get entangled with all the other processes of growing up. So now he comes like, let us say a pig, because only food has to be satisfied. Gathering of karma for animals is minimal, that is why naturally it progresses. The evolutionary process happens naturally for an animal because he does not gather any karma as such. It is only dissolution; it simply progresses; it advances by itself into higher and higher life forms.

SEEKER: *So Sadhguru, we are evolving, but we may go back and forth from human form to animal form?*

SADHGURU: You are going step by step, sometimes jumping, sometimes leaping, sometimes falling back. It's the *Snake and Ladder* game that is on. As long as the snakes are there, you climb one ladder and another snake will swallow you and bring you back to square one. You climb up for a few days and again go back down. It just goes on. That's how those boards are made, isn't it? You hit a ladder, you hit the snake, you hit a ladder, you hit the snake, and it just goes on. So here, we give you a device with which you can strip off all the snakes. If you just take the responsibility, there are no more snakes on your board. You cannot build any more karma; it is over. The moment you focus the whole attention on yourself, you will see you are the source of everything that is happening here. The moment this awareness comes into you, you cannot build any more karma; it's finished. Now only what is stored up, you have to handle. It's very simple. Otherwise you will go on emptying from one side and filling from the other side. There is no end to it.

Life has been going on like this. We don't know for how long. Many, many, many lifetimes it will continue to go on like this, unless your whole energy gets centered on yourself. Once the whole focus is on yourself, it not only burns up the past but also blocks the slide; you cannot slide any more. Now there is a new strength, there is a new freedom. Isn't it so? There is a new sense of well-being. Just in a moment, all these things happen, because the slide is stopped. By just being here, you have taken a step ahead. Please look at your own life and see, from the earliest age that you remember, until some time ago, let us say a year ago, just see the heaviness that you have gathered around yourself. Just see the life-negative substances that are slowly gathering around every human being. The slide is on, isn't it? Maybe some are sliding very fast, some are sliding a little slowly, but mostly, almost everyone is sliding, in terms of life. In terms of society, in terms of money and so many other things you may be going up, but in terms of life, from your childhood until now, definitely there is a slide. It is a constant slide. By the time most people are fifty or sixty, the burden on their head is such that it shows. It literally shows, on most of them. Some people are polished enough to hide it, but it shows on most of them.

Once some awareness seeps into you, working out the past, working your way through the past becomes simple. Going to the river with a bucket to get water is one thing. Going to the river with a sieve and trying to bring water to the ashram is something else. This is what you are doing with your life. Your mind is full of holes. Your life is full of holes. With that you want to catch something. What can you catch? You put whatever grains through the sieves only to catch impurities, isn't it? That is what you catch, nothing worthwhile in life. Whether you have one hole or one hundred holes, it makes no difference. Until you plug that, you won't bring water. You'll only come empty handed.

So in every life that you come here, whether you have one

hole or one hundred holes, every time people come, they go back empty-handed. Nothing attained, nothing gained, you are coming and going, birth and death. Punarapi Jananam, Punarapi Maranam. Only when you plug those holes you don't have to go to the river. The river comes to you; that is how it is. You don't have to go in search of God anymore. The moment your receptivity is right, God is. There is no need to search for God. There is no need to search for Truth. The moment your receptivity is right, Truth is. It is more essential than you and me. It is more essential than existence itself. It's not something that you search for; it is just that you are prepared to receive; that's all. It's not a piece of stone or a diamond or something to find. It's something that is everywhere, something that is always. So there is no question of finding it. It's just that you have to create the right kind of receptivity, and it is there. Plug all your holes and it is there. Are you plugging the holes? First of all, stop puncturing yourself; that's most important. If you stop punching holes into yourself, the holes that are already there are easy to close. If you stop creating new negativities, new karmas, the old holes are easy to handle. Your only problem is creating newer and newer karmas. That's the whole problem, do you understand? If that is stopped, you will see that the sense of buoyancy increases every day. Day by day, you will see that things are going up, not down any more. It cannot go down any more, because every moment, everywhere, within you, without you – God is; His Grace is. It is just that you don't have the right receptacle to receive Him, that's all. Watch yourself and do not make new holes. That is the most important aspect of sadhana.

SEEKER: *Master, you said that in the Indian tradition, the cow and the snake are revered. Does it mean to say there is no compassion for other animals?*

SADHGURU: No, no. Compassion should be there for the others, too. All animals are worshipped wholesale here (laughs). See, if you have to eat some animal for food, if you have to kill some animal and eat it, even towards that you should have compassion; there is no doubt about it. Even for a rudimentary man, the snake and cow have been a taboo only because these are the compulsory steps in the process of evolution of the soul. It should not matter; if you have the same compassion for everybody, but if you are a rudimentary man who kills, you spare at least these two animals, because they are potential human beings. It's like killing a man; it is so close. If you kill a chicken or something else, the police don't arrest you. Only if you kill a human being it is a murder and they arrest you, isn't it? Why? You should have the same compassion for all life forms – it's the same loss for all life forms, isn't it?

In the Indian tradition, the laws were fixed like this: if you kill a human being it's murder; if you kill a cow it's murder; if you kill a snake, it's also murder. That was how it was fixed, but they could not fix a law to say that anything you kill is murder, because the need to kill was there, maybe for man's survival, for his food. Now the cow is one animal that has human emotions. A cow will shed tears when you have suffering in you. People have very deep relationships with cows in India, and snakes are very sensitive to certain types of energies. Wherever there are meditative situations, or rituals are performed, snakes are drawn there.

SEEKER: *Snakes, or the symbolism of snakes, is predominant in this culture. They are worshipped here and seem to have a significant meaning in yoga also. How come they are seen as evil in the West, especially in Christianity? Can you explain this, Sadhguru?*

SADHGURU: Everybody is after my snakes; even you started now! (Laughs). Snakes, I think many times we have spoken why snakes, and what is the significance of a snake. Fundamentally, one aspect of this is that it is the symbolism for the Kundalini because of its nature, and its similarity with that of a snake in terms of movement and stillness. Another aspect is that the snake is at a very significant step in the evolutionary process of the being. As the monkey is at a very significant step in the evolutionary process of the body, the snake is at a very significant step in the evolutionary process of the being. It is based on this that in this culture, you are not supposed to kill a snake. If you happen to find a dead snake or if you happen to kill one, then you must give it a proper funeral and a burial in India. Are you aware that a snake always gets a proper burial, like a human burial, because in terms of its being, it is very close to a human being. So killing a snake amounts to murder. That is one aspect. There are so many things; and you know, for me, snakes have always been around me. People are complaining about my garden which is full of snakes, particularly about one of my close friends who is very big, and people are terrified of him. He is very beautiful. Nobody is seeing how beautiful he is. Everybody is concerned about how big he is! (Laughs).

About the Western culture having a very negative attitude towards snakes, it is fundamentally because of a gross misinterpretation of certain aspects of the Christian philosophy. One basic aspect about the snake being a negative factor, or it being presented as a Devil's agent is because the snake came and tempted Eve to eat the apple. Now two idiots were on this planet: Adam and Eve, and they did not even know what it means. See, a man or a woman going beyond their dualities of being a man and a woman consciously, by choice, and transcending their sexual identification is a wonderful thing; but not even being aware of it is a stupid thing. They were not Enlightened and free, they were ignorant, so ignorant that they didn't know what that even means. There was no possibility of life. The snake entered the scene and tempted Eve because he found Eve to be the easier nut (laughs), and induced life on this planet.

If you believe life on this planet is God's creation, and if the snake has been the agent to induce life on this planet, you tell me whether the snake is the Divine's agent or the Devil's agent (laughs). It must be the Divine's agent, isn't it? Whatever induces life on this planet must be a Divine agent. Only somebody who is dead against the very process of life, who is stupid enough not to even accept the fundamental processes of life – the basic biology of life – such a person will think of the snake, which induced the process of life on this planet, as the Devil's agent. Anybody who is for life will definitely see the snake as a Divine agent.

Here, in this culture, we see him as a Divine agent and Shiva Himself carried snakes, not at his feet, but above His head, because in many ways, the snake is seen as a significant step towards life, human life, human possibilities. Because of that, in this culture, whichever temple you go to, there are snakes. I don't think there is any temple without a snake. Somewhere, there will be a little snake in almost every temple. At least all the ancient temples have snakes. Many temples that are built these days are just like your shopping complexes, probably for the same purpose. They may not have snakes, but any ancient temple you will see there is a place for a snake, because it's a very important step in the evolutionary process of the being, and in many ways, it is the inducer of life. For us, in Isha, it is very significant for so many reasons; some of them you know, some of them you are yet to know because if I speak too much about snakes, people will get paranoid. For me, they need to be constantly around me. I am very comfortable with them.

It is painful ignorance to see the snake as an agent of the Devil. If you believe God is almighty and if He did create the Devil, if He is the Creator of everything, if He did create the Devil, then He must have a useful role for the Devil also! Otherwise, we would have done without the Devil. If you are a believer in God, and you believe that everything is God's creation, and if God had to create a Devil, then you must be mature enough to understand and accept that the Devil also has a rightful place in the process of creation and his agent also has a rightful place. They must have some purpose to serve, isn't it? It is a rudimentary mind which divides life into good and bad. Anybody who knows life will not divide life as good and bad. We still choose, we make choices, but choices are coming in terms of what leads you towards freedom and what leads you towards bondage, not because something is good or bad. We have not chosen to be in a certain way because we think another way is bad. We decided to meditate, not to drink alcohol today, not because we think alcohol is bad; we meditate because we see meditation as leading us towards freedom. Alcohol was leading us towards bondage, so we chose freedom; that's all. Any conscious human being naturally will choose freedom. It's not because we have a morality, "This is 'bad' and this is 'good'," that we have chosen this. We have chosen this consciously. It is rudimentary minds which always want to divide everything into good and bad. Once there is 'good' and 'bad', there is going to be a fight, and what is 'good' and 'bad' is everybody's cake. Everybody can decide what is 'good' and 'bad' for themselves.

See, right from day one, the snakes have distracted the Adams and Eves. Half the world believes that the snake is the agent of the Devil because, you know, it tempted Eve to eat the apple. Now this eating the apple was not an evil thing. If God did not want life to happen, he would not have done that. It is only eating this apple which induced life on this planet. It is the root of life. If life is God's creation, definitely the snake was a Divine agent. Only people who are against life will say it was the Devil's agent. Anybody who is for life will naturally see that the snake was the main inducer of life. So anything that induces life must be a Divine agent, not the Devil's agent.

The Only Bondage

SEEKER: *Is nature always working within us, Sadhguru, so that we unconsciously evolve?*

SADHGURU: Charles Darwin told you that you were all monkeys, your tail fell off and you became human. When you were a monkey, you did not desire to become human. Nature just pushed you on with your evolution. Once you are in this human form, you can only evolve consciously. Unconscious evolution is over for you. The unconscious evolution is the physical evolution of the world, but once you come in the human form, the evolutionary process is in your hands now.

SEEKER: *Darwin's theory says man has evolved from monkeys. Given the human population, by now, monkeys should have gone away!*

SADHGURU: No, Doug, too many monkeys are sitting here as humans with very minor modifications (laughs). That is what I am saying. All the process, all the steps in Darwin's theory are not essential for the being to evolve, but these two forms, the cow and the snake, are significant steps in the evolution of the being. Darwin only talked about the evolutionary process in the physical sense. He did not say every creature had to go through the form of reptile, bird, mammal and all that. He was only talking about the body, how it is evolving, how the whole of nature is evolving on this planet; that was all. Darwin was only talking about how the whole nature on this planet was evolving; how both the plant and the animal life are evolving. How, somewhere before they started, there was no plant and animal. It was a common life form, and somewhere they deviated. Plants became what they are and animals became what they are. He was only talking about the physical evolution of the planet as such.

SEEKER: *So Master, since there are more and more people all the time, doesn't that mean that other life forms are evolving into human form? If so, why aren't there fewer of the other forms? How does that fit into the evolutionary process?*

SADHGURU: That is simply because you are thinking in terms of quantities. Suppose one million life forms started. Now one million people are here; that means all the life forms should have been extinct. That is the logic, isn't it? That's not the way it is. It's not in terms of numbers. Suppose I create a billion bubbles and all the air is contained in them, where is there more air for other bubbles to come? That's the question, isn't it? Life does not happen that way; when we talk about the unbounded, there is no such arithmetic. Darwin never explored that sphere of life. He was not looking at how life came to be. He was only seeing how life evolved; he was only describing evolution that had been recorded on this planet, in fossils and this and that. He studied, he described, and he made a theory that said this is how life has evolved, how the physical form, the present sophisticated body has come out of that crude form that was created earlier, how it has evolved itself to this point of evolution. Darwin was only talking about that. He never talked about life as such. He was only talking about the natural evolution of physical life on this planet. Evolution and karmic laws are not against each other; they go with each other. If that is true with the body, if Darwin's theory is true with the body's evolution, a similar evolutionary process must be there for the being, for the inner nature also, isn't it? Maybe it does not happen in the same way as the body evolves, but a similar evolution should be there. Moving from the gross to the subtle is there.

SEEKER: *Dear Sadhguru, many times you have told us that we are functioning out of our intellect. If this is so, then how can we use this state to become more open and free?*

SADHGURU: See, when you talk about openness, being absolutely open means that who you are should not be. The limited identity should completely go away. Only then, you are truly and absolutely open. Right now, if you look at it from the limited means that you have, it is an impossible thing. People believing that, "I am absolutely open," is again illusory. As I have always insisted, never think of liberation; never think of freedom; never think of openness. Always think in terms of that which binds you. Your business is with that which binds you. Right now, your hands and legs are tied up. You thinking about freedom is of no use. You just see how to handle the ropes which bind you; your business is with them. This may look uninteresting for the romantic people because they want to visualize how it is in heaven, how free they will be, how they will fly through the skies. It's not romantic. It is realistic and it is workable. Very easily, one can work themselves out of the bondages that they have fallen into. The same goes for openness and being closed. What is it that has closed you up? Before we look at how to become open, what is it that closes you up?

SEEKER: *Emotions.*

SADHGURU: Not just emotions. There are four dimensions which could have closed you for so many reasons. Your mind could be closed because of the influences that it is subject to. Once the mind is closed, the emotions will also be within the closed circle of what the thoughts are – for the way you think is the way you feel. Your emotions are always guided by your thoughts. They may not be conscious for most people, but it is so. Another thing is, your physical body itself may be closed, and your energies may be closed. If you take two people who don't know anything about spiritual processes into a certain atmosphere, or let us say into a certain initiation, you will see that one person responds with absolute openness. Another person, even though he is mentally wanting to – even if he is praying for that to happen to him – it does not happen to him because he is closed either on the physical body level or on the energy level, of which he has no awareness.

This becoming closed has happened because of the structures that we have built over a period of time. These structures are what we are calling karmas. In India, we call them vasanas or samskaras. It means that you built limited structures around yourself. These structures were essential for your survival. Because your whole focus was on survival, you strengthened these structures too much. After some time, the same structure which was protecting you is now restricting you. You don't want it anymore, but then you don't know how to get rid of it, because that is how your whole orientation of life has been. For example, as we are heading to Badrinath in this bus, Suman has pulled the whole shutter down to protect herself from the sun and dust. After some time, when there is a change in the weather, she wants to open it but she is unable to do it; maybe the bolts are stuck. She cannot open it and now it becomes a desperation.

This is the situation of many human beings in the world – almost everybody – because of their security concerns, because of simply responding to their own basic sense of survival in the world. Their body, their mind, their emotions and their energy have created certain cocoons. These cocoons did, in limited atmospheres, help them to protect themselves, but when your longing reaches for other dimensions, the same things which were protecting you are a huge restriction. It is like, when you were a small kid, your parents protected you. It was nice; you enjoyed the protection. You enjoyed the comfort of being hugged and kept on their lap, but once you became a little bigger, you wanted to get off their lap and run. If they don't allow you and hold you on their lap, you will start struggling and hating that which holds you down. Karma is just like this. This is not a question of right or wrong. This was created with a certain understanding of well-being, which is limited. When that is fulfilled and naturally your being longs for the next thing, it becomes a restriction.

Whatever spiritual processes we start – on all levels of body, mind, emotion, and energy – slowly all these dimensions are handled, but one thing which is easily at hand for you is the mind and emotions. Making yourself mentally open is very fundamental and very crucial, because this is something that is immediately in your hands. Your energy is not in your hands; you don't know how to open it. Even your physical body, you don't know how to keep it open, but your mind is something that you can consciously open. That's why a lot of talk is going on about opening the mind, not because it's the most important, but because right now that is most available for people. For opening other dimensions, anyway sadhana is there. You don't have to understand how. You just do the sadhana and it opens up, but if the energy opens up – on the level of your energy, if your karmic structure opens up and becomes more receptive, then you don't have to bother about your mind, emotions or anything, because suddenly everything changes. If you go through the mind, emotion or body, it is a more accessible way, but a very long way. If you open up the energy, it is not so accessible, but if it is opened with a certain external influence, then it's a very quick way. You don't have to understand anything. What is happening is beautiful.

SEEKER: *Master, if you know that your focus in life is wrong, you know you have blocks inside of you, you don't know where those blocks are, but they are keeping you from seeing goodness in life and in people – what can you focus on to help remove those blocks?*

SADHGURU: You mean blocks that you are conscious of?

SEEKER: *I don't know, Sadhguru. I just know there are blocks there – energy, physical, mental – I don't know...*

SADHGURU: Fundamentally, the very karmic walls are always like this. They are like sheets of glass. If they were like walls of brick, you could see them and you could break them, but they're sheets of glass. Everything is open, but when you try to reach out you are locked in; that's how it is. Now, what can I do to break that? Why sadhana is always set up – apart from any teaching – is just because of this: any teaching, after a certain period of time, becomes a block by itself, in a certain sense. You will twist it to your convenience. You can twist all teachings in the world. Initially, a teaching has an impact on you because it's new and you have no clue as to how it works, so it works; but over a period of time, as you begin to understand, then you will start twisting it to your convenience. You will see how the teaching supports you. The teaching is not about supporting you; the teaching is about demolishing you, but you will start using the teaching as a support for yourself. Once that happens, the teaching is no good anymore. That is why a Guru is constantly talking from different dimensions. It is Truth, but they are so contradictory that he does not allow you to settle anywhere, because the moment you settle, you start using it to your advantage. Apart from this process, the sadhana is always there – just the simple things. A kriya – in the morning you sit and breathe in a certain way – can slowly decimate these blocks. If you don't understand any teaching, it doesn't matter. You just keep doing the practice; after some time, suddenly there is a new sense of openness and freedom in you. That's always the bedrock that you can rely on, because you can always twist teachings.

SEEKER: *Sadhguru, whichever way I try to be, my karma comes and bombs me out. How do I work off my karma?*

SADHGURU: Oh, really? Good, you admitted you have got a little bit (laughs). See, certain aspects of life are going in a certain way. Whatever the karmic structure, we're not trying to change the karma. We are trying to be free from the karmic structure. We're not talking about creating good karmas. Creating good karma still amounts to survival, a little better living. We're not seeing how to live a little better. We are seeing how to become free. So this freedom will happen, not because you are trying to change the trajectories of your karmas this way or that way. Let the karma go and bomb whatever it wants to, you are no more a part of it. That is the path that I am offering you. That is the awareness that is being created. That is the possibility that is alive right now. Let the karma go and bomb anything. You are not a part of it any more.

Once you know how to be aware, once the necessary awareness — to be away from your own body, to be away from your own mind — has come to you, don't even bother about your karmas. Just see how to deepen this awareness. Do you see, being here with me, or during the Isha Yoga programs, there have been many moments of awareness? This is the beginning of freedom. Your business is just to establish that, not to bother about your karma. Let the karmas go wherever they want to go.

SEEKER: *Sadhguru, if we are creating more karma just with our thoughts — to actions we can say, "It's not necessary," but the mind is not in our control. It is scary to think that even a single thought can give you a backlog of karma that you may have to work out for lifetimes.*

SADHGURU: As I have already said, you don't have to watch your actions; it's a wrong idea that people have. By watching your actions, you aren't getting anywhere. It is the thought process which creates the volition, the intention. If you do something with strong volition, either positive or negative volition, both ways you build karma. If you're looking for just creating a little more pleasant atmosphere for yourself to live in, then you try to create good karma, but being on the spiritual path is not about making life pleasant. It's about seeing how to transcend both the pleasant and the unpleasant.

You have had enough of both the pleasant and the unpleasant; now you want to just drop this bag and go beyond this present dimension of existence. So this must always be understood: karma is not in terms of what you do and do not do. Karma is only in terms of what you desire to do. It is attributed to Gautama, the Buddha, that he said 'desirelessness'. When he said 'desirelessness', he is not stupid, to think that people can exist here without desire; he knows that without desire there is no existence. You being desireless means you have no identification with your desires; your desires are only about what is needed. You have no personal identity with the desires that you play with. Desires are just things that you play with. Without desire, there is no game at all, but now the desires are not about you anymore. It is just the way it's needed for this moment, for this situation. Once that awareness is there – once you are desireless in that sense, there is no karmic bondage for that person. Whatever he does, even if he fights a war, there is no karma for him because he has no desire to do anything like that. It's not coming out of his love for something or hate for something. It is just coming because simply, that's the way. That is the whole Gita. See, Krishna is constantly talking about nishkarma – not performing any karma, but insisting that Arjuna should act. He is talking about the same desirelessness with a different language and a different connotation, but nevertheless it is the same thing. Here we are just talking about simply accepting. Just accepting everything is desirelessness, in a certain way. It does not mean you will become still and you will become incapable of activity or anything like that. It's just that, once you are truly accepting what is there, you're not identified with anything. Everything is there the way it is, do whatever you can do about it. That's all there is. You can be deeply involved with everything, but still not be identified with it any more.

SEEKER: *Dear Master, can karmas accumulated in a lifetime be done away with in a moment?*

SADHGURU: See, the karma has gathered in you in so many ways. This karma that is recorded either on the level of your body, mind, or physical energies is an accumulation, but once your awareness comes to a certain point, all of this is happening separately from you. In Shoonya, do you see, the mind is happening separately and you are happening separately? This can go so deep into you that if you sit here, everything that is not you and that which is you are separate. Once you are like this, it is all done. Your tape recorder where everything is recorded is there, and you are here. Whatever noise it makes has no impact on you. You are free from it in a moment.

SEEKER: *Sadhguru, is it true that karmas don't take effect upon children?*

SADHGURU: Yes. As soon as you are born, your karmas do not take effect immediately. They just wait for the right atmosphere. Karma can be compared to a seed. Before the rains, the whole land is barren. There would be nothing. It rains; suddenly all kinds of vegetation will sprout up. The seeds are already there; they're just waiting for the right kind of atmosphere. Until then, they are dormant, latent, waiting there. You were carrying it with you, but it had not yet taken effect. It was simply there. When you were just born, it did not take immediate effect. It was waiting. As the process of growth happens, it looks for the right kind of situation and takes effect.

SEEKER: *So we can dissolve this seed of karma. How, Sadhguru?*

SADHGURU: Yes, but not by chopping the plant; dissolving the seed is dissolution of karma. Otherwise there is no dissolution. Maybe it can be covered or converted into something else. You may make your physical suffering into mental suffering and vice versa; it is possible. You can convert one form of karma into another with certain adjustments in life, but it will come anyway. Only when you dissolve the seed, it is finished. It's very resilient.

SEEKER: *Is looking at past lives useful, Sadhguru? I heard that during Samyama programs, people were re-living past life experiences. Is it true?*

SADHGURU: In your memory, let us say you found out that the little boy next door was your husband in some previous lifetime. Many emotions well up and you would not know how to be with that boy. You would also disturb him with your emotions and in no way would it be liberating for you; it is unnecessary. Already with what relationships you have now, you are terribly attached and struggling with them. Just reminding yourself of past-life situations will not do any good, unless some specific memory is opened up for you for a certain kind of work. Otherwise, for your well-being, for your own liberation, it does not do any good. Why Gautama chose regression for the larger public is because it does not need any other preparation. You don't need any understanding, awareness or anything. The only thing that is needed is perseverance; you are willing to sit there and watch and watch. Even if you don't know anything, it does not matter. Other systems need understanding, some preparation; regression doesn't need anything. That is the reason why he chose that for the public, but in closer circles, he did not do regression.

What we handle in Samyama is much more than regression. We are not doing anything particular to regress the person. At the same time, when your awareness is heightened in a particular direction, as your awareness becomes deeper and deeper, the unconscious layers of the mind start flicking up and coming into your consciousness. It can happen physically. People can go through the whole act – whatever their past life – physically, within themselves, energy-wise or memory-wise. In the earlier Samyamas, too many past life memories were coming up, but now I have almost taken away the aspect of memory because later on, people can struggle. For some people it's very liberating to remember, but for many, this remembrance can be very entangling. Whenever this remembrance happens on the energy level, it is always liberating, although you might not be aware of it on the

The Only Bondage

mental level. You cannot call Samyama regression, because regression methods are generally psychological exercises. What people are generally calling liberation is mainly psychological exercises. It is only giving a different manifestation of your own present psyche. It's more of a psychological exercise. It's not really about past lives. It just brings in other dimensions of your psyche which are not in your normal experience, but that is not what it should be. If you go through such experiences, it is cathartic, but it's not at the level of bringing the unconscious into the conscious.

SEEKER: *Sadhguru, can regression therapy to recall past lives be beneficial in any way?*

SADHGURU: Psychological exercises have got nothing to do with past lives. It is all just a different projection of your present experience. See, your mind has different projections of the same thing. That is what Freud was talking about. What Freud says is that if you look at your mother, one thing is you see her as a caring, loving mother. Another thing is: you are looking at her sexuality. Another thing is: you remember her breasts from your childhood. Another thing is: when you were in the womb and coming out, you remember her reproductive organs. Because of all these projections, you have so many things mixed up in you, which make you into a complex human being. This is not past life.

There are so many images of the same thing, which are normally not in your perception. The psychological processes of regression can only bring up those things. Now, you think it's past life, but it is not so. It's another projection of your mind. Let us say you saw a film in positive. Now you see it in negative. It looks totally different. You are seeing it backwards, it also looks totally different. Let us say you saw your mother as a young woman or something else, which you have forgotten on a conscious level. When she delivered you, she was probably twenty. Today, you remember her as forty, or sixty. So 'my mother' means you have an image of a forty-year-old woman, or a sixty-year-old woman, but somewhere in your mind there is a twenty-year-old woman. So when that image comes mixed up with so many things you may think, "Oh, maybe I knew my mother in my past life." This is not the reality. It is just the layers and layers of recording that are happening in your mind. That's the significance of Freud's work. That is just a psychological exercise, and the regression processes that are happening around the world are just that.

SEEKER: *So Master, for instance, when I see a different time and I'm in a different place, is that still true? Say I am in France, in a cathedral, in front of monks giving me instructions, and as a result of not following the instructions, I see myself put to death by the Catholic Church. I am seeing all this happening! Even though this is not in my current experience, somehow it is coming up and I'm seeing this. What is this? What is happening?*

SADHGURU: On a certain day, a drunk got into the subway train and plonked himself next to a parish priest. After a while, the drunk asked, "Why are you wearing your collar backside front?" The priest soberly answered, "That is because I am a father." The drunk said, "So what? Even I am a father with three children!" The priest explained, "No, you don't understand, I am a father to my whole congregation." So the drunk said, "Wearing your collar backside front won't help then; it's your pants that you need to wear backside front!" So Patricia, keep your mind backside front, otherwise you will have a congregation of fancy hallucinations. Too much of a Catholic upbringing has gone into you! All this is just your mind playing tricks with you. I want you to understand one thing: there is one dimension of a human being which is longing to be unbounded; the rest of it is all limited – your body, your mind, your perceptions – because the only tools that you have are body and mind. This body and mind try to do funny things to project you as something more than what you are right now – always. Some people call

The Only Bondage

it romance, I call it hallucination. I don't want to take all the beauty of romance away from people's lives, but understand that if you are enjoying your dream, just enjoy it. If you are enjoying a movie, just enjoy it; that's all. Enjoy it. There is no problem about enjoying it, but don't create any significance to it. People who see such things, you will notice, are seeing so many things that don't even exist. Slowly they have become senseless about their life, about what is in front of them. Have you noticed this?

A lot of these new-age people and others who are talking about past lives and all this have no sense about the life that they are living right now, isn't it? This is simply because you are going into hallucinatory states. You are not realizing it. If Realization comes, you will become absolutely sensible with what is here now. This is the significant difference between something that comes out of your awareness and something that comes from a hallucinatory state. Awareness spreads into every dimension of your life; not just the way you eat, the way you stand, the way you sit, but everything, the very way you exist. You will become absolutely sensible. If you are moving into hallucinatory states, you are always having huge visions of great things, but in your physical reality, you are becoming more and more senseless. This is a clear indication that you are hallucinating.

SEEKER: *But Sadhguru, during this Karma Samyama, it has been spoken about how people remember their past lives, and how real everything is in their experience. What is the difference between what is happening with Patricia and what is happening in Samyama?*

SADHGURU: In Samyama, there is no input. There is no psychological exercise that says, "Do this, see this, say that", you know? Nothing. It is just meditation. It's simply meditation. The meditations and the processes are just aimed at pushing your energies up to such a point that your body will explode. Now, why are we pushing the energies up? To put it very simply, a very rudimentary example would be, let us say there is a light bulb here. It needs two hundred and forty volts to be fully lit, but here, in this rural power supply, we are only getting one hundred volts. If it's one hundred volts, you see only that much. If it becomes one hundred and fifty volts, you see a little bit more. If it becomes two hundred and forty volts, it will show you everything that is in the area, isn't it? So all we are trying to do is raise your voltage. We are not trying to make you see anything. I'm not saying, "Look there. This past life is there. God is coming; Jesus is coming; something else is coming." No, we are just cranking up your energy to the highest possible pitch, full voltage. In full voltage, everything that is there, you simply see; that's all. This is not suggested to you. We are not making an attempt to see anything. By wanting to see something, you will only go into imagination or hallucinations. Right now, it's dark. Let us say in the evening you come into this garden. It is pitch dark. If you try to see something, you'll imagine many things which are not there. Isn't it so? Trying to see is a stupid thing. There is no such thing as trying to see.

Samyama is not trying to see your past life. It is just cranking up your energy to the highest pitch. If your voltage is full, your awareness will spread. That also is limited to the kind of bulb that you are. Okay? Let us say you are a big halogen bulb. It lights up a whole big space, but if you are just a little bulb, at full brightness it sees what it has to see. No matter how much we crank up the energy, this bulb will see only that much, but the business is to crank it up to the full pitch, so that whatever is possible, it will see. Once it sees and dissolution happens, this little bulb, next time it meditatively sits, it will become a little bigger bulb, a little more potent. Do you see this happening every time you go into very intense processes of meditation? Have you attended Samyama?

SEEKER: *Yes*.

SADHGURU: The first day, when you came and sat in front

of me, with what clarity did you see? Since then, are you beginning to see many other dimensions of life? This is simply because slowly, your wattage – not the voltage, the wattage – is being upgraded. As your wattage increases, your vision is increasing, but if I tell you, "See, see, see," you will hallucinate. The moment I say, "See," there is no way to see, please see (laughs). Did you get that? I want you to know that there is no way to see by making an effort. You can see only because of the light and your open eyes; that's all. You are not willing to come to terms with the simple facts of life. That's why spirituality seems to be so complex. It is not complex. You are not willing to come to the simple facts of life. You have silly ideas; that is the reason why it seems to be so complex.

So why they say that if you surrender it becomes easy is because by surrendering, you keep all your fancy ideas aside. Surrender does not mean falling at somebody's feet. Surrender simply means that you have kept all your fancy ideas aside. Everything that you consider as 'myself', you kept it aside. That is surrender, isn't it? "No, I surrender to you, I fall at your feet, but I don't like this." That is not surrender. Samyama meditations do not happen as a regression process. It is just a meditative process. Once a person moves into a higher level of awareness and a certain direction is there, naturally layers of the unconscious become conscious; that's why we call it Karma Samyama. It is an enormously liberating experience.

SEEKER: *Sadhguru, is it better to handle past life memories energy-wise rather than memory-wise? And if a person is energized, does past-life memory come up quickly?*

SADHGURU: Right now, what is your experience in life? This moment you are experiencing life; you are sitting here and talking. This moment, what you are experiencing on one level is in the awareness of your mind. In the general awareness of your mind, if you were asleep, you would not know what I'm talking about, but since you are awake and alert now, you know what I am talking about. That's one level of experience. Another level of experience is the physical body sitting here. It has its own experience, but generally, most of it is not in your awareness. Another level of experience is your sensations. Most people are not aware unless it touches them in a certain way; energy-wise also, certain things are happening which are not in your experience. So you can bring back this situation that you are living right now, either in the form of memory, or in the form of body, or in the form of energy. Like this, you can bring it back. Energy-wise if you bring it back, people will not remember, but they work out the same karma on a much deeper level. Memory-wise if you bring it back, some people will work it out, but some people will get even more entangled than before.

SEEKER: *Master, are you saying that actually on all four levels, the play of the karma's manifestation is going on?*

SADHGURU: It's like it is getting imprinted. Everything that happens here is constantly getting imprinted, which is having an influence on what you do next. It is easy to understand the imprints on the mind. That you can see, but people are not aware of other imprints that are also there. This memory, first it is in your energy, then in your sensation, then in your body, then in your mind. In yoga, it is said that one who has mastery over his ring finger can rewrite anybody's destiny. If I just touch my ring finger in a certain way, I can rewrite your destiny if I wish to. It is a whole science by itself. See, your finger can be divided into three portions by the lines drawn on it. The first portion of the ring finger, from the tip onwards, carries lifetimes of experiences. Everything is in this. Everything is written into this, whether you touch here or here or here (gestures), every bit, every milli, milli, millimeter is rich with life. Every micro millimeter is different.

There is a whole lot of sadhana for this. If you just know how to handle your ring finger like you handle a computer mouse, you can scroll all your lifetimes just right here. If you have mastery over it, you can do miraculous things to yourself and to the external situation. The second portion of your ring finger has elaborate detail of your prarabdha. The base digit can be used to predict future possibilities, based on the past accumulations of karma and the present expressions of the prarabdha.

Always in our tradition, for everything that you do, you must use the ring finger. All the nadis are activated by touching certain portions of the finger. If you want to take vibhuthi or kumkum you use this finger to apply it, simply because these are all different ways to defuse the karmic structure. Even unknowingly, if you touch something sacred that has a certain energy quality to it with your ring finger, it dissolves some karma; you get to shed some of it. Now this powerful vibhuthi here, when you take it with your ring finger, unknowingly you will drop some karma right here. The whole tradition was built like that – whichever way, you must be slowly moving towards your liberation.

SEEKER: *So if I just touch this finger like this…?*

SADHGURU: Once you raise your energy to a certain point, in a certain direction, there are certain nadis which are keys to the karmic structure in the physiology. Not all the nadis are like this. Some are keys to physical life, and others are keys to different aspects of life. Certain nadis are keys to the karmic structure. So the moment you touch that, if you are aware, the moment you touch those nadis – now with great intensity, the karmic substance just pours in. If huge volumes of karma pour into your life when you aren't sufficiently prepared, or when the necessary awareness is not there, then it could lead to huge upheavals in your life. If the necessary awareness is there, when it pours in, the energy just works it out in a certain way. So the old karma, whatever it is, begins to work itself out at rapid pace. Right now, just sitting here, talking, living, breathing, is working out some karma. This is happening at a very slow pace, because in the process of dissolving, you are also creating new karma. In heightened states of awareness, you have stopped creating, and dissolution is happening at a rapid pace.

SEEKER: *Sadhguru, this yoga system, the pranayama, this also comes into our energy memory?*

SADHGURU: Yes. Nothing has been taught mentally. Once it's a question of energy, everything that you know on the mental state is also there on the energy state. Do you see that many things you have learned are there in your body without even thinking? For example, if you know how to swim, it is in your body. You don't have to mentally think about it. Almost everything you have learned is on the level of your body, on the level of sensation and on the level of your energy. If I have to teach you something memory-wise, what I know will take ten lifetimes for you to learn because it has taken that long to acquire, but if it has to be transferred by energy, it can be transferred in a moment. That is what an initiation is. Initiation is not a bundle of instructions.

SEEKER: *I may not know how to receive this, Sadhguru!*

SADHGURU: Now transmitting and receiving is on many different levels. If we teach people certain kriyas, in the very process of teaching the kriyas, we also offer a certain amount of energy. That's why I am repeatedly saying while we are teaching yoga kriyas, "Don't try to learn mentally; we will put it in you some other way. Just be patient and receive it," but people want to write it down. It is just that energy-wise, it can be put in differently; the whole dimension is different, and it works in a different way. People think the only way to learn is to write down and memorize. This is done on the pranic level, but on the level of your etheric body also, there is memory. The subtler parts of your memory are always in the etheric body. It is very subtle energy. Right now, suppose you take a seed, or now you have genes, isn't it? Do you know genes have a memory? A gene is just a memory chip; it has generations of memory in it and it is manifesting it. That is not in your mind. If you had to remember all that in your mind, you know what a burden it would be.

If you take an apple seed and put it in a mango grove, it will not give mangos. It will only produce apples because the memory that it is an apple is deeply written into it. No matter what you do, it will only produce apples. You cannot confuse an apple tree to produce mangos or peaches, or something else. The memory is so perfect. That is what karma means; it is a deep-rooted memory. You cannot confuse it. Similarly, it does not matter where you put the man, you make him a king, or you make him a beggar, or make him whatever, his deep-rooted memory is constantly taking effect. There is a story in the yogic lore. One man loved his dog very much. So his ambition became that somehow, he had to make this dog into the king of that country. Anybody that you love, you want to put them up, isn't it? He loved his dog, so he wanted to make his dog into a king. He played some trick, and the dog ended up marrying a princess. Then they put him up on the throne. Now the dog sat on this throne, dressed in all regal clothes with the whole pageantry serving him and everything; but one day, he saw a bone out there and ran straight for it. That is what they say about the karma. What is in your deep-rooted memory, no matter where we put you, you will only go after that. Unless you move into an awareness that takes you beyond these limitations, your karma will work compellingly.

SEEKER: *Sadhguru, you tell us not to create new karma, but how? You say don't judge, but how not to judge?*

SADHGURU: Even in the basic Isha Yoga program, the first

three sessions are all about not creating a new stock of karma. Only later, we are talking about dissolution. What is more important than dissolving karma is that you learn to stop creating new karma. If you don't create a new stock, the old stock will go in its own time, or if you are aware enough, you can drop it in a moment; that's different. The important thing is to stop creating. With every reaction, you are creating more karma. Especially you, Indu, you have strong likes and dislikes.

SEEKER: *Yes, very strong, Sadhguru. Only you should save me! Sadhguru, I am very tempted to come to the Samyama program, because I heard one acquires the knowledge and the sakshi not to create new karma if one goes through this.*

SADHGURU: Indu, if you sit there with this attitude of getting something, you will only gather more! (Laughs). Samyama is an extremely rapid way of dissolving, an almost violently rapid way of dissolving. When your karmic structure begins to fall apart at a very rapid pace, you will see violent things will happen in the body, because it's just going through lifetimes like that. What would take many lifetimes is just happening in moments, so it takes on a violent form sometimes. The very way the teaching goes is about not reacting. Just accepting and not reacting is just to stop creating new karma. As you become more and more aware, natural acceptance of what is there becomes so much higher. One important aspect of Samyama is to teach you to become meditative with your eyes open. We start with eyes closed and we slowly move people to a state where they open their eyes partially, then fully, then get active with everything, just maintaining the same awareness. So once you are able to maintain that awareness with eyes open and with activity, then the question of creating karma does not arise. It is just a rapid dissolution. If one establishes himself in the Samyama state, dissolution happens. The question of creating does not arise at all.

SEEKER: *Sadhguru, there is a lot of teaching out there about positive thinking and how it can transform your life. Is it that simple? Can positive thinking help you get rid of karma, or at least keep you from creating more karma? Yet there's something about people who are always repeating positive affirmations that seems shallow.*

SADHGURU: The reason these people have lost depth to their life is that they have become frivolous by focusing their attention on only what is convenient for them, which they call positive. They want everything quick, quick, quick, quick (snaps fingers). There is no dedication to anything. Suppose somebody has to become a scientist. He has to study for years, isn't it? Maybe he will forget his wife, his children, his nonsense; he forgets everything and gives himself. Only then something opens up for him, even on the physical plane.

If these things have to open up for you, it needs enormous focus. That steady focus is not there in the modern world, because somebody is going about teaching all the time, "Don't worry, be happy; just enjoy yourself! Enjoy yourself! Everything is fine; be happy! Laugh! Ha! Ha! Ha!" People just become frivolous and that kind of happiness will crash. One day it will crash. They'll go into mentally sick situations. One big thing that I see that is happening in the West especially is, "Be happy, be happy, live in the moment, live in the moment." Everybody will quote, "Live in the moment," because books have been written about it, all the programs have talked about it, without understanding, especially without experiencing what it is. Everybody is saying, "I am happy; I am always happy. I am always laughing." You watch those people. The moment they start this 'I am happy, I am happy' business, depending upon their lifestyles, within five or six years they'll come to a depressed state. One day, it will hit you very deeply, because your energies, according to your karmic structure, are apportioned for different possibilities. There's something for your pain. There's something for your grief. There's something for your joy. There's something for your love. This is prarabdha karma. It is not just in your mind, because the data is like that; the energy is flowing in those directions. If those things don't find expression, if you deny them, they will take root in a completely different way.

Accepting is so important because accepting means you simply see everything the way it is. You don't deny anything. If grief comes, grief. Sadness comes, sadness. Joy comes, joy. Ecstasy comes, ecstasy. When you do this, you are not denying anything; at the same time, everything is happening, but you are free from it. You're not trying to stop anything; but if you just say, "I am happy, I am happy, I am happy," this positive thinking – do you see that all those positive-thinking people went crazy? Most people who promoted all this went mad. They committed suicide. The 'Don't worry, be happy' people have committed suicide! It's bound to happen, because energy is apportioned to your prarabdha karma in different ways. Karma is data. According to this data, your energy is functioning. If you deny it, it will take root in some other way. It will find expression in some other way.

SEEKER: *The other day, I saw this space around you, and when you were moving, it seemed to be filled with these small, small, small… I don't know what to call it, but is that energy? Can I call it energy, Sadhguru?*

SADHGURU: There are particles, the fundamental particles which constitute the basic construction materials for the atom. Today, modern science clearly says that the whole existence is just particles, moving in different patterns, but these particles have given way to energy. Even for a particle to move around there is energy behind it. So the most fundamental thing is energy. On that the particles happen, the particles become an atom, the atom becomes matter, you know? Then the other dimensions of creation happen, but the fundamental thing is absolute emptiness. Today, they have studied the radioisotopes that come from what are called black holes, which are total emptiness. They say they are very powerful. There seems to be another kind of energy there, the kind of energy which is not physical. Energy is always physical – electric, electronic, whatever – it is physical. It is a flow of electrons. In those black holes there is no flow of electrons – no electrons, protons and neutrons, but still it is very powerful. It's a different kind of energy. It is that which we have always been calling as Shoonya. It's that which we have been calling as the core of a human being, whatever it is. That is the most fundamental. It is that which we are referring to as mukthi also – to become that which is non-physical. Whatever you see, a particle or an atom, is still physical.

There is another dimension which is not physical. In that non-physical state, there is no memory. Memory is only in the physical state. That energy, that prana, is still physical, just like electricity. Once you move into the non-physical, there is no memory, so there is no karma. That is why Shoonya meditation is so important. If you move into Shoonya, you are completely free from all karmic structures, because in that state of no-thing – you will understand it better if you put a hyphen between no and thing – it is no longer physical. Once it is not physical, there is no such thing as karma because this whole karma, or the cause and effect, belong to the physical reality. Either you can sit here and start working out your karma step-by-step – which may take we don't know how long – or you just move beyond your physical reality and all karma is gone in an instant.

SEEKER: *So my energy also is pure power?*

SADHGURU: What do you mean by pure power?

SEEKER: *Electricity cannot carry the memory. It goes to the refrigerator and makes it work. It can go to the heater or to the cooler. Similarly, energy is pure. In my body, somewhere this energy is heat, somewhere it is anger, somewhere it is greed, whatever. That pure energy,* one might discover as a black hole. Pure means it is not passing through the boxes. All my boxes have become neutral. The body has become very cause-and-effect-less. So the energy flows...

SADHGURU: You are talking about Ultimate Nature flowing as energy. No, Ultimate Nature does not flow as energy. It cannot flow, because it is nothingness. It can only flow from something-ness. Only because this is something it can move from here to there. How can nothingness move from here to there? It is not that which is moving. Everything that is moving is physical. Maybe it is very subtle, but it's still physical. Memory is built into that physical energy, not into the Ultimate Nature. There, there is nothing. That does not carry anything.

SEEKER: *So the purest of pure is not even the awareness; awareness is one type of sakshi.*

SADHGURU: One of the manifestations.

SEEKER: *Now I got it.*

SADHGURU: Oh, you keep saying that, every day. What can be of ultimate purity? Only nothingness can be absolutely pure, isn't it? Everything else has a duality. The closest manifestation of nothingness is blissfulness. It is so much easier for you to understand this if you look at it in the way yoga describes the five bodies. The closest creation, the first creation is blissfulness; from blissfulness to awareness, from awareness to energy, from energy to mind and from mind to body. It is the simplest way of putting it.

SEEKER: *That awareness, we were told, is the intellect.*

SADHGURU: No, this is the big mistake that people make. People always mistake mental alertness for awareness. Mental alertness is not awareness. A dog has better alertness than you do. A dog or a cat has got much better mental alertness than man, isn't it so? That is not awareness. Mental alertness is still an instrument for survival, but awareness is not an instrument for survival; it is an instrument for creation.

SEEKER: *Sadhguru, will I shed a lot of karma in Shoonya dhyana as well?*

SADHGURU: It is not a question of shedding the karma; you are learning to create a distance with your karma. You're not trying to shed karma.

SEEKER: *Okay, so karma will not be a part of me anymore?*

SADHGURU: Right now, you're carrying a big bundle on your head, a basket of karma on your head and you want to sell it to someone. That someone is not going to buy the whole basket, but anyway you will sell them one handful. If you sell them one handful, they will give you something in return. It may be smaller or bigger; it depends on the situation. You drop something, you pick up something else; this goes on. Now we're seeing how to put the basket aside. We are not interested in what is in the basket. We just want to put the basket aside; that's all. Once, Shankaran Pillai had to travel by train with a huge bundle of luggage. He carried it on his head, went into the train, found himself a seat, and sat with the bundle on his head. The co-passengers curiously looked at him sitting with a bundle on his head and they thought, "Okay, maybe he will put it down later," but he didn't, and he sat there quietly, as if everything was normal. The train started and still he sat there with the bundle on his head. Then one passenger, feeling concerned, thought that maybe he needed some help. So she asked him, "Sir, can I help you with anything?" Shankaran Pillai replied, "No, no. I am fine, thank you." And he just sat there. Ten minutes passed, then half-an-hour, and this man sat like this with the bundle on his head. Now the co-passengers' necks started paining looking at this. Totally flabbergasted, they asked him, "What's the problem? Why don't you put it down? If it has something very valuable and you are scared of thieves, please put it down and sit on it! Why are you carrying it on your head?" Shankaran Pillai said, "No, no, nothing valuable inside, just some clothes." "But then why are you carrying it on your head?" "Oh! I just don't want to burden the train." So Indu, please keep your basket aside.

SEEKER: *Then Sadhguru, that is called sakshi. I am the seer of the basket; I am not the basket. That awareness, I am awareness. I am already 'me'. This, which is reflecting, is not 'me'.*

SADHGURU: You thinking, "I am not karma" is karma because you are doing all this sakshi business only to avoid the karma, isn't it?

SEEKER: *No, I am keeping distance from the karma.*

SADHGURU: How?

SEEKER: *By just watching it, Sadhguru; and I have kept the basket down. I see the basket is not dissolved and I say to hell with it. I am not this basket, I am not this karma. Nothing can touch me.*

SADHGURU: Your saying, "I am not this karma," is still karma. When you say, "I am not the karma," what is the intention? You want to be free from the karma. You want to avoid the karma. That itself is karma. If you sit here, your body is here, your mind is there, and you are somewhere else – it is not that you are trying to watch this or that; you are simply here – a clear space has come. Now, whatever karma that is in the mind, whatever karma that is there in the body or energy – everything has become separate from you. For a few moments, if there is a separation, you know it is possible. Once you establish this in your life, it becomes a living reality. If you sit here, the body is here, the mind is there and you are here. Once this distinction comes, now there is no karma for that person. Whatever he wants to do, he can do. Nothing touches him.

SEEKER: *Sadhguru, this is philosophy...*

SADHGURU: Are you okay for a joke? One day a bull was grazing in the field and a pheasant was picking out the ticks off the bull's body. They are used to each other; they are sort of friends, so it's going on. Then the pheasant became nostalgic and said, "When I was young, I could fly and sit on the topmost branch of the big tree out there, but now I can't even get to the first branch." The bull said nonchalantly, "Oh! What's the problem? Just eat my dung, and it will give you all the nourishment that you need to go to the topmost branch." The pheasant said, "Really? You mean just eating your droppings will get me to the top of the tree?" "Yes, try and see!" he replied. So the pheasant hesitantly ate some of the dung, and that very day he flew up to the first branch! Every day, he started eating more and more of the dung. In about a fortnight's time it reached the topmost branch, and went and sat there. The pheasant was so thrilled, having eaten this dung and being able to sit on the topmost branch. Now when the farmer, who was sitting on his balcony, saw this fat pheasant sitting on the topmost branch of the tree, he just pulled out his shotgun and shot the pheasant off the tree! The moral of the story is: bullshit may get you to the top but it will never let you stay there. Your philosophies will not get you anywhere. Mentally if you do it, you're only trying to avoid it more and more. You are only acquiring more karma, because it is resistance. It is craving and aversion which builds the karma. You have an aversion to karma, so you're trying to push it away. In the effort to push it away, you are only building more karma.

SEEKER: *But if I am detached, Sadhguru, and have kept myself so distant, even if I am having an effect of karma in my body, I say, "It is not me"; I don't react to it. There is negativity but I don't say, "Oh, why this negativity?" and shift toward the positive. If it is there, it is there, but it is not me. I am just trying to accept it.*

SADHGURU: Now I must tell you a story about this Vedanta. Once it so happened, Shankaran Pillai went to the Vedanta classes. The speaker, the teacher of Vedanta, was going full swing. "You are not this; you are everywhere; there is nothing like 'yours and his'; everything is yours; after all, everything is maya. What you see, hear, smell, taste, touch, is not reality; it's all maya. There is no such thing as yours and mine; it's all one." This is Vedanta. This really sank into Shankaran Pillai in a very deep way. He went and slept over the Vedanta. He got up in the morning, totally fired up. Usually he loves to sleep but because of this Vedanta, now, first thing in the morning he started thinking, "There is nothing here which is not mine. Everything is mine; everything is me. All that is in this world is me, and everything is maya." Like this he went on. Then, you know, whatever philosophy, hunger comes. So he went to his favorite restaurant and ordered a big breakfast, and he ate saying, "The food is also me, I am also the food, the one who serves is also me, the one who eats is also me." Vedanta! He finished his breakfast, and with his stomach full looked around. He saw the owner of the restaurant sitting there. "It's all mine, what is mine is yours, what is yours is mine." With the same Vedanta thing going on, he got up and started walking out. When everything is yours, where is the question of paying the bill? And when he just happened to cross the counter where the cash box is, the owner got distracted by some other work and left the place, Shankaran Pillai saw a huge heap of currency in the till. Immediately, the Vedanta told him, "Everything is yours; you cannot differentiate between this and that." So because his pockets were quite empty, he put his hand into the box, took some cash, put it in his pocket and continued to walk. He is not out to rob anybody, he is just practicing Vedanta. Then a few people from the restaurant ran behind him and caught him. Shankaran Pillai said, "What are you going to catch? What you catch is also you, the one who catches is also you, what is in my stomach is also in your stomach, so who can I pay?" The owner was bewildered! He only knows idly, dosa, vada! See if a thief tries to run, they know how to catch him, beat him, thrash him; all this they know. But when he said, "The one who catches is also me, the one who is caught is also me," they didn't know what to do, so they took him to the court. There, Shankaran Pillai continued his Vedanta. The judge tried in many ways to make him understand, but Shankaran Pillai continued his Vedanta teachings. Then the judge said, "Okay, sixty lashes." First lash...reality hits. Second lash... a shout. Third lash...a scream. Then the judge said, "Don't worry, the one who lashes is also you, the one who is lashed is also you, so who can lash anybody? It's all maya. So sixty lashes on the backside." Now Shankaran Pillai cries out, "Please, no more Vedanta. Leave me alone!"

These teachings will only deceive you. When you come to a living experience that, 'This body is not me,' then there is a different kind of wisdom in you. There is a different kind of understanding in you. When you intellectually understand, it leads only to these deceptive states. When you experientially know, it's very different. Why you are saying, "It's not me," is because you don't want it to be you, isn't it? A philosophy like that will just give you some semblance of balance in your life, but it does not liberate you from the deeper karma, because you're only trying to avoid it, and in that avoidance you find a little balance in day-to-day life. But slowly, if a person does this philosophy, you will see, slowly they will become joyless. They will become reasonably balanced and stable; at the same time they will slowly become lifeless.

If you bring lifelessness into you, that itself is a very negative karma because you are just suppressing life. That is karma. The most beautiful thing that has been said about this is: Krishna said, "Hesitation is the worst sin," because with hesitation you kill life. Anything that suppresses life is the worst sin. Suppression doesn't mean, "Okay, now I want to eat; I do not eat." This is not suppression. People always think, "If I don't do what I want to do, it is suppression." No! It is just that you are not allowing yourself to experience it totally. Whether hunger or food, if you sit here and experience hunger totally, it is wonderful, it is releasing; or if you experience food totally, it is releasing. But you neither experience hunger fully, nor food fully; this is karma. It is saying, "This is not me." See this 'not me, not me' nethi process is a very different process, but denying what is happening within you is like self-denial. If you deprive yourself of any experience – whether it is pain, suffering, joy or whatever it is – if you avoid it, that is big karma. If you go through it, it is not so much of a karma.

Today, in the name of civilization or whatever – etiquette or education – educated people are not able to experience any of their emotions fully. They cannot cry fully; they cannot laugh loudly. For everything, they have got etiquette. With this you'll see, slowly they will become joyless. A deep sense of frustration will establish itself. You will see simple people who laugh and cry as it comes, they are so much more free. They have not accumulated heaps on them yet; but people with practiced etiquette accumulate heaps on their head. The very process of life is dissolution of karma. Every living moment of your life, if you live it totally, you dissolve enormous amounts of karma. Living totally does not mean just having fun. Anything and everything that comes, you just experience it fully, intensely.

Body's Plight

This toy of elemental ploy
Deceptive in its ability for joy
The pain and bondage of these miraculous five
If broken, you in liberation will fly.
— Sadhguru

The human body is the pinnacle of the physical evolution of life on this planet. The intricacy, complexity and the sophistication is unmatched by anything that modern science can hope to comprehend, far less imitate or compete with. To pack each minute cell with such an enormous amount of intelligence and to infuse this mass of billions of cells with prana (or the subtle life force) of such prodigious potential, is truly the ultimate miracle.

In the spiritual lore, the human body is considered supremely sacred, as this is the only mechanism that can take a being from the limited identification of the self to the unlimited, from a bounded existence to the realm of the unbounded, to the final plunge into the vastness of the Infinite.

Growing from a meeting of two cells, the body, before it

withers away, goes through a series of experiences of pain and pleasure, of disease and deformity. Helplessly entangled in the tentacles of maya, the celestial illusion, the body is also the source of untold fear and suffering. Yet, it is the body that becomes one's deliverance. Thus the seeker's affair with the body runs a full spectrum from trauma to Bliss.

In Body's Plight, Sadhguru dwells at length upon the very nuts and bolts of the mechanics of the body – the karma that dictates its creation and dissolution, of health and healing, of diseases and miraculous cures, of depression and madness, of psychic surgeries, of death and after-death, of birth and rebirths, the choice and the choicelessness of it all.

Walking the seeker through a maze of beliefs, rituals, superstitions and myths, Sadhguru reveals the play of life culminating in what is known in the tradition as Mahasamadhi, Mahaparinirvana, Nirvana, Moksha or the complete liberation of the self, sharing insights on the necessary sadhana to transcend the trap of the body.

SEEKER: *Sadhguru, everyday I see so much disease and suffering around me. Many times it has deeply bothered me as to why a human being should suffer like this at all. It seems so unreasonable that one human being enjoys good health and another one suffers. Can you tell us, why disease? What is it? Where does it come from?*

SADHGURU: There are many aspects to disease. The word 'disease', if you look at it more closely, is dis-ease. You are not at ease. Your body does not know how to rest. When it does not know how to rest, the energies become chaotic. People with asthma attend Isha Yoga programs and begin to do their yoga kriyas and meditate. For many of them, the asthma is completely gone. For others, it is partially gone. For a few others, there is no change. This is because the causes are different. With one person, it is chaotic energy. After three days of practicing yoga kriyas, the energy becomes more organized and their asthma is gone. With another person, one part of it is chaotic energy, another part has deeper karmic reasons, so it is only partially gone. For those where there is no change, there are very strong karmic reasons that are causing the disease. There might also be external situations, which have not changed.

Now how can karma cause disease? There is something called prarabdha. Prarabdha means the allotted karma for this lifetime. There are many aspects to this. To make it simple, prarabdha karma is written into your mind, body, sensations, and your energy. It is most basic on the level of the energy; it is the fundamental recording. How can information be recorded on the energy? It can be recorded. I'm not sure if it is being explored scientifically, but I know that some day science will find a way of recording information on energy. At one time, whatever we wanted to record, we had to write on stone tablets. From there, we moved onto books. Now, what could be written on a thousand tablets can be written in a single book. What could be written in a thousand books can be recorded on a compact disk. What could be put onto a thousand compact disks, we can now store on a small chip. Someday, what we now store in a million chips will be recorded on a little bit of energy. This is a living experience within me. I know it is possible because it is happening within me all the time, and it is happening within you also. The energy itself functions in a certain way. Everybody's energy, or prana, does not behave the same way. It behaves according to their karmic bondage. So the deepest recording is in the energy. This is like karmic back-ups. If you lose your mind, it is still in the body. If you lose your body, it is still in the energy; it remains in the backup systems. So energy has allotments.

There are many complexities to this. To put it very simply, there is a certain amount of energy dedicated to action, another amount to your emotion, another to your thought process, and yet another for the experiential dimensions within you. Let us say you have this much energy dedicated for emotion. Today, in modern life, in the present way of living, people's emotions are not finding their full expression. That part of the energy, the unexpressed emotion, cannot become something else. Either it has to find an emotional expression or it will turn inward and do funny things within you. That's why in Western countries there are so many mental problems. It is said that one out of every three Americans is suffering from some form of mental illness. Think of two of your best friends, Frederica. If they're okay then it must be you (laughs). One of the major factors for this is that there is no room for emotional expression. Anything emotional is looked upon as a weakness in those cultures, so it is suppressed. People are emotional, but there is no free expression for their emotion. Ninety percent of the people in the world, or even more, never find full expression for their emotions. They're afraid of their love, they're afraid of their grief, they're afraid of their joys, they are afraid of everything. To laugh loudly is a problem, to cry loudly is a problem; everything is a problem; and they call this 'modern culture'. I would say this is a restrictive culture, which causes you to behave in a certain way. So if your emotions never find full expression then that energy can turn around and do many damaging things to you.

The major portion of your prarabdha karma is the energy that is allotted for activity. The physical body is the major thing in you, even today. So the maximum amount of prarabdha goes toward activity, always. Ninety-five percent of the time, the maximum allotted energy goes towards activity. This proportion may vary from person to person, but usually it is like this. Now, the activity level in modern life has come down dramatically because people do not use their body the way they used to. If this unused energy stays there, it could easily cause disease. The modern mind is going through a unique kind of neurosis which was not there in the past,

Body's Plight

because man has stopped using his body to a large extent. When you involve yourself intensely in physical activity, a lot of your neuroses are worked out because your nervous energy is used; but modern man has become more inactive and more neurotic than ever before. It has become a common phenomenon in society that everybody is in some level of neurosis. This is simply because the energy allotted for physical activity is not worked out. It is trapped because the physical activity is so low. Today you can see this; people involved in high levels of activity in the form of a sport – like say, a mountain climber – because of the full utilization of physical activity you will find him or her in a different level of balance and peace. You will not find such a person so entangled in sexuality and other physical drives. This is simply because one aspect of him has found full expression.

One result of this inactivity is disease; and above all, the lack of activity and trapped energy cause restlessness. It causes agitation in the body. This agitation may become a physiological disease in some people. In many people it may not become disease, but they are agitated; they are anyway at 'dis-ease'. Their energies are always struggling within themselves. There is no ease in them. They cannot even sit quietly. Even if they just sit, there is no ease. If you observe people, the very way they sit and stand shows they are not at ease. They have brought practiced gracefulness to themselves – how to walk, how to stand and how to sit. If you take away the unease in your movements, it will build into your energy, because it's not finding expression there. It shifts to yet another dimension where it is easy for it to find expression. So disease is happening because of this, because the energy turns inward.

This is one reason why our bhramhacharis are into so much activity. Anybody seeing their level of activity would ask, "Why are these people who came here to pursue their spiritual practices or sadhana working twenty hours a day?" In people's minds, spirituality means someone half-dozing under a tree. This is not so. Their work is part of their spiritual growth. Now that Isha is expanding – we want to bring in a significant transformation to the rural areas of Tamil Nadu – our life will become twenty-four hours of activity. Right now, it is already twenty hours; it will increase to twenty-four hours.

The reason for this is, I want them to finish all the allotted energy in their prarabdha karma, let us say, in five years' time. So we keep them this active. If they expend this karma, then there will be no need for action. The action will be by choice. There will be no compulsion to be active. Now if you ask him to just sit here, he will simply sit. There will be no struggle. That's what we are doing in the higher level programs, Bhava Spandana and Samyama, immense activity, body-breaking activity, because you use up that allotted energy for activity faster than you would in normal life. This gives you a space to sit, unmoving. Then meditation will come naturally to you. When there is still unused energy allocated for activity, you cannot sit because the energy is trying to do more.

There are other aspects also to disease. There are karmic reasons why your energy functions in a certain way and causes disease. If people are diseased for karmic reasons, that's different, but many people in the world need not have disease. Today, medical science is more advanced than ever before, yet people have not become free of disease. So both the physical and emotional energies, though they are large allotments, are not being used. The only thing being used is mental energy. What is allotted for thought is being used to a large extent in today's world. For example, let us say there is money allotted in your country's budget: this much for education, this much for development, this much for industry, and this much for power. The major allotment goes toward energy, but it's not used. If you do not use it, your economy

Body's Plight

suffers. That is all that's happening in the body.

SEEKER: *When somebody is incapacitated, like for example my mother, who has a severe disease, and is dependent on others for even simple bodily functions, she suffers so much because somebody else has to do all this 'dirty work' for her. She also feels indebted to them, and at the same time questions why this should be happening to her. How is her karma being worked out, Sadhguru? Is she adding to it with all these emotions and feelings?*

SADHGURU: See, why a certain work has become 'dirty' is not because there is anything wrong or improper. It has become dirty in your understanding because of the embarrassment it causes you, and the sense of helplessness and hopelessness it brings to who you are. There never was any problem about somebody helping you, somebody doing your 'dirty work'. All these years when you were well, you had no problem with somebody doing your dirty work; in fact, it felt good that somebody was doing your dirty work. Only now this feeling and emotion has come because of your helplessness. There are various aspects to this. The helplessness is not just physical; it is much more.

Why the world is going the way it is right now – why people are pursuing life the way they are right now is – the only things that are important to people are wealth, power, and pleasure. These are the things which have become the whole guiding force of life. Somewhere in their foolishness they came to this conclusion that if they have enough money, enough power, life is going to be okay, life is going to be fixed for good. It's because of this that people are putting their whole life energy behind it. Then you see that somehow everything that everybody would wish to have, you have, and still your suffering is simply untold. It is not any different from the man on the street. Actually people who have nothing but their four limbs seem to be better than you. Then, there is shame in you, there is a disappointment in you, there is a shock in you, there is hurt in you which makes you feel hopeless. Above all, your pride is totally mauled by this.

This is not a problem of somebody doing your 'dirty work'; this is the problem of you being helpless, and your ego hurting so badly. So if somebody is doing all this work, what you should feel for them is extreme love, compassion and affection. What your own children or grandchildren would not even do, somebody else is doing, for whatever reason, and they are doing it pretty well. You should become extremely loving, but you become irritable, you become angry; you become all this simply because the problem is just that you are helpless. So definitely with these emotions you are adding to the karma. About this particular person – your own mother – though she handled her disease quite gracefully at one point, it is becoming more severe and more demanding. Slowly it is beginning to hurt, emotionally and otherwise. This is not because the disease is hurting more, but because she is not able to maintain her dignity and pride, which she managed even in a wheel chair – to some extent – earlier. That's what is hurting right now. So that definitely adds to the karma.

SEEKER: *Sadhguru, it's very easy to say what should be welling up in you is love and not irritability. This is more easily said than done. I mean, how can this love happen in the individual unless they have risen to such a state within themselves that they are free from all this?*

SADHGURU: This is a mistake that people always make. They think that to handle life properly, intelligently, you should have risen to some height. It is not so. The moment you have come here as a human being means you have risen to a certain level of intelligence. That means you have risen to a certain level of capability to handle. That means you have risen to a certain level of freedom and awareness. The moment you come in human form, it is so. You have just gotten entrenched in your own trap that you built out of your pride, your dignity and your egoistic approach to life. Somebody is doing something, which you consider to be dirty, without even making faces about it. If you look at it with openness, only love and affection will come towards that person, nothing else.

I have known many people who were very debilitated with illness; they really had to be helped with their toileting and whatever else. Suddenly, for them – their child, their wife, their husband – nobody really meant anything. That one person who was taking care of them became their everything, and they loved him or her immensely. There have even been situations where they willed their whole property to them because they felt such immense love for that person, for what they were doing. So if you just look at what somebody is doing for you, that is what will happen to you; but you're not even looking at it. You are only looking at what is happening to you. When you look at what is happening to you, pain and hurt will arise in you. If you look at what somebody else is doing for you, then definitely love and affection would arise in you, but you are not at all looking at the other person. You are only looking at yourself: "What is happening to me? What is happening to me?"

SEEKER: *Master, isn't it unfortunate that not even one percent of the terminally ill get this kind of realization, and use this as an opportunity to grow? In that context, what about the remaining population? I am probably very fortunate to have come in contact with you, but what about people who go through life so blindly? How is it possible for them also to get this kind of an opportunity?*

SADHGURU: Whether you come in contact with a Guru or not, whether you come in contact with spirituality or not, it doesn't matter. I'm not even talking about somebody being on a spiritual path. Once you have come with the human form, life has given you a certain sense of intelligence, a certain sense of awareness and freedom to choose what you want to be right now, in this moment. Everybody, literate or illiterate, spiritual or non-spiritual, every human being has this within him.

With the whole process of teaching this yoga, that's all we are doing, so that he gets to stand up and exercise his choice in this moment as to how to be, just reminding him that what he is doing, whether positive or negative, is still by choice. The very process of my whole teaching is just this, to make a person aware enough, to knock him on his head and tell him that whatever he does – whether it is love or hate, anger or peacefulness – whatever he does is still by choice. He is doing it by choice, but he has made his choice so one-directional – he has made himself the centerpiece of everything – that he has just discarded the other choices about life. So when you get diseased, when you get severely ill, though physically you are not wishing it upon yourselves consciously, one way or the other you have created it; knowingly or unknowingly it has happened to you, for so many reasons. Now it has come, and when you see someone doing things for you, that you yourself would not do for anyone, if you see what this person is doing, extreme love and compassion will naturally come forth in you. You do not have to create love.

"When I am in pain how can I create love?" You do not have to create love. If you just see what this person is doing for you, love will arise within you. Nature has not put this burden upon you that you have to create love when you are in pain. If you just see what somebody else is doing for you, love will arise within you, affection will arise within you; but right now your whole mental structure and the way you are looking at life has become so self-oriented, you do not want to look at anything else. You are only seeing what is happening to you; you are not seeing what somebody else is doing.

SEEKER: *Sadhguru, that is because somewhere it's like, "Okay, they are just doing it for money; that's their job."*

SADHGURU: No. The thing is, "Okay, I paid you money, so you clean up my shit," with this attitude you will definitely suffer. If you had seen, "Money or no money, that is not the point; this person is doing this for me. Without him or her, my life would not exist." If you see it this way, definitely love and affection will arise within you and even this diseased state, though physically painful, can become a liberating experience for you in so many ways. It can become a great realization within you, because in your normal state, the body itself is a big barrier; it is constantly distracting you. When you are diseased, suddenly you realize that your body is not permanent, that it is perishable; so all your focus and energy should shift to a higher dimension. It is a great potential. It has a great potential in it.

Now you don't have any exposure to spirituality, that's not an excuse. Everybody has the intelligence, the awareness and the freedom of choice to do this for themselves, but how many people do it is always questionable. Unfortunately, not many people do it. Even for the person who does the dirty work, instead of seeing what she is doing for somebody else, if she sees what she is doing and how, "What I would not do for myself I am doing for somebody," she will become such a wonderful human being, you understand. But if she is thinking, "Oh, I have got to do this because of this person. I have got to do this because of my economic situation," then she will also create karma. Your mother will also create karma endlessly.

SEEKER: *That is so in ninety-nine percent of the cases, Sadhguru. Even that one percent I am not too sure... That's how the world is right now; that's how it's happening.*

SADHGURU: It's not one hundred percent. I think most of them are off and on. Sometimes they are this way, sometimes they are that way. Some moments they are Realized, some moments they are blind; that is how they go on. That is why they have some moments of joy, some moments of pain, because they are always off and on. If they constantly create misery for themselves, then it will lead to something else. They will become ill in a completely different way. An extended negative karma for a certain period of time will create a different kind of suffering for people.

However, most people are on and off in creating suffering, and most people are on and off in creating liberation also. To stay on consistently is the whole thing. If you stay on with suffering for too long, it will take you to Realization in some way, or it will destroy you. If you stay on with liberation, it will definitely liberate you, but people are always on and off, they are fickle. That is why Krishna says in the Gita, "The worst crime in the world is indecision." Mainly it is the fickleness, the unsteady attitude. There is no nischala tathwam, no 'one direction of energy'. You are going in different directions all the time. So the life energy is confused; it does not know where to go or what to do. Only with human nature has this freedom been given to you, that you can decide the direction of your life energies. For animals it is not so; the direction of their life energies is decided. It just goes that way, whichever way they go; but for human nature, this freedom has been given. It's a benediction, but you're using it as a curse.

SEEKER: *I have, in my own family, people who were ill and I have handled them. When I'm with them part of me does not react to anything; it does not touch me. It is not that I'm indifferent to their suffering. I can respond to life-suffering around me, but I just do what is best and leave it at that. I wonder at times what people think about me. Can you say something about it, Sadhguru?*

SADHGURU: (Laughs) What they are thinking about you? I will answer the last question first: heartless. They are not even thinking; they made the conclusion long ago. Now the thing is, what is it that you are responding to? Is it responding to

Body's Plight

just some life-suffering?

SEEKER: *No, it could be more because it is someone in my family.*

SADHGURU: Oh, "It's my family, it's my thing." That's what is causing the suffering.

SEEKER: *But Sadhguru, can't they see that I become dispassionate because something in me says that all emotion is only because one gets identified with someone or something as their own?*

SADHGURU: Every suffering that you see – whether a worm, insect, bird, animal or human being – if your whole system, your energy or your emotions, everything – responds to it, that is wonderful. Once you start responding to everything, you will see that your response has to move into deeper dimensions within yourself. It cannot be psychological and emotional anymore, otherwise it will only lead to madness.

SEEKER: *Yes, exactly.*

SADHGURU: See, now this tree branch is broken; my energy responds to it, but my emotions do not. Sometimes I allow myself the luxury of responding emotionally also. It's a luxury for me. Once in a while I allow myself to respond emotionally also to some type of suffering around me; otherwise, I don't emotionally respond to any suffering around me. This is coming because there is enough control over the situation. There was a time when, if I just looked at anybody's face on the streets, just seeing that they are not happy enough would bring tears to my eyes. Once it becomes so deep that you start responding to every life and whatever is happening, then there is no way to exist here. You have to dissolve; that's all there is. So naturally you will come to a deeper understanding within yourself, that psychologically and emotionally you don't respond anymore. On a much deeper level you naturally respond, but it is no more emotional and psychological, and it is good. It's a big step ahead in life, not responding to things emotionally and psychologically, not because you are putting up a barrier between you and their suffering. You're very much open to their suffering, you are very much a part of it, but still, emotionally and psychologically you do not suffer, or you are not disturbed on that level. It's a huge step to take. Now for people, the suffering is not about life going on like this. If that was it, if they had that sense, the world would be a different place altogether; but now the thing is, my father, my mother, my house, my something is suffering; that's the whole problem. So this has nothing to do with them. It's only about you.

When I was just about eleven years, maybe twelve, a certain situation occurred between my mother and me. See, an Indian mother would never come and tell her child, "I love you," or something like that. Maybe today you do it a little bit, but an Indian mother would never – at least my mother would never. Such a necessity was not there at all. Everything she did in her life was for us. We knew that, so she never had to say it. It's almost a sacrilege to say it. That's the kind of situation it was. Now something happened and she expressed herself in a tender way to me – not exactly telling me, "I love you." It's a rare thing to happen. Then I asked her a simple question – you know, my thoughts were in a certain way by then - "If I was born in the next house, would you still feel this way about me?" She felt so hurt, so offended, and with tears welling up in her eyes, she went away. I didn't think anything about it. I just asked a simple question, which was not an issue for me within myself. I knew very well that if I had been born in the next house she would not be feeling like this about me. I knew that very well; it was very clear to me in my mind. So that was why I just asked her. Then after half an hour, she came to me and not knowing what to say, still in tears, she touched my feet and went away. That also did not mean much to me. I knew she was trying to come to terms

Body's Plight

with it. She saw the point of what I was saying, but her emotions were struggling to come to terms with it. She knew it was true, but at the same time there was a struggle within, because it would have brought up many things, maybe about all her other children, her husband, her house, her father, her mother, everything. Probably it would have all come up in her mind and the whole struggle and turmoil was because of this.

So this is all about 'mine'. What is mine is just an extended me. Isn't it? The very reason why, on the spiritual path, all possessions are taken away, is so that what is 'me' becomes small inside this flesh. Right now, this big house is me, this car is me, this property is me, you know? These acres of land are me. Everything is me actually. If somebody damages the house it hurts me, as if it is me, isn't it? If somebody damages the car, it hurts me. So you're just extending the ego, extending this 'me', trying to find extensions to what you call as 'myself' outside, which is a falsehood. This is happening with a wrong identification with many things, which is the fundamentals of ignorance, which is the very foundation of all ignorance in the world – your wrong identifications. The whole spiritual process is to remove the identification even with the physical body. So extending your identification to many things outside is absolutely stupid.

Your feeling hurt because, "My mother or my child is ill" is coming from sheer ignorance. Does it mean you do not care? Does it mean you should not take care? Does it mean to say you do not do anything about it? No. You do everything that you can do about it, and there is only so much that you can do about anybody. It does not matter how much you love them, there is only that much you can do; whether they live or die is not decided by you. You will do the best you can do with what means you have. It's not even the best in the world. With the available means, accordingly you will do your best. So all this is happening. It's just that emotionally you are not greatly hurt. You're still laughing, you're still enjoying your food, you're still going to the cinema, you're still doing everything and you're still meditating peacefully. This offends people who are emotionally attached. They will get so offended, they will think you are heartless. They will think you're a stone or whatever else, but I would say stones are better than stupid human beings, because they do not cause any harm to anybody. They are just there, not doing anything. Maybe they are meditating, because people who want to meditate always go to the mountains to be infected by the rocks. They go to the rocks to learn meditation.

I heard that an actress had said that one place which is truly spiritual for her is some rock in Bombay. She said, "This rock, I sit near this rock and I find so many answers to so many of my questions." Definitely a big rock seems to be wiser and better than any stupid human being.

SEEKER: *Sadhguru, how would the human race perpetuate itself if total dispassion arises? Isn't that why people fear spirituality also?*

SADHGURU: People have understood dispassion as becoming dry and senseless. Dispassion is not dry and senseless; dispassion means that the bondage with life is gone. Freedom has come. Once freedom has come, how you respond to life is in your hands, isn't it? If freedom has come, in terms of your thought and emotion, you can respond. You don't have to become like a stone; you will respond as it is needed. There are situations where even if people are in extreme suffering or pain, I don't even look at them. There are situations where, for the smallest things, I will shed tears with them. So this is by choice; this is what dispassion means.

Whether it is your family or anybody else that you are taking physical responsibility for; or if there is somebody lying ill on the street, in terms of my life response, it's still the same. If my mother is ill or this woman on the street is ill, it is the same response. As far as I'm concerned, as a human being, my response is the same, but in terms of what I can

Body's Plight

physically do, it may alter depending upon my capabilities. What I could do for my mother, if I had the capability to do it for everybody physically, I would love to do it. I'm sure most human beings, or every human being who is willing to look at himself with a little openness, is the same, is it not so? If you had the means to take care of the whole world the way you take care of your mother, everybody who has looked at his life with a little sense would naturally do that; but right now it's a question of capability.

That is so even for your mother, isn't it? Even though you feel so much for her, what you can do may be limited. For many people here in India, if somebody is ill with cancer, they may not be able to do much because they cannot take their mother to America or they do not have the economic means even to seek the local treatment. So it doesn't mean that they love them less than somebody else who is capable of providing all those things for their mothers; it's just that they cannot do it. So maybe they will just give them plain water, hold their hands, sit through their pain, do whatever else they can do and allow them to die.

In terms of their karma, in terms of life, it's not any different. They let them die physically, but still everything that can be done for a human being has been done. Your life response need not change. It does not matter who it is or what it is, whether it's an apple, potato, chicken, mother, father or a tree, your response is still the same. But what you do physically is at your discretion, depending upon your capabilities, energies, possibilities, inclinations, time, life – so many aspects are involved.

SEEKER: *I was thinking more in terms of human perpetuation. Won't the human race come to a halt with dispassion, Sadhguru?*

SADHGURU: No. Wouldn't it be very, very beautiful if human beings conceived consciously, because it is needed for the human race rather than out of their own physical compulsions? Wouldn't it be so much more beautiful if they created this very consciously – this being is needed for human life to happen and you produce it with that consciousness, rather than out of your compulsions? Is it not in many ways an indignity to the person who is born that he or she is born out of your compulsions, not out of your consciousness?

SEEKER: *But Sadhguru, it is not that everybody goes for a child with a compulsion. For some it is out of love for a child – maybe because it is their child, a little extension of their womb, something of theirs.*

SADHGURU: See, when you say, "love for their child", where did you get love for your unborn child? When you have no love for life around you, it is still a compulsion. When I say 'compulsion', the compulsion need not necessarily be just physical; the compulsions can be psychological and emotional. There is a need to extend yourself, something that is you. Most people want to have children because they want an extension of themselves. They want something to leave behind when they go. Children are their greatest property.

SEEKER: *So it is more instinct, isn't it, Sadhguru?*

SADHGURU: Physically it is an instinct. Emotionally, psychologically, it's not an instinct; it's a trick that you play. Physically it is an instinct, but emotionally and psychologically it is a trick, it's a ploy that you're creating to extend yourself. Do you see, when people who take up some cause in their life, whatever cause – they are fighting for the freedom of their country, they have a political cause or some other cause – when they get too intensely involved in that, they have no need to produce children because they are extending themselves in some other way where their involvement is much more?

Fundamentally, bearing a child has become such a big experience in people's lives because only by bearing a child can most people know a certain sense, or a certain depth of involvement and inclusion with life. With nothing else are they so deeply involved. They are incapable of being deeply involved with this tree. They are incapable of being deeply involved with the air around them. Their only capability is to be involved with a child, because a child does not have so much personality, or does not have personality at all when it comes into your hands. Another thing is because your identification is so much with the physical body, something that comes out of your body is definitely yours. You may say, "My house is mine," but you know you can lose it. You may say, "This property is mine," but you may lose it; but this comes out of your biological body and you cannot deny it. Even if your son denies it, still you know he's anyway yours. So it's a sure-fire extension of yourself.

People are seeking children only because of that; that's the only way they know involvement. Otherwise, they are incapable of being involved. Why, especially for a woman, bearing a child has become such a big experience is just because of her involvement; otherwise, she is never really involved with anybody for that matter. Very few people can involve themselves to that extent in their love affairs also. Even there, the involvement is because bodies touch. Because their identification is with the physical body, the only way they know to involve themselves is by opening their body. Only when a person rises to another level of experience, their involvement with something else or somebody else goes to great depths without physical involvement, because now identification with the body is receding. Identification with the other dimension of yourself is building momentum.

So a child is a deep involvement. People are hankering for children because they are seeking involvement; otherwise, what is life? If you have never tasted life, by bearing a child you're getting involved with life. With nothing else are you involved; but if you know how to involve yourself with everything around you, you will see a child is not an emotional or psychological compulsion any more. It would be very wonderful if people chose to have children, rather than bringing them through physical, psychological or emotional compulsions within themselves.

SEEKER: *Jaggi, when it comes to women and children in India, it is considered very inauspicious for a barren woman to attend some of the social gatherings and celebrations, so isn't it also a social compulsion for a woman to bear children?*

SADHGURU: What is auspicious? What is auspicious in the society is decided by certain people and you know how sensibly those people are living their lives, first of all! Those women who have a dozen children, in what way are they more complete than somebody who does not have children and is still happy?

One person does not have children by choice, and maybe someone else is incapable of bearing a child due to some biological reason; then she suffers, since she is incapable of doing something that is a simple biological function of being a woman.

It's like Joe, who was eighty-four years of age; he went to the doctor. The doctor asks, "Joe, what's your problem?" Joe says, "Doctor, I am not able to pee!" The doctor thought for a while and then said, "Joe, you are eighty-four years old; have you not peed enough?" It's just a simple biological function. So if the woman has chosen not to have children, she has no problems with it by herself. It is just that social stigma can come for anything that you do. Even if you sit and meditate you may get a social stigma! (Laughs).

SEEKER: *Sadhguru, could this stigma also have come due to the social structure? Just like a barren land is no good, in the same way, a barren woman is no good?*

SADHGURU: In Indian society, the social structures were

Body's Plight

mostly agriculture based. This whole society was agriculture based at one time. For a very long time – for thousands of years – India has had an agro-based society, not a hunting-gathering kind. Only small tribal segments have been the hunting-gathering kind. Agriculture is always labor-intensive. Today we hire labor to do things, it's a different situation, but back then everybody was working on their own lands and making their own food from the land. So, how many children you had was a great asset; especially if you had male children, it was a great asset. As you know, women who have only girls are also considered inauspicious. Only when she bears a boy is she auspicious. The king determined this, because without a boy there is nobody to take over his position. He wants only his blood to take over this position, which is just an extension of himself. His son ruling the kingdom is just like him continuing to rule the kingdom after his death. If somebody else takes it, it's not good enough; that's the mentality.

So, children were a very important part of life for survival and for economic and social situations. Also, people did not experience life to any depth with any other aspect except by bearing children. It's as if you have not experienced life. Like our meditators will go and talk to somebody: "Oh, you did not experience Samyama? It is no good for you to be living." Just like that, a woman who has borne a child has experienced some intense moments of being involved with another being in some way. When she sees another woman who does not have children, she thinks that the woman has not known this involvement with life at all – it could be true. This involvement matures the person in so many ways, so the other is scoffing at the one who does not have a child, "You have not known involvement; you are barren with life. Not only as a physical body you are barren, you are barren with life! You have not known life." Like people are saying, "If you have not known Bhava Spandana you are barren with life," or "If tears of joy and tears of peace and love have not washed your cheeks, you are barren." Just like that they are speaking to the childless woman.

There are various aspects involved – social, economic, emotional, physical and biological aspects also. Over a period of time, if such a natural function as child bearing does not happen, she is a freak in some way, as far as the society is concerned. So whatever you are incapable of, people have always made fun of. If you cannot hear, they will make fun of it. If you cannot walk, they will make fun of it. It took a lot of time, evolution and culture for people to understand that if someone cannot walk, it is not a laughing matter. He needs love, compassion and support. Similarly, if somebody cannot bear a child, she needs love, compassion and support. It will take a lot of time for people to understand that. I think people are beginning to understand that now, which they did not in the past.

SEEKER: *Master, I have seen many people who are afflicted with different kinds of diseases come to the ashram. They are put on various practices and regimens alone, without any medication, but their conditions improve dramatically. For example, how was the physician from the US, who had an ischemic heart condition, able to trek in the Himalayas? Doug's knee, which showed torn cartilage on the MRI, is now fine and he is no longer in pain. How does this happen?*

SADHGURU: The life energies within you created a whole body, isn't it? Even your brains were created by that. When you were born, your body was so small and today it became all this. Nobody is stretching you from outside, are they? Whatever is creating the body is within you. Your whole body, all the bone, all the blood, all the flesh and everything, including your brain, was created by this energy. So when it can do so much, can it not fix a little cartilage? Of course, it is not true for everybody. See here, Gina, her mother fed her with sheep brains (laughs). So even sheep brains can be a contributor! The only reason why it is not fixing it is that you're not in touch with it. You're creating a distance from it

Body's Plight

because you have formed such individual nonsense within yourself. You have identified yourself with your clothes, with your house, with cars and people - all kinds of stuff except your life energies. The more you identify with these things, the less and less of energy you become and the more and more inanimate you become. When certain things happen and that person completely gives himself to me, at that moment, it's very easy to activate his energies in a certain way and whatever is not proper in the body will be corrected; but this energy is capable of doing that all the time. This energy is what is running your life. It is not you running this life; it's being done by this energy. Now you have read a textbook about digestion and assimilation and you think you are doing all that. Where are you doing it? At least Americans think they are, because before each meal they are reading labels about how much magnesium, how much calcium there is in the food – they are not reading the Bible anymore, they are reading labels – because they think they are doing everything. You're not doing it; this life energy has always been doing it. So if you just allow it for a moment, it will do anything.

SEEKER: *Sadhguru, when you say, "If somebody gives themselves in one moment," what the hell does that mean?*

SADHGURU: Drop your hell! That's what it means. Right now, you are identified with everything you are not. You are functioning within the limitations of your likes and your opinions. You're sitting here, listening to me because what I'm saying is still appealing to your logic. Though we are going into the realm of the mystical, which is mumbo-jumbo to you, still it is perfectly logical. If I do not speak logically, you will not sit here. I know that. That means you have not given yourself totally; but there are moments when all your logic falls apart, you stop identifying yourself with things that you are not and you have just given yourself. In one moment, in bowing down to me, they kept their identities aside and that was all.

SEEKER: *Where are those moments, Sadhguru?*

SADHGURU: It does not matter; don't look for those moments, because you cannot create them. When you are completely overwhelmed by someone's presence, you do not exist. Otherwise, you have no way to dissolve yourself. It's a waste of time trying to do that.

SEEKER: *Sadhguru, I am always overwhelmed by your presence.*

SADHGURU: Yes, but not enough, not to a point where you do not exist. Not enough yet. You can only be overwhelmed by that which is beyond you. You will not be overwhelmed by that which is you. So this talk is just that, without demanding any kind of faith or belief, we're still trying to overwhelm you. Normally, overwhelming you was done only with faith. The whole world always has been talking about faith, just to overwhelm you. Do you understand? People have been talking about miracles just to overwhelm you. Whether the miracles are true or not, consciously false miracles are also being created just to overwhelm you.

Once, a magician was on a cruise liner and he had a parrot that had seen all the magician's tricks a zillion times. He had figured out long ago how the magician made everything in the act disappear. The parrot grew to be bored, his owner growing stale and not developing any new tricks that the parrot could not figure out. One night, in the middle of the magician's performance, the ship hit an iceberg and sank. Everyone sank except the magician and the parrot. The magician managed to swim to a piece of wreckage and climb onto it. He immediately collapsed from exhaustion. Soon afterwards, the parrot flew there, and perched on the edge of the makeshift raft. It stared at the magician, and stared at the magician and stared at the magician. For a whole day, the magician was unconscious and all this time the parrot did not take his eyes off him. Eventually, the magician started to stir. Looking up, he saw the parrot eyeing him intently. Another

Body's Plight

hour went by and finally the parrot squawked, "All right, I give up; what did you do with the damn ship?" Here, we are not using those methods. With thinking and investigative minds, it will not work, so we are overwhelming you in a completely different way. Only when you are overwhelmed, you do not exist. When you are totally overwhelmed, when you do not exist, you become available in a completely different way.

SEEKER: *Sadhguru, if someone is ill and they give themselves to you and you activate energies in a certain way and their condition is corrected, is that true for just some people whose condition you have become aware of or for everyone?*

SADHGURU: That's true for everyone. With these people something was noticeably wrong. With so many other people, just like that they're feeling so much younger and better. Is it not so? It's because the same thing has happened, but there is no specific damage that shows, that has been rectified.

SEEKER: *Sadhguru, is it not only with physical disease but with mental illness as well?*

SADHGURU: It is with mental illness also, but mental illness is at a deeper level than physical illness, so it takes much more.

SEEKER: *Then what does it take, Sadhguru?*

SADHGURU: You are dropping your identifications only in installments. Jeanne probably had seventy-two pairs of pants. I told her, "You just keep six pairs of pants. The rest, you just give them away." She cried, "How can I give them away? They are good ones; I paid so much money." I said, "You give them away; just keep six pairs of pants. Anyway you can only wear one at a time. Six will do for you; seventy-two are not needed." Why is giving away your pants so difficult? It is because you are identified with them. When she gave them away, the first pair or two hurt, but as she gave away more and more, her identification became less and less. Now with six pairs the identification is not gone, but it is lowered. If you completely drop your identifications, you will become Realized.

SEEKER: *Sadhguru, I have heard that this doctor with the heart problem has recovered miraculously and trekked in the Himalayas. What was the significance of having her sleep in the Dhyanalinga temple before she left on the Himalayan trek?*

SADHGURU: The general and the fundamental dimension of the Dhyanalinga is spiritual, but all the other dimensions are there in it. There are temples and situations which are made for certain specific purposes. Suppose I take certain people to such places; I always make them receptive in a particular way, to that particular energy which is present in that place. Suppose I take somebody to some Devi temple, which is a feminine aspect, which is very powerful. If somebody needs to receive that in a particular way, then I do certain things with them so that they can receive that dimension very well.

This doctor's problem was in a specific dimension. So we just made her in such a way that she was more receptive to that dimension alone, when she slept there. You saw, the very first day, or the second day probably after she came to India, we took her off the breathing support device she was using. She thought this was impossible because of her tracheal collapse problem. When she would lie down, her trachea would collapse and she'd suffocate. Without the device she slept here at the ashram, for about a week. Then she traveled on the train. No chance of having the device there, and in the Himalayas, no possibility at all. She went through the whole trip without it. Now if she starts descending from that which was offered to her, you will find, probably in a few months' time, she will need the device again. If she does not descend, if she has sense and she enhances what has been offered to her, then she will never need it; but if she just drops from that, probably in a few months' time... How long has it been?

SEEKER: *Three or four months, Sadhguru.*

SADHGURU: Any time now, we cannot really gauge it exactly, but I would say anywhere between three to six months she may start needing the breathing aid again if she does not handle that situation sensibly within herself. I hope she does not do that to herself, but it's very much possible.

SEEKER: *Master, when you say, "handle that situation," what do you mean?*

SADHGURU: (Laughs) Handling it improperly or handling it properly, what it means is: in a way, you were made receptive to certain energies. That energy did things that you could never imagine doing. This doctor's case is quite dramatic. With many other people it may not be so dramatically there, but it is there. Every time this happens, the first day they are all grateful, tears flowing. Within three days they just think, "It's me." The moment they get identified with that and think it is all them, then you will see it will recede, because it cannot stay in your identification. Once it recedes, all your problems will be back. The change is still only on the level of her energy. For it to manifest itself physiologically, it will take a while. If that time is not allowed, very easily people can revert themselves back to their old ways. Already, somebody told me Doug's knee is paining again.

SEEKER: *Sadhguru, when something is offered to any one of us and we are receptive enough to receive it, should we keep it as a gift we can use, as something we don't identify ourselves with?*

SADHGURU: It's not like that. It is not like it's there as a gift to be used. Right now, you are breathing. The air that you breathe is not you; it is coming from outside, isn't it? But you never acknowledge it. So many of your diseases are just because of that. The food that you eat, it's not you, isn't it?

You never acknowledge that. If you go like this, what is it that is you? There is nothing in you that you can call 'you'. In some way, the food that you eat, the air that you breathe, has gotten integrated and has started functioning as a physical body, and you call that 'me'. Because you call that 'me', it is functioning in a limited way. If you do not call it as 'you', if it's really not in your identification, then it will function in an enormous way.

For example, in Doug's case or anybody's – there are many other people like that – we have made them receptive in a particular way, a receptivity beyond the normal sense of eating food or breathing air and whatever else. It's a little above that. Before this, you were still taking in physical quantities and making them into physical quantities. Now here, you are receiving an energy situation, which changes – it's not that it changes everything, but it just triggers things in a certain way. So your whole system begins to function in a different way because of this influence. The first three days you understood it as, "This is not me; this is Grace;" but within a week's time, it becomes, "Okay, it is me and Sadhguru;" then in a month's time, "It's all me!" This is happening, isn't it? The moment you go this way, Grace recedes, because it cannot be there once you bring in your identification.

SEEKER: *Today, we are seeing so many people going to psychologists for treatment. It seems every single person has a shrink that he sees at least once a week. Why are we becoming so troubled? Are we all going crazier by the day, Sadhguru?*

SADHGURU: Today, ninety percent of the people are in different states of mental sickness. It's just that the level of sickness is sometimes manageable, sometimes unmanageable. Let's say you have asthma. Sometimes your asthma is manageable, so you do not consider yourself as sick. You take some syrup or some tablet and you manage. On a particular

Body's Plight

day, you become really sick and you either totally collapse or are hospitalized.

Only then you consider yourself as sick, isn't it? That does not mean the other days you were not sick; you were sick, but it was manageable.

Similarly with the mental states, almost everybody is sick. It's just that they are in some manageable level of sickness. Once in a while, they flare up for some time and then they settle down again. They are managing, but the madness is very much there. Now all the psychologists and the psychiatrists have only studied sick people. People like Freud never found a meditator or a Buddha to study. He would have studied only those people who are in different states of mental sickness; either manageably mad or unmanageably mad, whichever way. They only studied mad people, and the one who is studying is also mad. He is equally mad. It's not that he has transcended his limitations.

On a certain day, it happened like this. Three psychiatrists were traveling together on a train from Germany to France, to attend the annual all-psychiatrists seminar. Sitting there, they started confiding to each other their greatest secrets. The first one said, "My greatest weakness is compulsive gambling. Every weekend, I take off from the clinic and let myself go full blast. Of course, I put all the money that I earn from my gambling spree into some charity box, and mind you, I don't start stealing from another charity box until I go drinking. Then I get sodden drunk and finish the night in the gutter." The second psychiatrist nodded his head in understanding and said, "Well, my greatest secret is that I am so dependant on taking anti-depressants all the time, and I have to gulp down an extra double dosage before I sit in consultation with my patients." The third one sat there very smugly and quietly. So the other two prodded her, "What about you? We've told you our deepest secrets. Now you have to tell us yours." The third psychiatrist said, "Well, I'm a diagnosed gossiper, and I can't wait to get off this train!"

Whatever problem you have – anxiety, fear, psychosis or anything – according to that, they put you into the corresponding category and they have a treatment for that; and what kind of treatment it is! Somehow adjusting the whole situation and making you manageably mad, not making you sane. Nobody can make you sane, please know this. From unmanageable madness, they can bring you down to manageable madness. Everybody has learned the trick to manage the madness. Now this process of spirituality is not about moving into manageable madness. It's about going so mad that you become sane. Okay? You cross the limits of madness, then you become perfectly sane. See, you're born with the madness; the karma itself is madness. The very bondages that you have created for yourself, the limitations that you have created for yourself, are they not madness?

If there is a mad man who thinks he's tied to this column – there is no rope, there is no chain, but he thinks he's tied to the column – he will only go around this, round and round. Whatever you tell him, he will not listen, because he feels he is tied to the column. Isn't this the way everybody is living, tied to some column? So it's the same madness. Being manageably mad or unmanageably mad really makes no difference. At least, if you become unmanageably mad, you can enjoy yourself in the asylum. You don't have to be ashamed of being mad anymore! You can just freak out the way you want to. You don't have to bother about controlling it. It's such a big strain to control that madness. Do you know why a person growing on the spiritual path looks totally crazy? It is because he is pushing himself to the point beyond madness, where it cannot touch him any more.

These meditations at Isha are not about you becoming peaceful. They are about blasting yourself into bits until there is no peace and no disturbance within you; only that can be called as peace. If you get disturbed and then make yourself peaceful, that's not peace; it's just a lull. This peace is like the eye of the hurricane where everything is calm. The hurricane is blowing like mad and in between, suddenly there is total calm. Do not be fooled by this calm, it's just a small respite. The next gust will come again and it will be even worse than before. Hurricanes always move like this; because of the centrifugal and centripetal forces and the forward motion, the front end of the hurricane is less forceful than the rear end. So what you see first is nothing compared to what's going to come. That will be much bigger. The same goes with your mind.

Everything in existence is like that. Whatever blows with force is like that. It will blow, then give a little space and then again blow. The mind is also like that; it goes through a phase of disturbance then it comes back to peace. Don't ever think it is peace; it's just a break in the madness. Even mad people are perfectly sane in some moments in their life. Don't think they are twenty-four hours mad. Sometimes they are very sane and perfectly okay, and sometimes they just go off; they are more spontaneous than you. See, the man who has lost his so-called mental balance is a lot more spontaneous than you, isn't he? But you are also doing what he is doing.

SEEKER: *Sadhguru, does spirituality have a treatment for our depressions, our neuroses, and our madness?*

SADHGURU: The way of treating madness on the spiritual path is very different. Generally, if somebody goes really mad, especially with psychological problems, what they do is take him to the master at a monastery or an ashram. See, if this person remains in the family, they try to attend to him too much, do everything for him. Now if they take him to the hospital or the asylum, there also they will attend to him, guard him, do many things. If they take him to a Buddhist monastery for example, there, they will just leave him, ignore him completely. He shouts, raves, throws stones; whatever he does, nobody reacts. Everybody just goes about doing their own work, not reacting to any madness. Within a few days this person will settle down and become peaceful, because without attention, his madness cannot go on.

Madness is just a trip of the ego. It's like a power trip, or electrical trip; it overflows. Similarly, madness is simply an overflowing of your ego. That's all it is. So just ignore the man. Put him in a corner. Don't bother about him. Don't even call him for food. Just leave him. If the fellow is really hungry he will come and eat; otherwise, he will just work out his madness and become okay. The atmosphere is right, the energy is high. Slowly, that man will settle down and then he will come and say, "Teach me meditation." Ignore the madness and it will die by itself. Your madness also, you attend to it too much. You should not.

SEEKER: *Master, I hope I never go mad.*

SADHGURU: What makes you think that you're not mad right now? The limitations that you have set upon yourselves, are they not madness? Madness does not necessarily mean that you have to take off your clothes, go on the street and run. Mad people are of different varieties. They need not necessarily be laughing and rolling or ranting and raving. Some mad people are very serious. Others are in some other way. Madness is just the ego. It needs some expression. Now a tremendous amount of time and energy is spent to cover your madness. One way of handling it is to cover it up. Another way is to transcend it. If you cover it up, you will only fool other people who will think that you're a perfectly balanced person; but you suffer for the madness that you cover up and keep within yourself. It will grow and you will pay the price for keeping it within. If you transcend this madness, there is something else which opens up, a new fragrance, a new light.

Everybody has become a great master in cover-up jobs. Do

see, you are a fantastic actor all your life. You fool the world, you fool the people close to you and you fool yourself. You tell your friends, "I think I have found inner peace. My therapist told me that a way to achieve inner peace was to finish things I had started. So today, I finished two bags of potato chips, an extra large supreme pizza with all the toppings, a lemon pie, a big box of chocolate candy and drowned it all with half a case of beer. I feel better already." Maybe you can only fool yourself like this and to that extent you can put up an act, isn't it? So much negativity you think you can drown with a beer. You cover it up so beautifully.

It is layers and layers of madness. This is not just something you gathered in a few years. It's an accumulation of many lifetimes. Layers and layers of madness have been accumulated. It has to be worked out. There is no other way. Either you drop the whole thing and walk away or slowly you cleanse the bag. The moment you lose your madness, if you really lose your madness, you are meditative. How else can you be? That's all meditation is. For a while, during meditation, you are bypassing your madness and experiencing a little bit of sanity. The mind settles down and you are just there. Otherwise it is going non-stop. The moment you're out of your madness, you are always meditative; there is no other way to be. Your mind itself is madness. Whichever way it is, it is madness. Transcending that is sanity.

SEEKER: *Sadhguru, are action and psychology connected? Since I was a kid, I always got into intense activity to such an extent that I would exhaust myself. I would go swimming, biking, trekking, all-night dancing or running intensely if there was nothing else to do. Was I working out my madness, unconsciously?*

SADHGURU: They are connected in many ways. So Tina, if you had not been into all this activity, we know where you would have landed up by now! (Laughs).

SEEKER: *In the loony bin!?*

SADHGURU: Yes! During the Isha Yoga programs, when you really let yourself go, you saw that the madness is a part of you and not something being put into you by anyone. Maybe it is hidden, or covered, but it's very much a part of you. All your effort in life, conscious and unconscious, is to cover this madness, this insanity which is there within, to give it a nice outlook, a nice image.

The whole world itself is going through a unique kind of neurosis, which was not there in the past. This is simply because modern man has stopped using his body to a large extent. In the past, when you intensely involved yourself in physical activity, a lot of your neurosis was worked out. Your nervous energy got spent. I know many people, especially young people, who had psychological problems. They just started swimming or playing some sport daily and then everything became okay; because of enough activity, the energy was expended.

Today, man has become physically inactive like never before – he could not afford to be so physically inactive before, he had to do so many things physically, just to survive. So he has become more neurotic than in the past. As a general phenomenon, there were neurotic people then also, but not in these numbers. Today, it has become a common phenomenon in society that everybody is in some level of neurosis. This is simply because your energy is not worked out; it's trapped. You have not transcended your madness and at the same time you're not working it out. The therapy also is not there. If you went out and chopped wood for the whole day – if you chopped a hundred logs a day – a lot of your energy would be spent, and life would be peaceful; but today it's not like that. You are not using your body the way it used to be used, so you go on generating all kinds of diseases, like never before.

This builds up into your system over a period of time. Then your physical and emotional energy need some outlet. That is how your bars, your clubs and your discotheques have come into place. People have to work out their neurosis somewhere, somehow. These discos look like madness, you can't even breathe inside. They are full of smoke and sweat but people are just going wild. You can't even dance; everybody is bumping into everybody else, but it doesn't matter. You have to work it out, otherwise you will go crazy. So on Saturday, you go work out your neurosis for the week. Then the piling up starts once more and once again the Saturday night fever comes. There is another way to drop this madness and go ahead, completely leaving it behind and going ahead where you are no more a part of it. This is what meditation is all about. Now, if you dance, you simply dance for the joy of it, and not because there is something to work out. If you're dancing to work out something, maybe it is therapeutic. It is good therapy all right, but there is a certain ugliness about it. It is lusty; you cannot dance out of love. You can only dance out of lust.

Do you know the difference between love and lust? Lust is a strong need. Love is not a need. When you love, you settle down; nothing more is needed. You can just sit here for a lifetime. With lust you can't sit anywhere; you either get into some mad action, or you are bound to go crazy. When there is a certain neurosis, a certain madness within yourself, you can only be in lust. Your lust can be for sex, for food or for some particular activity or some hobby, it doesn't matter what it is, but you develop lust for something. Without that lust you cannot live. Even your work is an effective way of throwing out your lust. It's just that it is the most popular and accepted way in the world. Today people just go on working, working and working. Not because they are creating something fantastic, but simply because they have to work, otherwise they don't know what to do with themselves.

You have to guard that madness cautiously. Nobody ever knows that you have this within yourself and you yourself would like to forget it. You do everything possible to forget it. All the entertainment in the world has come just to hide your madness. If you were perfectly sane, you would not need entertainment. You need entertainment just to cover your madness. If we take away your entertainment, you will go crazy. Do you understand? Man needs entertainment simply to hide his madness. If he was perfectly sane, he would not need entertainment. He could just sit and watch this bamboo grow. He does not really need entertainment.

SEEKER: *There are various types of healing going on around the world. Does the karma that is appeased through this take effect in some other way? Also, Sadhguru, in what way is psychic surgery, that is sort of getting popular now in India, different from the various other healings?*

SADHGURU: See, everything always functions between cause and effect. Physical existence is always happening between cause and effect. Suppose there is an infection and the cause was bacteria. You eat or drink something somewhere and get infected; so the cause was bacteria. Now there is an effect, infection. For this you're trying to take away the cause by taking antibiotics. There, you kill the cause with medication because it is external to you. With other diseases that are not externally caused, but are happening from within the body, the cause is so much deeper compared to an infection. For this type of disease to manifest, there is an imbalance or a malfunction in the energy body, which is manifesting itself in the physical body, or sometimes in the mental body.

Now with pranic healing – or any kind of healing for that matter – you are only appeasing the effect. In a way, what you're doing is that, with a little control or mastery over your own energies, you are able to put a screen between the cause and the effect. So the effect dies out, but the cause is buried. It's like this: one sunny day, the owner of a drug store walked in to find a guy leaning heavily against the wall. The owner asked the clerk, "What's with that guy over there by the wall?" The clerk replied, "Well, he came in here this morning, to get something for his cough. I couldn't find the cough syrup so I gave him an entire box of laxatives." The owner yelled, "You idiot, you can't treat a cough with a box of laxatives!" The clerk said, "Of course you can. Look at him, he's afraid to cough."

So as far as nature is concerned, as far as this life energy is concerned, the effect was only its way of telling you that there is a cause inside of you. What we call as 'cause', the disturbance of energy, is trying to manifest itself in a certain way. Let us say you have asthma. Today I just remove your asthma. Without asthma in you, but still with the same type of energy, you may become some other type of calamity in a moment. The disease may not be there, but you may get into an accident. Your asthma was only an indication of a deeper disturbance. If we take away your asthma, it may manifest in some other way, in some other calamity. This may happen simply because your energies are still in the same situation, but its effect is gone; so it will take effect in a deeper or more acute way to inform you again. If you bring awareness to your disease, you are trying to get connected to the cause of it.

When we talk about bringing awareness to your disease, when we talk about accepting what is there, it does not mean becoming defeated by your disease. If you truly become aware of the disease, then you become aware of the cause also. The moment you bring awareness to any part of your body, in terms of energy, it will immediately become active and different things start happening there. Just as an experiment, if you carefully attend to any part of your body – not necessarily the chakras, any part of your body – put your attention there and just be with that. You will see that so much energy activity will begin to happen there, because if you bring awareness and consciousness to that part of the body, naturally life energies become enhanced. Like this, one could heal something and change the energy situation to some extent.

Now you are asking about the popular healing business that is going on right now. See, one aspect of pranic healing is trying to focus your mind on someone or something, which you intend to heal. This is only one part of it. Why did the energy body get disturbed, first of all? For the energy body to be disturbed, either there is an improper lifestyle, improper thought patterns, improper emotions, or all these put together. There is a certain karmic structure that you have built which is causing a vacuum, some kind of turmoil to your energy, which is manifesting itself in the physical body as disturbed energy. So, even if you settle the energy situation to some extent with healing, or mental focus or with a certain sense of awareness, still the karmic substance which is causing this is not gone. The karmic substance is recorded in your energy as the fundamental software. It can work only within the ambit of the programmed software.

SEEKER: *Excuse me for interrupting you, Sadhguru, but I thought pranic healing is not about using the mind, or any such thing. It's like using the natural force that is around us, an energy force that is all around us, which we are also part of. The healing is said to be done like that, not by the mind or any such thing.*

SADHGURU: If that is what somebody is claiming, ask them to focus their mind on the mountain or on the sky and do healing to the person in front of them. It will not happen. You have to focus your mind in that direction. Without focusing your mind, nothing will happen.

SEEKER: *But, Sadhguru, healing is done even long distance. That person could be even outside of India and I can sit here and do it. That is what is being said.*

SADHGURU: Mental focus need not necessarily be within the physical limits of perception. Your mind can be focused on anything, irrespective of distance. It is not confined to the limitations of physical spaces. There are all sorts of healing processes in every town, but still the load on the local hospitals has not come down in any way. I would say fifty to sixty percent of the people are not even ill in the first place. They imagine illnesses. When I say imagine, it's a self-created situation. Medical science experimented with this just by giving placebo medicines, placebo surgeries. People became perfectly well. That means they never really had any illness; it's just a certain situation. All they need is just some placebo effect. This placebo effect was very effectively used in our tradition in India because the wise of the past understood that most people are ill by choice. They have chosen illness as a kind of defense against some other life situations within them. So all they need is a placebo. I'm talking about that segment which only needs placebo treatment and nothing else. So if somebody is praying for you and calls you up and says, "I have done healing for you. Don't worry, everything will be okay," it may just make you okay. See, people always need psychological support. Many people cannot step out of their house in the morning unless they get a phone call from somebody else saying, "Everything is okay. I'm blessing you, I'm praying for you." This is their psychological condition.

So what happens long distance is really not relevant to the earlier question that you brought up. Healing can be done, people can be relieved, but if you truly want to heal, you must be willing to take their karmic substance upon yourself, because as far as nature and life energies are concerned, where this karmic substance is does not really matter; life is life. The distinction between you and me is only in your mind. As far as life energy is concerned, one part of life energy is getting rotten right now. That's all it is. So you can shift it upon yourself, into your own energies, and it will naturally manifest in your body.

Now, suppose somebody has serious asthma, or a cardiac problem or something else and I take it away. In my body, it need not necessarily become asthma or a cardiac condition. Sometimes it can manifest the same way, but many times it will manifest in some other way, depending upon how my body reacts to that particular energy and karmic situation. All I am doing is taking that karmic substance into my system. Now this karmic substance in the other body, for that level of awareness, may take ten years to dissolve, if he does not add anything more, but in my body, I might be able to work it out in ten days.

As a preparation for the Dhyanalinga consecration process, we had drastically altered the karmic structures of a few people – physiological and other kinds of disturbances in them – so that they could be part of the work. As a result of this, you have seen on that particular initiation day, I vomited more than three-fourths of a liter of blood. This means my liver was in a complete mess and as per medical advice it needed emergency treatment without which one cannot recover; but you know very well, within forty-eight hours or a little more than that I was perfectly okay; there was no need for any doctor. So when a situation comes like that, what is being done is a certain kind of psychic surgery. See, surgery can be performed with various instruments. In ancient times, they did crude machete surgeries, then surgery evolved using finer instruments like scalpels. Now technology has taken surgery to the realms of the laser, which is a certain kind of light beam, which does the work more effectively than a machete. So without blood, without gore, without opening up wounds, surgery is performed and the body goes through all that it would during normal surgery except for the physical pain.

Similarly, with the sharpness of your psyche you could cut

through and perform a surgery. Certain people have certain inborn psychic capabilities that allow them to perform such an act. It can also be developed through a certain type of yoga sadhana. It is always more reliable when it has come to you with conscious sadhana; otherwise this capability in you may be on and off. So psychic surgery is a completely different thing compared to healing which is so much on the surface. See, with surface healing, the karmic substance will always take effect in some other way.

Another part of this whole activity of trying to heal somebody is, in some way, you are trying to play God, trying to manipulate energies in a certain way. Here we are teaching yoga kriyas to people with which healing is naturally happening. The objective is not healing, but it's definitely happening; but this involves sadhana, which is karma by itself. In the so-called healing processes or clinics also this is being done, but with a lack of understanding and depth. Just laying your hands on somebody and relieving him of pain and things like that, is not a good thing unless you are capable of taking the causal substance of it.

SEEKER: *Master, you were explaining earlier how you have taken upon yourself somebody's karma and how it affected your energy system. You knew how to handle it. What happens to that individual whose karma you affect? What happens to his energy form, his karmic structure? Is it being altered?*

SADHGURU: It is just like he is completely free from it because the fundamental cause of trouble itself is taken away. It's like you have a bad engine in your car and you sold it to your enemy. It's not there anymore, that's all.

SEEKER: *Master, why do you need to do it? Shouldn't everybody work it out themselves through sadhana?*

SADHGURU: Yes, that's what I said. In normal conditions we will never do it. It is not just to relieve him of his disease that it was done. This was done in a very special condition where we were working towards the Dhyanalinga consecration with certain time limitations. What objectives we wanted to fulfill had to be fulfilled within a certain time span, so many things had to be pushed. If there had been more time, so many more things that we did, we would not have done. We would have handled it with much more ease and in a different way; putting people into longer stages of sadhana and not having to take these drastic steps.

SEEKER: *Sadhguru, Jesus performed many miracles to create faith among his followers. He even raised someone from the dead.*

SADHGURU: This is all your nonsense, because when Jesus asked the fishermen to follow him and they started following him, one of them – I think it was Peter – said, "My father is dead; can I bury him and come, Master?" Jesus said, "Leave the dead to the dead. You come. You just come; follow me." He is saying his father is dead, and he is saying he will bury him and come, but Jesus says no; leave the dead to the dead. Do you know what this means? It means leave the dead to the dead in the village; those people are dead anyway. Leave the dead to the dead and you come follow me. Such a man, would he bring a dead body back to life?

SEEKER: *Maybe it was for some other reason, because he wanted people to have some faith?*

SADHGURU: How did Lazarus die? Did he have leprosy? See, in those times, whenever people became ill, the tradition of the Jewish culture was to put them into seclusion in caves; it was their way of avoiding infections. Food and water was just dropped inside. So they thought Lazarus was dead. When they told Jesus that Lazarus was dead, he went to see – I am just trying to reconstruct the situation; it may not be true. So Jesus went to see and probably he found that Lazarus was still alive. Jesus was brought up by the Essenes and other people who were healers; he might have nurtured him back to health.

Jesus went into the cave and came out after some time, isn't it?

SEEKER: *Yes. He stayed inside for some time.*

SADHGURU: Probably, he nurtured him and then he brought him back. So people said, "Oh! He has brought the dead back. Lazarus was dead and now he is back." In people's perception, maybe it was so. I am just saying how things can get, you know... A miracle means, raise the dead. So much for miracles and healing.

SEEKER: *Sadhguru, I have a phobia – a fear of disease – and I run away; rather, I am repulsed by diseased people, sick people. This is quite a hindrance for my growth, isn't it?*

SADHGURU: Nobody wants disease, of course. Nobody would choose to be diseased, isn't it? Nobody wants to be ill; everybody wants to be healthy. It's okay, but at the same time, you must understand that once you have a body, illness, old age and death are natural processes of life. You are not choosing to be ill, but you know that once you have a physical body, illness may happen at any moment. All right, you take care to see that you're not ill, but if you become excessively concerned about illness or health, that itself becomes an illness. Just trying to avoid illness is an illness. Illness restricts you, that's why you do not like it, isn't it? Why you do not like illness is that in some way it's going to restrict your life; but just the fear of illness also restricts your life and maybe your life span too, isn't it? It's an illness by itself.

This is not just you, there are so many people who have this fear. Especially once they cross forty, forty-five, their fear of illness becomes huge. When they were young they did not think so, because they thought they were immortal (laughs). Until they are forty or forty-five they are immortal, isn't it? Only after that the fact that you are mortal comes to you. Your fear is not of illness. Your fear is of death. Illness is the passage. You know illness is the first step towards death. So the fundamental fear is always of death. Now you're still not addressing death directly, but you're addressing illness, because you know, if illness comes, the other will follow.

Generally, in social situations, people have been telling you, convincing you, that after all, fear of death is natural. The problem is whatever the majority is doing, people say it is 'natural'. If the majority of people were smoking cigarettes people would say, "Smoking is a natural thing," yes or no? Certain groups of people, even now they say so. "What's wrong with smoking? It's just natural." A human being is not made to smoke; you're not an automobile or something! (Laughs). It's not natural for you to smoke, but people will make it natural. So the fear of death has been made natural by social situations, but it's not so. Fear of death has come because of a certain sense of ignorance and unawareness. It's not natural. Maybe the majority has ascribed to it, but it's not a natural process to fear death. If life happens, the natural process is death. Being afraid of a natural process is unnatural. Isn't it? The fear of death comes simply because you're not in touch with reality. The fear of death has come to you because you've gotten deeply identified with this body. Your identification with this body has become so strong because you have not explored other dimensions. If you had explored other dimensions of experience, if you had established yourselves in other dimensions of experience, the body would not be such a big issue; but now your whole experience of life is limited to this body. No matter what kind of teachings other people give you, this is me, isn't it?

It doesn't matter if somebody tells you, "You are not the body," somebody tells you, "You are atma," whatever nonsense they teach you, in your experience, this is you. Whatever Gitas they may read to you, your experience is limited to the physical body. The fear of losing it is natural, but if you reach other dimensions of experience, if you establish yourself in other dimensions of experience, the body will become an easy thing to handle. Life or death will not make so much of a difference. Life or death is only in terms of what you are doing. For example, you started a project. It's only in terms of whether you'll be able to complete your project or not before you die. That is all it is for me, at least. Right now, I have a project on my hands. Whether it's going to be completed or not, whether I should start the next project or am I going to shed the body before it is complete, that is all my calculation about death. My calculation of death is only in terms of, "Okay, for the people involved, can we do this for them within this time frame or not?" That's all. The question of shedding the body is not a big issue, because if your experience of life is established beyond the physical body, it's a very simple affair. When you want to change your clothes, you change them, isn't it? Or if you do not like them, you throw them away and walk naked. It's up to you; both are possible.

Once, when I was in the ninth standard of school, this girl, my classmate, during the Dussehra holidays, died of pneumonia. This just left me wondering, where could she have gone? Somebody who was just about my age died. How could someone just disappear like that? The way I was made, my nature was such that I would explore everything that came my way. Even on my way to school, I would at least climb up half a dozen big trees, look at the eggs in the birds' nests, eat the fruit on the tree; only then would I finally reach school. I just wanted to explore anything and everything that came my way. Now this death, I just had to see for myself, so I acquired ninety-eight Gardinal Sodium tablets from my father's medicine cupboard, as he was a physician.

In preparation for death, I distributed all my property to my friends. My property was a lot of small, small things, my prized catapults which were most difficult to part with because I held them very high and valuable and did not allow anybody to even touch them, my pet birds, the pet turtle that I released into the local Kukkarahalli water tank, the pet cobra which I released on the Chamundi hills. You see, I had a whole zoo going on the terrace of my house. I also gave away all my money, about one hundred and twelve rupees – in those days, a fortune for a young boy of my age – which I had earned through my self-employment as a snake catcher from house gardens, college and institution grounds; all of them I released on the Chamundi Hills. I distributed all these and one fine day told all my friends that today I was going to die. They thought this was one more joke. That night, I refused to take my supper and on an empty stomach, took all these tablets and went to bed. I wanted to know what would happen.

After three days, I woke up in a hospital bed. Everybody was anxious as to why I resorted to this step because until the last moment, I was that boisterous, crazy boy who was going around, doing all kinds of strange things. Even if my father scolded me or sent me out of the house, I just waited for that, and then I would just go away for a trek into the forest for a few days. That's how it was with me. If I had to find out something, it did not matter what was the price. About dying also, I never thought I was going to lose something, that I had to look into my parents' eyes one last time, nothing. I just took the tablets, closed my eyes and slept. The only heartache of this whole episode was that I could not get back all my possessions. Half the money I did get back after a lot of threatening and fist fights.

When your wanting to know something is so intense that you're willing to die for it, then knowing is not far away. So now you know what kind of crazy man you are with. When life and death make no difference for you, nothing is needed anymore. When life and death make a lot of difference, only for that fool there are so many problems. For someone who does not differentiate between life and death, there is no problem; he can live with a lot less limitations. Once this body has run its course it will go anyway, whether you like it or you do not like it. Whether you approve or disapprove, it will happen. As long as you retain your body, taking good care of it is definitely your business. Isn't it? Now if you are paranoid about ill health or death, you will not take good care of it. In your anxiety you will destroy the body. The very anxiety that says, "What may happen? What may happen to this body?" will destroy the body.

Now this fear of illness – even on seeing a dead body people are terrified. Is that so with many of you? Just by seeing a dead body you are terrified. Every day people die, all right. I am not saying it's a small thing for the people who love them, for people who care for them. For them it is a big thing, I understand, but why are you afraid just seeing a dead body? Living bodies are dangerous. They can do many things to you. What will a dead body do to you? A dead body is the safest thing, but you're afraid of it! (Laughs). Just look at this: living people are capable of so many things. They can put up very good pretenses, but tomorrow they may kill you, they may do something else to you, they may do anything. Dead bodies are so safe, but still people are afraid of them.

When I was about fourteen or fifteen, I spent an enormous amount of time in the cemeteries in Mysore. Something, somehow, drew me there. I would go and sit in the cemetery the whole night. People would set fire to their relatives' bodies which would go on burning; it's a long affair, you know. They don't have the patience to wait, so they wait for half an hour or one hour and then leave. I was the one attending to all those dead bodies. Somebody's head falls off, I would pick it up and put it back in the fire. Why I'm telling you this is because it's good to expose yourself to death. It's very good. I know that in your homes they have told you, you should not even utter the word 'death', because they have a stupid hope that if you don't utter the word, it will not enter your house. Do you think that if the word death is not in your vocabulary, it will not come to you?

I would like you to practice death. If you are willing, tomorrow evening we will set up a situation where you can consciously practice death. Are you willing, Indu? If every day, or at least for a few times in your life, you practice death consciously, then you will see that it is not the way you think it is. It's very different from what you have known. Death exists only for ignorant people. If you are in awareness, there is no such thing as death. The process of yoga is all rooted in death. In fact, you will become spiritual only if you start facing death. If you think of God, you will not become spiritual; you will invent stories. If you think of God, you will seek more survival and well-being and prosperity. Isn't it? Why are you thinking of God? Because you think he is easy currency for well-being, yes or no? Thinking of God is not spirituality; it's just another desperate attempt to live well somehow. Only when you are confronted with death, you start looking: "Okay, beyond this body, what the hell is there?" What is beyond the physical body is what we are referring to as spiritual. Your ideas of God are not spirituality, they are just another tool for survival. Only when you truly start seeking what is beyond the physical body, the spiritual processes open up for you.

Everything that we have been doing here from day one is just that, to somehow give you an experience that is beyond the limitations of the physical body; but every time something new comes up, fear and resistance is what you see within yourself. That's why the process is so slow. If you had just given yourself to me, many wonderful, liberating things could have happened to you. Right now, you want to go very cautiously. You don't want to step into anything that you don't know. At the same time, you want to know new things. There is no way. You are just defeating yourself all the time. You don't want to step into anything new without knowing it.

Body's Plight

How will you know it if you do not step into it? There is no way to know it unless you step into it, but you're not willing to step into it unless you know it. "You tell me what it is; only if I know I will step in."

Every day, just spend five minutes reminding yourself that you are mortal and today you may die. It is possible that today you might fall dead, isn't it? Just remind yourself; wonderful things will happen to you. Have you heard of Gurdjieff? Gurdjieff was a wonderful Master, but he was known as a rascal saint – a rascal, but a saint. His methods were so drastic; he did crazy things, terrible things with people. So Gurdjieff gave a solution to the world. He said, "If you want to have the whole world Enlightened, we must plant a new organ in everyone's body. Every day, twice a day, this organ will remind you: you will also die." Every day, twice a day, it reminds you. That is what the Shoonya meditation that you are initiated into is. It's not implanted; you have to make it happen. Every day, if you sit for meditation, you will see, everything that is you will die. The fear of death is not in the body, I want you to understand. The fear of death is in your personality. You, as a person, are going to die. That's the problem. Suppose you have grown old and God offers you a deal: "Okay, you give me this old body. I will give you a new body." Won't you take it? You will, won't you? So the body is not really the problem. The problem is that based on this body you have created a personality. That's what you are really attached to. When you sit in Shoonya meditation, do you see that your personality has dissolved and just a certain presence is there? Like this, every day, twice a day, you die consciously. The personality is dissolved. Just the presence is there. This will release you from everything.

This happened to me. A few years ago I was in Bangalore city and I went to the vegetable market, just taking a walk. I like walking through vegetable markets, so I'm just walking there, talking to the vegetables...why, Poornima? Why do you look so shocked? You think I am only capable of talking to your kind? Suddenly, I see this one vegetable vendor who is all bright and lit up. I can't believe a man like this is selling vegetables. I look at him, and instantly our eyes lock and I laugh and he also starts laughing. I could not believe this man is selling vegetables. Then I went to him and we started talking. I asked, "How come you are here selling vegetables, a man like you?" He said, "No, I am doing my work here." I said, "What do you do?" We were just bantering. In his life he was selling vegetables, just a plain vegetable seller. Then one day he became ill. He became so ill, he thought he was going to die. For over four months, he remained so ill that every day he thought, "Today I'm going to die." He went through this process of, 'Anyway I am going to die' for four months, and then he recovered. Then, something wonderful happened to him. He got Enlightened, I am telling you. So he says, "Anybody who comes to my shop, I bless them to have a long illness." (Laughs). I said, "That's great, but if people ever come to know, you've had it!" He blesses every customer who comes to him, "Let them have a long enlightening illness."

Whatever it is – illness, death, calamity, anything that happens around you – you can either use it to liberate yourself or you can use it to entangle yourself. Especially these calamities, illness and death, are a tremendous opportunity to look beyond the limitations of what you normally understand as life, isn't it? You thought that getting up in the morning, having a coffee, having breakfast, going to work, doing this, this, this, again eating, doing that, that, that, throwing yourself around on everybody, and coming back in the evening, you thought this was life. If one day you're bed ridden, suddenly you'll see, life seems to be something else, something very different from what you thought it was, isn't it? This need not happen to you. If you're intelligent, do learn from other people's experiences. Everything in the world need not happen to you; you must learn from other people's experiences.

Body's Plight

You have heard about Gautama, isn't it? He just saw one sick man, one old man and one dead body and he Realized that any day, this could happen to him. There is no point in running away from it. Let us look at it and see. If somebody is ill, I want you to sit with them and see that this could have been you and could be you any day. The most horrible illness that somebody has – we do not want it and we are not wishing for it – you could get it any day. It doesn't matter whether you are eighteen or eighty; it could be you today or tomorrow, isn't it? It's important to face everything with a stable and balanced mind. Avoiding it is not the solution. If you avoid it, you only get entangled. So do not avoid illness or death; face them. See that it could be you. Remind yourself. Tomorrow we will put you through an experience, but you must allow it to happen. If you are constantly resisting, it will not happen. It's a very subtle, simple process that can happen easily if you are willing.

SEEKER: *Sadhguru, you are saying you can make us experience death?*

SADHGURU: I am walking death in so many ways. 'Guru' means 'death'. Do not take death in the negative connotation. It is the death of the limited, always, because only the limited can die. Can the unlimited die? So 'Guru' means 'death of the limited'. In His presence it is always like death. Why you are uncomfortable but at the same time you want to be there is because you know He is death and on another level you know He is liberation. Still, there is not enough maturity to come to terms with it. So my presence always influences the death meditation simply because all the time, my very energies are like that, to release you from the limited or the physical.

SEEKER: *Sadhguru, in many ways we have been a witness to a drastic deterioration in your health and body in a short span of time since you started the Dhyanalinga consecration work. We believe you can do something about it. Don't you want to stay back and see us through?*

SADHGURU: Nobody will stay back. Everybody goes (laughs). Don't have hopes like that. For all you know I may live until seventy, you never know. In the next four or five years, after the Dhyanalinga consecration, I want to attempt this and see, literally recreating life. Theoretically, it's very much possible. It's just a question of whether we make it happen or not. The formula is right. I know that if I put all the ingredients in a proper way it is bound to happen. We will experiment with that. If it succeeds, I will live on; otherwise, I will go without regret.

There is one aspect which is unchanging, which is always there. In Isha, we don't usually talk about it because words like being, atma, consciousness, whatever, have been badly misused. I made it a rule not to talk about it. Here, it is always referred to as 'the beyond'. What is beyond limitations is reality. So that is absolute. The physical body, we know, is very transient; it's changing every day. Prana is also physical in nature, but very subtle. It is this prana that connects you to what is being referred to as 'soul', and to that which is the physical body. Prana is life. Prana is the liveliness that you see, the flowers blooming, the birds singing, us sitting here. All this is because of prana. The soul cannot do this. The soul has no quality of its own. It cannot do anything.

SEEKER: *Master, what exactly do you mean by 'prana'?*

SADHGURU: What you are referring to as a 'soul' is not an entity. Just to bring an understanding to people, the Hindu culture used a word to describe that which is unbounded, which is unfortunately misunderstood. That which is unbounded is never an entity; it cannot be. But the moment you put a name on it, it becomes an entity. Whether you call it atma, soul, self — whatever you call it — the moment you stick a name to it, it becomes an entity. That's where the misunderstanding and the struggle is with people. Why we are making jokes — if somebody says 'soul', I immediately look at

Body's Plight

the soles of my feet and make fun of it – is to make them understand that whatever they have thought about it, is not it. It cannot be like that. I just joke about it and destroy their concept of what the soul is.

People say 'good souls'. In the West, they say, "Oh, he is a good soul." There is no good soul or bad soul. Soul is beyond all identification, all entity, all everything. Another way to look at this is that there is no soul as such. That's why Gautama went about saying, "You are anatma. There is no atma." If asked, "Then what is it?" he would say, "Ah, it is nothingness." He's just giving another name, just to deceive you out of your misconceptions. To get you out of one, he's getting you into a new word, that is all. So tomorrow you go about saying, "I am nothing, I am nothing, I am nothing." That also becomes an entity. When that happens, we use another word. See, it's not that the word is trying to describe what it is. The word is trying to destroy your misconceptions about what it is. That's all. My life and my work is just that – to destroy all your misconceptions. Just trying to destroy one concept and giving it another name will not take anybody to reality. The Master's role is to just demolish everything that is untrue. That's all. One can never get anybody to reality, but if you're ready to have all untruths destroyed, you'll arrive at it.

Now you're asking about prana. This has been looked at in yoga in a very wise and wonderful way, just looking at everything as body, this physical structure as body, physiology as body, mind as body, energy or pranic system as body, and etheric substance also as body. Everything as body, even the soul as body. It is a very wise way to look at things. When we say anandamaya kosha, still we are not referring to the ultimate; but even that is seen as a body, because that's how it is right now. That's the only way you can grasp it. You do not talk about anything there (pointing in the distance). You talk about how to transcend one limitation and then go to the next one. When you transcend all limitations, what happens,

happens. Why should you think about it now, because whatever you think, you think only from your limitations. Nobody can think of anything which is not in his present dimension of experience. Nobody! There is no point talking to you about something which is not in your present level of experience. So in yoga it is said, everything is body. Mind is body, prana is body, etheric substance is body, everything is body. In other words, as I have been describing this, if you take your body as a whole model of creation, it's like a paint smear – starting with a very gross substance, becoming subtler, subtler, subtler – becoming nothing. So from the physical body, to the mental body, to the pranic body, it gets subtler and subtler. The physical body and mental body are more substance. The pranic body is the energy which fires all this. So that's what keeps you in touch with the body. When prana drops, you drop. Your body drops dead, or in your experience, you drop dead – whichever way. So what you're calling death is only that the prana has lost its vibrancy. Either due to old age or disease or some other damage or injury, prana has lost its vibrancy.

Now, another way is, if I shoot you in the head, your prana may be vibrant but still you will be dead. The physical body is broken and so the prana cannot immediately reconstruct it to keep it going. The physical body collapses. Suppose I shoot you in your thigh muscle. In cases where the body is not broken enough, it will allow enough time for the prana to reconstruct the damaged part. Why it is said that if somebody dies in an accident, his ghost will be going around, is simply because that man is moving around with more substance than one who dies a natural death. So there are more chances that people may feel him. Do you understand what I am saying? Suppose somebody died of old age, his prana would become very weak, the vibrancy would be lost, and then the body would fall apart. So you will not feel him. He is too subtle.

SEEKER: *So the prana of this person who died in an accident is felt more? And that is again the subtle body, isn't it, Sadhguru?*

SADHGURU: No, let me come to that. As we saw, there are five bodies. We know that. Now, the pranic body is fully vibrant in a person, but as he becomes older and older, the pranic body loses its vibrancy. What you're doing with your kriyas and pranayama is just keeping the vibrancy. No matter what your age is, just keeping that vibrancy. How vibrant it is, that is how the mental body and the physical body will be. So we are just trying to keep the pranic system in proper vibrancy, always. Now somebody is young and vibrant, but the body is destroyed – the physical body. Either by an accident or a gunshot or whatever, the physical body is destroyed. The pranic body is still very much vibrant and intact. So now, anyway, he has to part with the physical body because it's ruined. It is physically damaged. He can't do anything about it. Now when he leaves, the vibrancy of the pranic body is still intact. So he's felt much more easily by people.

SEEKER: *Yes, Sadhguru, but for how long would he be able to keep this pranic body which is still intact? When you say "still intact", is it a subtler body?*

SADHGURU: No. Even the person who dies of old age has a subtler body, but it is too subtle for people to feel.

SEEKER: *So Sadhguru, this pranic body will stay intact until rebirth?*

SADHGURU: Yes, until it's capable of finding another physical body.

SEEKER: *Finding or creating, Sadhguru?*

SADHGURU: In a way, creating. In one way, creating, because without the pranic substance, the body cannot form itself.

SEEKER: *So Master, does creating mean when a woman conceives?*

SADHGURU: A woman conceives just because two physical cells meet.

SEEKER: *Yes Sadhguru, one of these energy bodies finds its way to the womb at the time of conception.*

SADHGURU: No, it's not then. At that time, it is not there. As the physical body slowly starts developing within a woman's womb... see it's just like there was a nest. Some bird built the nest; some other bird came and laid its eggs and made a life there. It's just like that. Some two fools came together and they started creating a body. Somebody else who is ripe for that is always looking for a body; he finds it and in that there is some choice. Depending upon how consciously he has lived, there is a little bit of choice as to what kind of body he chooses.

SEEKER: *Is that choice always there, Sadhguru?*

SADHGURU: There is a little bit of choice, always; but when I say choice, it is not like you go into this shop and buy this shirt or whatever. It's not in that sense. There is a karmic choice. There is a natural tendency for the person to go in a certain direction, towards a certain womb, towards a certain body. That natural tendency is there. See, even when you're alive here in the physical body, you have a natural tendency to seek out certain people, because that's how your karmas are. So, similarly, when you do not have a physical body, it's much more unconscious, but still the karmic substance that you carry with you seeks out a certain type of body. So once it has found that body, it is the vibrancy of the prana which enhances the quality of the physical body. It's not just the mother who is making the baby. See, there are millions of instances where probably the mother is weak, undernourished, on the street, and yet she delivers a very healthy baby. Any number of situations like this are there. Somebody coming from the best of families, where everything is taken care of and who is very well fed, gives birth to a very fragile child. This is the pranic substance, pranic vibrancy of the being who has taken on that particular body. That's why this distinction is there. Depending upon the kind of vibrancy the pranic body has, accordingly it creates a certain type of body. So the creation of the body is not just the mother's work. What kind of being came there, also creates this in a certain way.

SEEKER: *So Master, when exactly does this prana enter the body that has been conceived?*

SADHGURU: See, until about forty to forty-eight days after conception, it's still a body. Why it is said that if the woman has gone over forty days past conception, it should not be aborted is because the being has come in by then. Before that it was not a being. Not only because of the smallness of the body, but the being is not yet there. It is just a bundle of cells. Now this bundle of cells becomes a being, maybe not yet a person, but in many ways a person. His personality might not have manifested in the sense that we understand, but the very way the baby kicks around in the mother's womb is different from baby to baby. You had two; were they the same?

SEEKER: *Definitely not, Sadhguru.*

SADHGURU: They were not the same; the very way they kick around is different. They already have a personality. Depending upon their karmic structure, they have a certain personality. It's not so manifest, but it is there. To what extent that little person can manifest, to that extent he's manifesting. The very moment he's born, he has his own personality. Isn't it?

SEEKER: *Oh, very much Sadhguru.*

Sadhguru: The very way he yells, the very way he demands things is different. It's different from one baby to another.

Because their area of activity is so limited, people think all babies are the same. It's not true. Every baby, the way he cries, the way he behaves, the way he looks up, the way he goes for food, everything is different from baby to baby. You just see four puppies, they're all different. All four of them, though delivered from the same womb, just see the way they are. They're different. It depends on the kind of vibrancy that he has come with, the kind of karmic substance that he carries; accordingly it is. So the diminishing of the karmic body, the diminishing of the pranic body, is what is called 'old age'.

Now the karma, as it is impressed into your physical body and mental body, is also impressed into your energy body. As the allotted karma or prarabdha is reaching completion, the pranic body's ability to hold on to the physical body recedes. Life, as you know it, which is physical, will begin to lose its vibrancy, but at the same time, the subtle body gathers more vibrancy because the physical body is losing its grip on the subtle. This is the reason why many of you might have noticed, even a person who has lived a gross life, the last few days before his death, seems to carry an ethereal peace about himself.

SEEKER: *Sadhguru, how does a decimated pranic body regain its vibrancy before it acquires a physical body again?*

SADHGURU: One thing that we are doing through yoga kriyas is rejuvenating you when you are here, in the physical body. It could happen in so many other ways. Just a walk in the forest can rejuvenate you. Good food can rejuvenate you. Yogic practices can rejuvenate you. That's a different dimension. All this is when you have the body. Now, after you leave the body, if the pranic body is too vibrant, let us say it's in full life when it died, he cannot find another body for some time. He needs a certain settling down of the pranic body. Only then he can find a body. That's why we are saying that if they die now in an accident, they will remain disembodied – what normally people refer to as ghosts – for a long time.

SEEKER: *Is that why the rituals, Sadhguru? To appease them?*

SADHGURU: Yes, to pacify him, because he's still vibrant. His pranic body still carries desires, longings, everything – so it will not settle. It remains in that form for a long period of time. It has to run its course. Initially, when they die because of an accident, they're very vibrant. That's when they are felt very strongly. Then when the prana loses its vibrancy they just hang around. In the Indian way of life there are certain practices and processes to hasten the course so that he does not have to hang in there. He's in limbo. You want to hasten that process of being in limbo for that person. Some of it is true. If somebody who is doing it knows what he's doing, it can be done. Some of it is just psychological solace for the living, so that they feel that their son or husband or child is not hanging there. "We've done something; he will find a good space." Still, it's also true that those who know what they are doing, if they do it, they can hasten the process for him so that he does not have to be around for too long.

If these pranic and subtler bodies have to take another physical body, they should come to a certain sense of sedateness. Only if they come to a lower sense of vibrancy or sedateness can the being find another body; otherwise it will not find it. If it is fully vibrant like this right now, it cannot find another body. It has to become sedate. Such a process can also be set forth willfully. Samadhi states can be very intense or very sedate, almost like death. Beyond a certain level of subtleness, the structure is not so firm, so it is easy to mix things; but when it's like this, with the proper structure of the physical body, when the body is firm, you cannot do this because it is vibrant. So samadhi is almost like death. With natural death that's what is happening. When somebody lives a long and proper life and dies peacefully – people are always thinking of dying peacefully – it is understood that his prana has run a full course and has simply gotten disentangled.

It's just like a ripe fruit fell off a tree. The moment it falls off, with the ripe fruit around it, the seed will immediately find root with the necessary food around it. See, the fruit has the necessary manure around it. Fruit is actually manure. We are just eating it before it actually becomes manure. So now there is a mango. The flesh is created by the tree. One thing is to attract animals so that they will take it elsewhere, carry the seed and drop it in other places. Another thing is, when the fruit falls down, it has the necessary food in it so that it works as manure. We call it manure, but it is the seed's food. It comes with packaged food, so that when it falls on the earth it has food from which it grows. So when a person goes through a full cycle and when he comes to that point, we say he died peacefully, because he has run his full course. There is no struggle, there is no disease, there is no injury. There is nothing. The prana has reached a certain level of sedateness and disentangled itself, without any struggle or disturbance. Now what we call Mahasamadhi is the same thing: to bring the prana to a certain state of passivity with a certain level of intensity in the structure, a certain level of maturity, so that it disentangles by itself. We are looking forward to that kind of death, because when you die like that, it is proper, because it is just a simple disentanglement, it is natural. If you die with a disease, if you die from an accident or an injury, there is violence in it. That violence is carried in so many ways in the subtler bodies.

SEEKER: *Jaggi, we say when a person dies of old age, prana loses its vibrancy. Then let us assume that it takes another body; does it mean to say that the prana starts getting vibrant again?*

SADHGURU: Yes, it is rejuvenated. To enter the body it must be in a certain state of passive inertness. Only then it

Body's Plight

can find a body. Once prarabdha karma runs out or wears itself out, prana will lose its vibrancy, its dynamism, without a karmic substance. Once the prarabdha or allotted karma completely wears out, after a short span of time, the new installment of prarabdha will begin to manifest itself. As this new prarabdha begins to manifest, the prana regains its vibrancy and by then it will regain a body again.

SEEKER: *When one reaches Mahasamadhi, isn't that person's prana in full vibrancy? And if it is in full vibrancy, how is it that it dissolves by itself, that it does not seek a body again? What is the basis of that, Sadhguru?*

SADHGURU: See, when you die of old age, you die peacefully. If somebody dies in his sleep, people say it's so wonderful because he got disentangled from the body naturally, without any violence. In a way, it's a good way to die. Now we are trying to create the same thing consciously, because it's not necessary that when it happens naturally, it will happen consciously. It may happen in your sleep. It may happen here when you are sitting. It may just happen to you, and along with that life will dissipate. Because prana is dissipating, when it comes to that stage, you may just become senile, lose your memory and not be conscious of what is happening. All these things may happen with dissipation of prana. Why an old person is becoming senile or getting lost is simply because of this. It is again like a second childhood because his prana is losing the vibrancy that it had in youth. It's again becoming like a baby. So he is going back to the same state where he took on the body. In what level of passivity his prana was, if he reaches the same level of passivity, he will die. He will leave the body like he took on the body, very naturally. All other forms of deaths, whether you die from infection, accident, suicide or whatever, all are considered unnatural. Now, what you're talking about as Mahasamadhi is to bring about that stage of dying naturally, consciously. So now one thing is, with yogic practices, it's becoming more intense. Your energies are becoming more intense. Now how can this person's energy be inert? If you know anything about energy, that which is of tremendous intensity is always stillness. Yes? This is a scientific fact. If any vibration reaches tremendous intensity, it will become still. In that stillness, the person will leave. It is in absolute stillness, not inertness, that he leaves. Once again it looks like the prana has become inert or passive as far as the physical body was concerned. In a way, you can say you deceived the body. The physical body thought that your energies became totally inert and it dropped. In a way, consciously, you deceive the body by creating a high pitch of vibrancy. This extreme vibrancy can be set with awareness; with razor-sharp awareness one can get there. One can also come to this with bhakthi, intensity of emotion. One can also come to this by doing the necessary practices like you are doing now. Let us say tomorrow morning you sit and do one million kapala-bathis; at the end of the day you may leave the body. It's possible. If your energies become so intense, they'll become still. The physical body cannot contain it. It will think it's over and it will drop.

SEEKER: *Sadhguru, would that be Mahasamadhi?*

SADHGURU: Yes, it is! For twelve years you do kapala-bathi, at the end of it you reach one million, okay? If you raise it to that pitch, it becomes absolute stillness. The physical body feels that it's over and disentangles because your energies become vibrant but still, because of the practice. That's very good for you. Right now, you may think you have taken on the body. That's true in one way, but in another way, the physical body is holding you. You can't leave it. Many people, when they get into the first stages of sadhana, they say, "The hell with this body," but it will not happen. All the spiritual-thinking people believe they have taken on the body. It is true in one way, but the body has taken over you; that's another thing. It will not release you even if you want to be released.

Body's Plight

So if you push your energy to a certain pitch, with whatever method you know, then it will become still. In that stillness, the body may be deceived and dropped. Stillness is the most intense aspect of life.

SEEKER: *So Master, this prana which is in full vibrancy, will it not seek another body?*

SADHGURU: It will not seek because it has come to that level of vibrancy.

SEEKER: *Realization! That is Realization!*

SADHGURU: You can call it Realization, but usually we use the word 'Realization' only if somebody realizes and lives on. You can call it Enlightenment. It's the same, but you use the word 'Realization' because he is Realized. Realizing is a sort of knowing. Mahasamadhi is not necessarily knowing. He became free, that's all. The moment of freedom is also a kind of knowing, but there is nobody to know, so the knowing does not arise. Dissolution of the individual means joining the unbounded, and that's the ultimate knowing also.

SEEKER: *Sadhguru, when we die, the prana we carried dissolves, disintegrates and just sort of gets mixed up with something?*

SADHGURU: It is just like a bubble. The bubble burst; where is the bubble? What happened to the air inside? There is no such thing.

SEEKER: *Sadhguru, why is the population always increasing? When you are saying that everything is one...*

SADHGURU: That is because all crawling and climbing creatures have become human beings. The insect population is coming down compared to the human population, isn't it, Kiran? (Laughs). This question itself comes from the ignorance of believing and thinking of existence numerically. It's not like that! Life does not happen that way. You must understand this. Now if I say, "The bubble in the air," suppose I create a billion bubbles and all the air is contained in them, where is there more air for the other bubbles to come? That's the question, isn't it? When you are talking about the unbounded, there is no such arithmetic. Don't take the example literally, but I think it clarifies many things.

SEEKER: *The question, Sadhguru, was like, if you sum up all the beings or all the...*

SADHGURU: The thing is, you are thinking there is a being. What if there is no being? That is why Gautama went on saying you are anatma. It was total sacrilege for the Hindus; he is saying, "You are anatma." So if it is anatma, how many anatmas, how many non-beings can you create? If it is atma there could be any number; if it's anatma, how many can there be? How many non-beings can you create? How many 'emptinesses' can you create? That's the question. You're always thinking materially, which comes only from the dimension of your experience, which is very limited.

If you go on producing bodies, they will get occupied anyway. If you produce bodies, life will happen. So where will the karma come from for them? Where is the karmic substance for them? Where is the mental substance for them? There is plenty of this substance. In reality, if you want, this person who is sitting here right now as one person, can take on a million bodies with the same karmic content that he has now. It's possible. There are many situations where yogis have taken up two bodies and gone around – the same karmic substance has taken on two bodies. In a way, producing our teachers is just this. I'm trying to take on a hundred bodies and go around the world. Their individuality is intact, their intelligence is intact, but just one aspect of their life, one part of their karma is superimposed. So the numbers, the population, that's not a relevant question. It's a very logical, mathematical, arithmetical question. Life does not happen like that.

Body's Plight

SEEKER: *Sadhguru, what do you mean by recreation of life?*

SADHGURU: Let us say this life has run its full course, which means the prana has lost the necessary vibrancy to keep the body and the being together. This can happen either due to old age or disease or as it is with me, excessive usage of the pranic body. Now you recreate it once again. It is almost like being born again, but not going back to the womb, right away. The normal way is to go back to the womb. The natural way is, if this is over, to leave it and again go back to another womb. Now without going back to the womb, recreating it here itself; same body, but a different life force. Same body, same mind and same awareness, but that which supports life, that energy has to be completely changed. We started a small process towards this kind of rejuvenation a few weeks ago and it worked well. It really worked well, so let us see. We'll make it work but we need fourteen people. We need seven Idas and seven Pingalas, masculine and feminine energies; which does not necessarily mean man and woman. They need a lot of preparation to go through a process like that. They need a tremendous amount of preparation.

We have to work on these people to bring about heightened levels of vibrancy in their system and energy body. A kind of vibrancy that will disentangle them from their physical form, except for a small connection to avoid disembodiment, or in other words, to maintain certain levels of samadhi and still have enough mastery over their systems to maintain physical activity. With such people, their energies will be so fluid that you can recreate another one. It is like I've said, if you are making clay pots, let's say you make ten clay pots; before they are dry or yet to be burned, you can again reduce them into clay and make eleven pots out of it.

What we did right now was a small thing, but it worked well. It shows on me. It has worked well. I have not heard about it anywhere, but somehow, within me, the details are just falling into place as I look at it. I can see what has to be done. The formula is clear, quite clear. It's just that, let us say, you know the recipe, but still the cooking may turn out bad. It all depends on how we put things together. It needs an expert cook. Just the recipe will not make the food tasty, but the recipe is a proof that we know it is going to work like this. So making it happen is always in our hands. We make it happen or we do not make it happen. Maybe it also depends on something else, which is beyond us; it also depends on that. It depends on the existence also, about how badly the existence wants you; but it's possible. I see it is possible. More than wanting to live more, just the challenge of making it happen excites me.

SEEKER: *Sadhguru, you just said it depends on how badly existence wants you back, what do you mean by it?*

SADHGURU: See, existence is not interested in any person. When the energy is mature, it takes you back, it will absorb you into itself. That's all. This question comes up in your minds because of your emotions and your insecurities, because there is a whole spiritual career in front of you. You feel you have to safeguard what you have invested in. All this is involved in the question. We will do our best. Still, it is subject to many things. It's not one hundred percent foolproof. You're not like a god who (snaps fingers) like that, it will happen. It is not so. Things have to be done. For example, we can promise you that we will lay the garden in a year's time, but it is subject to many things. We know if you plant this bamboo here, it will grow in a certain time, but still it is subject to so many things, isn't it? One day an elephant may walk in and take away your bamboo. Similarly, life is subject to many things.

SEEKER: *Sadhguru, how badly does Yama want you?*
Another audience member: Amma???

Body's Plight

SADHGURU: Somu, Yama, Yama, not Amma! Existence and Yama are not the same, he is only the recycler. Yama is just a dispatcher – from here to there and there to here. Amma is the one who delivers you here. Yama is the one who delivers you there.

SEEKER: *And why would the existence want you? Is it because the existence loves you so much, you are so precious that the existence feels you are better off there? And why would it want only you, not any of us? In what way are you so special, Sadhguru?*

SADHGURU: Somu, as I said just now, existence is not interested in anybody. Existence does not know any love. If you look up in the sky during the day, you see the sun. That becomes most dominant in your experience. In the night, if you look up, the stars become very dominant in your experience, but both the sun and the stars – and the sun also happens to be a star – are very puny little things when compared to the vastness of the sky. Generally though, that is never in your perception. So true existence is the vastness of the sky. The sun, the stars, you and me, are just small happenings, brief happenings really.

Today, modern science is telling you that even the sun has a life span. It's going to burn itself out. As you are burning your life out, similarly, the sun is on fever and he's burning his life out too. Your normal temperature is ninety-eight point six degrees Fahrenheit or whatever; his normal temperature is some ninety-eight million degrees, but he also has a life span. He is also burning up. One day he will do himself in. So whatever you see as physical existence is just a small happening. The true existence is the vastness, the emptiness that is there, the space. So when I say existence reclaiming something which is right now sitting here as a person, it's just that what you call a person is just like a bubble. This bubble doesn't have any substance of its own. The air was around. It just created a shell around it, so suddenly it has a different quality of its own. There are thick bubbles, there are thin bubbles, there are strong bubbles, there are weak bubbles, there are big bubbles, and there are small bubbles – just like people. Just like every other creature too, but when the bubble bursts, the substance that's inside the bubble, where is it? The air has reclaimed it; the atmosphere has reclaimed it. Similarly, a bubble is formed in the form of an etheric body, in the form of a pranic body, a mental body and a physical body. The physical body we can shoot down any moment we want to. It is within our power to just cut the physical body in two if we want to, but the other bodies we are not able to cut. Only what you call as existence, only that can do it.

What you are calling the spiritual process is just that. It's a deeper way of suicide. This is not about killing the physical body. You're trying to destroy the very fundamentals of creating the body within you. You're trying to destroy the very fundamental structure over which a body can form. The physical body is possible only because of the necessary karmic substances that are there in the form of etheric, pranic and mental bodies. So you are trying to destroy that through the spiritual process. With your awareness, with your practices, with your love, with your devotion, all you are trying to do is destroy the possibility of taking on another body, destroy the very foundation over which the physical body can happen. Or, in other words, you're trying to take away the possibility of going through the recycling bin over and over again. A mother's womb is only a recycling bag. Again and again... (laughs) going through the same process. So you want to take that away.

Once energies have matured to a certain point, where the other substances – the necessary foundation for another physical body – have been removed from it, energy has become just pure energy. It becomes more malleable. It is no more within the structure of the physical body. So now, even when the person is alive, he begins to experience himself in many ways beyond physical limitations. Once this energy starts maturing this way, now existence reclaims this energy. It is not that existence reclaims it, this energy is mature to a point where it cannot take on the limitations of any form any more. So naturally, it merges with existence.

To what extent your energies mature, that's what we're talking about. Or in other words, when we want to do certain work – even if the energy is mature enough to leave, you still want to retain your body and perform certain activities – then you consciously create a certain amount of karma. You create a certain amount of sturdiness to your physical, mental, pranic and etheric bodies by doing certain karmas and kriyas. Karma is the way of bondage. Kriya is the way of release. Karma is outward action. Kriya is inward action, but both can be used either to bind or to release. Both internal and external action can be used either to bind you strongly or it can be used to liberate you. Like for example, us. We are teaching basic programs with certain kriyas, and we are reassuring the participants that this is not about leaving your life and going away. This is about being more effective at what you're doing, because we are teaching kriyas only to that extent which sort of roots them in their life, makes them more effective, makes them more capable. Many more possibilities of life open up for them. The kriyas and the physical processes are taught only to that extent where it roots them in the body. The same kriyas, if they are practiced in a different dimension, with a different understanding and a different intensity, will start loosening you from the body.

So these kriyas and karmas, the external activity and internal activity can be used either to liberate you or to bind you. Once your energies reach a certain peak or certain level of maturity, when holding on to the body becomes an effort, then you start doing karmas and kriyas to hold on to the body, because you have some unfinished work. See, as karma can be binding and releasing, yoga kriyas also can be binding and releasing. Both karma and yoga kriyas can be used either to bind you or to liberate you. So this is the problem, or this is the situation that a Realized being who continues to live always has. His energy is always disentangling itself; it cannot be associated with the body, but he is doing everything to keep it rooted in the body, because he still has something to do. What we are talking about, re-creation, is to re-manifest those areas of the pranic body which are destroyed. Another thing is to create the necessary karma and kriyas within yourself to root the energy into the body so that this form of life can continue for a while longer.

SEEKER: *Sadhguru, how come even some Enlightened beings have physical afflictions? Why don't they cure themselves? For example, Ramakrishna Paramahamsa had cancer.*

SADHGURU: Ramakrishna Paramahamsa was not interested in all this physical business. He was in the bliss body; simply blissful. The physical body, he was not bothered, mental body, he was not bothered, pranic body, he was not bothered. When a person is like that, the body may rot. He does not care. When Ramana sat for meditation, he just sat for fourteen years and his whole body was full of sores and insect bites. Animals came and bit him and he just sat because he had nothing to do with the body. If it heals, it heals. If it doesn't heal, it doesn't heal. He treats the mind and mental body the same way. If cancer comes, he doesn't care. He doesn't even feel he has cancer because he feels it is not in him.

Only people on the path of kriya yoga are capable of attending to the body in a scientific way. Others do not pay attention to it. Usually, they are incapable of too much activity. A Ramana or a Ramakrishna would not be able to trek with me to the Himalayas, let alone at my pace. Physically they are very incapable, because they were not bothered about taking care of their bodies. Their growth did not

Body's Plight

involve building a certain body. So they never attended to those things. They attained through their own intelligence and their own intensity, not following any system. Only people on the path of kriya, the Realized yogis, are physically very fit and their bodies will be properly kept. For them there is no problem. They cross the border and they come back. They smuggle things across (laughs). For them, it's a daily affair. That's the difference between a saint and a Guru. Saints somehow cross the border. They are wonderful people. They will bless you and their blessings are good to receive.

A Guru is not somebody who is just a saint. A Guru is somebody who has the methods and technologies for everything. He's somebody who is good both ways. A Guru's ways will not be saintly at all. One moment he's this, the next that. He can be in so many ways. He is just playing a role because he has all the technologies in his hand. He's not always a good man; he can do anything, but a saint is always a good man, always gentle, always loving and always happy. A Guru is not like that. He will do what is needed. If needed, he can stand up and fight.

SEEKER: *Sadhguru, in the past you have talked about how pranayama helps with death. Would you please explain this further?*

SADHGURU: The pranayama that you are doing is a way to transform your life energies from just manufacturing a mass of flesh to manufacturing something so much subtler and so much more enduring than flesh. I'm sure you have no illusions about this, that the nature of life is such, this body is on loan for you from the earth. Mother Earth has loaned it to you, isn't it? She doesn't charge interest, but the loan is one hundred percent recovered. Not a cell or atom you can take with you; it's one hundred percent recovery.

Now when you have this body, you can manufacture something else, which the earth cannot reclaim. So the whole spiritual process is just that, trying to earn yourself something that the earth cannot reclaim from you. Whether you do pranayama, meditation or something else, all you're trying to do is to earn something that the earth cannot reclaim. If you do not earn that, then when the loan collection comes, the earth will take everything and will not leave anything with you. Then, you know, the next part of the journey will not be good. If you have cash in your pocket you travel more comfortably, yes? Otherwise, you'll be in trouble.

You are preparing for the journey of your life with qualifications, with money, with clothes, with homes, with families, with relationships, fully knowing that all this has only a brief existence. It's needed, right? It is fine, but it need not be made into such a big issue. It should not be a life-consuming issue. A certain part of your energy you can dedicate to take care of your well-being, your physical and mental well-being, your comforts and your things, whatever you need. You are capable of that. You have the necessary intelligence and energy to do it. It's only because your life is all messed up that it does not produce what it has to produce. If you streamline yourself, you will see, earning your living and living well is very much possible without twenty-four hours of dedication; but you know very well that you have to drop all this. If you sit here for a moment with eyes closed, you can see that you seem to be something a little more than this body. You may not know what it is, but you can feel that you are something a little more than this body, isn't it?

If anybody just closes his eyes for two minutes and looks, he can see that what he calls as 'himself' is something more than the body. When the body is reclaimed, if you do not have anything with you for the next part of the journey, it won't be good. This is not only about the next part of the journey, but right now, this part of the journey also won't be very good. You may have many valuable things, you may have many people with you, you may have everything, but you, as a person, will never know one moment of peace if your energies are not good. So both for this journey and whatever may be beyond it, it is important that you begin to manufacture subtler dimensions of energy around you. The pranayama that we teach you here is for this. This morning and evening practice, if you keep on doing it, slowly you will find every breath becomes a source of manufacturing subtler forces around you. Pranayama does not only mean breath. This must be understood. Pranayama means to control the vital energies. Control of vital energies need not necessarily mean using the breath.

Even if I move my fingers like this, I can have total control over my energy. I can shift my energy wherever I want it. Not just in the body, anywhere, literally anywhere in the world. Whenever you wish, you can have your energy anywhere once you have certain mastery over your energies. Initially, you are using breath as a means. Breath is only a tool, but it's not about the breath. Even without the breath it can be done. It has nothing to do with the breath really. The breath is just used as an initial tool, but once a certain amount of mastery is there, it just does not matter. So pranayama is not just about morning and evening. As you keep the practice going, you will see that the very quality of your breath throughout the day is different. Do you feel this? The very way it is, is different. In a way, yes, pranayama is a way of preparing for the last breath and beyond.

SEEKER: *Can you do anything at the moment of death to help someone who has not completely reached the point of liberation? I know a meditator who told me you helped her sick father who was painfully dying of cancer with his death. What did you do, Sadhguru?*

SADHGURU: Deepika, where do you collect all this information from? Now if he has run his full course of prarabdha, which is not true for most people, we can help him die consciously rather then in an unconscious state because there is a conducive atmosphere. Dissolution is possible. He is liberated. When they die of disease before the prarabdha is complete and prarabdha is still due, if I try to dissolve him, it's not going to work, nor am I going to do that. All we can do is help him to die with awareness; then he will have a little enhanced life somewhere else.

SEEKER: *If he has run his full course and you help him, then he's liberated for good? How is that possible, Master?*

SADHGURU: Yes, he is liberated for good and this is possible only when someone has run the full course of prarabdha. Now everything is over, he's in a certain space where there is a karmic break. There are many people who die of old age; they may have lived as utter fools, but the final few days, suddenly there is a new sense of wisdom within them, a new sense of awareness about them, because their karma allotment has finished.

Just the minor things are left and the next quota of karma has not come in yet, so that's a blessed period. Even for a person who lived an ignorant life, you'll see that suddenly he knows, "In the next three days I will die." Do you know this? Aged people, who are perfectly healthy, they will just know. Such people we can dissolve very easily because they have come to that blessed state where there is no karmic bondage. There is a stock somewhere else, but here there is a little space of no karma. No karma means no individuality. Do you understand this? No karma means no substance for individual process to happen. It has come to a point where you're almost like dissolving because the next quota has not been released yet. The current quota is over and in that space, dissolution is very simple. If one has not reached that space, if one is approaching death because of a broken body, either because of injury or disease or whatever else, such a person we can help him to die in a little better awareness so that he has a little enhanced life elsewhere.

SEEKER: *Is that so even for somebody who doesn't know you, Master?*

SADHGURU: There is no one who does not know me; I want you to understand this. As a person, whether you know me or not, is a different thing. There is nobody who does not know me because, when I'm talking on this level, I'm not talking about myself as a person, myself as some bundle of habits and patterns and things. That which I call as 'myself' is you also. There is nobody who does not know me. We are talking about that dimension. In that dimension there is no individual person.

SEEKER: *So Sadhguru, every time someone is born he just gets a pack of karma to work out in this lifetime?*

SADHGURU: The warehouse is there. One truckload has been taken out, to be worked out now. The warehouse is always sitting there in your head. Now what we're doing with Samyama, you're not going into the prarabdha. You're going into the sanchita aspect of your karma. You're bringing out, you are opening up the warehouse. That's the reason why, when a person walks the spiritual path, in many ways –if they don't handle the situation properly – they will suffer much more than someone else, because they are bringing up large volumes of it. Others are just handling what is allotted to them. Now you're trying to take up the whole portion, you want to get your Ph.D. today, so you're not going step by step. That is the reason why so much discipline was always brought into yogic practices, so that when things overwhelm you, you are able to handle that situation. Otherwise, if you open up things for which you are not ready, karma can just smother you completely.

SEEKER: *So Sadhguru, people come in this life to work out some karma, a part of karma, but end up with even more karma?*

SADHGURU: Yes, that's why it's like an endless circle!

SEEKER: *In many cases you have said to your disciples, "I can only show you the path. I cannot liberate you. If somebody says, 'I can dissolve your karma,' do not believe him; no Master can do it." This means that all these people who are with you - thousands of people who have given themselves to you - just because they die of natural death without pain, their karma will not dissolve, but somebody who is sick and suffering, say my mom or dad, you dissolve theirs? Why not mine, Sadhguru?*

SADHGURU: Yours also. Now I'm teaching you programs and I'm asking you to take your life into your hands so that you live gracefully and sensibly. I am not talking about death when I talk to you about these things. I'm talking about your present life so that you can live this life fruitfully. Do not wait for me to pull the plug and live a stupid life until then. I'm telling you to take care of your own life, work towards your own Realization so that you live an elevated life here. Now those who have given themselves totally to me, even for a single moment, they do not have to worry about their liberation. Liberation is assured. To live gracefully or not, that's not assured. That is something that you have to earn; there is no other way.

SEEKER: *Sadhguru, let's say my neighbor, who is a crook, is dying and you dissolve him just like that. Here I am doing this sadhana day in and day out. I would feel very cheated.*

SADHGURU: The sadhana is to live gracefully, to live beyond the present level of limitations. I told you that dissolving you comes only when you have given yourself totally. Now the reason why sadhana is done is that life is not one hundred percent in your hands. Many people may not run their full prarabdha, either because of injury, accident, disease or for any reason. Most people may not run their full course of prarabdha. Most people die in hospitals today because they are not running their full prarabdha. How many people die every day, without any ill health, just out of old age? It's a small percentage, isn't it?

Body's Plight

Sadhana is done so that you create a certain sense of awareness and you're hastening the process of the dissolution of karma so that your prarabdha gets finished faster and faster. If you dissolve some aspects of your prarabdha, generally you're working towards the mental and emotional dimensions of your prarabdha so that you can live in a blessed state for a longer period of your life. If you dissolve them, your physical prarabdha is still there, so you continue to live, but without the struggles of the mind, without the struggles of the emotions. That's a blessed state. When physical prarabdha is over, the body will drop itself. The possibility of liberation is so much higher.

SEEKER: *Sadhguru, what happens to all the layers of bodies that contain this being at death?*

SADHGURU: The physical one drops back here because it was picked up from the earth. It has to go back there. The next one is the mental body. The grosser conscious part of the mind also, you drop here. It's only the karmic part of the mind which travels with you. So next is the energy body, or the pranic body, which is the pranamayakosha. This is still physical, like electricity is. That goes. This is why we are working on your pranayama, to make the pranamayakosha so vibrant that when it leaves this physical body, it still has a good existence, a mind of its own, some amount of choice. Once pranamayakosha is functioning by choice, not by compulsion, evolution is very quick. When your energies are just functioning unconsciously, they function one way; but when your energies become a higher level of consciousness or awareness, suddenly you have a choice. Now, where you need to be born is your choice. Destiny slowly begins to come into your hands, if your energies are completely aware.

As I have been telling people, do not mistake mental alertness for awareness. That is not awareness. If you look at it that way, the birds are more aware than you are, isn't it? Physically, they are more mentally alert than you are. If a snake comes here, you will not know, but if you just put your foot down here, all the snakes within one hundred meters will know. So they're more alert, both mentally and physically. That alertness is only useful for survival. You'll survive better, but that's not the awareness we are talking about. If your energy becomes aware, your life begins to move from compulsions to choice. That's the first step you have to take, to move your energies into higher levels of vibrancy. How you get there is not the point. You may get there singing, dancing, breathing, or you may get there with your love; whichever way. If your energies are high, in a high pitch of vibrancy, your life naturally is no longer a compulsion. Everything slowly becomes by choice, to such a point that death and birth become a choice.

SEEKER: *Sadhguru, you stopped at the energy body...*

SADHGURU: The spiritual body and bliss body cannot hold form by themselves, in the sense that they have no structure of their own. Only because there is a karmic body – which has manifested itself right now in your physical body, in your mental body and your energy body – only because of karma, the other two inner bodies are there. If you take away the karmic body, even the mental body and the energy body cannot hold themselves. That's why we're calling karma the only bondage. If you remove that, your other bodies will just spill. Like if you're carrying fluid in a plastic bag, and if the bag bursts, then it's all over, finished, back into the ocean.

SEEKER: *Is that what you mean when you say 'dissolve', Sadhguru?*

SADHGURU: Yes. You just burst the karmic bag. Once the karmic substance is taken away, it just goes. It is the karmic substance which is giving you the sense of individuality. The individual experience is there only because of the karmic substance. Even now, when you're in the physical body, if you just forget your karmic structure for one moment you will

Body's Plight

not know who you are on the level of the mind itself. Suppose you got drunk, then you don't know who you are. See the sense of freedom, how joyous you become? You become joyous because just for some time you forget who you are. At least your identities have melted away a little bit. That's why you like to sit there in meditation so much, because sometimes your identity melts away. In a way, you become free of your karmic structure for a moment. It's not totally gone, but it is somewhat gone. Just that 'somewhat gone' stage itself is so beautiful because it is imprinted in other dimensions. It's still there, but on the level of the mind. If you forget your karma, it's an enormous freedom, isn't it? If all the karma is removed from all levels, then it is total freedom. Now you are playing a game, but you forgot it is a game. You think you're this and that, missing so much freedom. If you put down all aspects of the karma, it is dissolution, total freedom, the end of bondage.

SEEKER: *So Sadhguru, when I reach the level that I can decide when I die and where I will be born, is this earth the only choice that I have?*

SADHGURU: Yes, and also no, in a small way. Yes, in a huge way; I would say ninety-eight percent.

SEEKER: *Tell me about the small way, Sadhguru.*

SADHGURU: It's only two percent; don't bother about the two percent. Leave it alone. If your concern is your liberation, you just learn how to dissolve that which binds you. Don't go on a curiosity hunt.

SEEKER: *Sadhguru, after the physical death, can people who have known each other in this realm reunite in another? Is there some recognition?*

SADHGURU: Most relationships are either of the body or on the level of the conscious mind. Very, very few relationships cross that. Once the body and the major part of the mind are dropped, you don't know anything about the other being. It may so happen that all the people that practice kaka pranayama, their energies have become a certain way. It is true, in a way it's true, but I'm telling it as a joke. Suppose that by practicing this kaka pranayama, your energies have become a certain way, which is not the case for most human beings on the planet. When you leave your bodies and if you're not fully liberated, then all these kaka pranayams' bodies may come together. Not because they recognize that all of us were in Isha yoga, it's not like that; but because of a certain tendency of the energy, they may cluster together; it is possible. Not just possible, in certain situations it's very much a reality. As we were talking earlier, beings are clustering here because this kind of energy draws them – because somewhere, when they lived, they were into yogic practices, which naturally attracts them here. So in that way, yes, but not like, "This has been my wife, my child," no, because the deepest thing that you know about your relationships is just emotion.

SEEKER: *Yet in some of your other publications Sadhguru, you talk about determining specific individuals' place of rebirth and things of that nature. When you talked about the Dhyanalinga, you related that you had some individuals born in certain wombs. My assumption from that is you have the ability to take someone who has died, their energy, recognize that energy and direct that they go there for a specific purpose. Or, did they decide?*

SADHGURU: No, they did not decide. It is just that with the kind of contact that they had in that life they could have easily been dissolved, but for them, their Enlightenment, their liberation, did not mean anything. Their Guru is everything for them. They are not even interested in getting dissolved or anything. They just love him, that's all. These people do not care for liberation. They aren't even looking for Enlightenment. Such beings have no quality of their own. They have just become Him. So it's easy to plant them where you want because it is just you, in a way.

SEEKER: *Master, what is it about people doing something at death to negatively influence a person's death and rebirth?*

SADHGURU: When people curse somebody else they say, "Go to naraka. Go to hell." So when the moment of death comes, at that moment, they want to create some kind of desire or some kind of situation around him so that he goes to the worst possible hell. At this final moment of death, any kind of man, simply because of the disentangling process of the body, tends to become peaceful and empty. They want to disturb that. So they will create all kinds of situations where he will get desire, so that he'll suffer for a long period when he leaves the body. You don't know all the sciences. Many times they want to create the desire of lust or revulsion in him because these are very strong physical emotions. If his eyes are open, they get people to copulate in front of him. Seeing this, a little desire arises in him. Suppose someone hates you, now they are putting you to death. Now they don't just put you to death, they torture you to create revulsion within you. If someone dies with a strong desire, all evolution is gone. They just go back to the most basic state.

When the moment of death comes, no matter what kind of life you may have lived, it gives you an opportunity to settle certain things. A certain space is created no matter what kind of karmic baggage he carries. Now these vicious people want to take away that opportunity because they know that if they create a desire, he will carry his suffering beyond his physical body. There are people who can access this and tell them what kind of suffering that man is going through. So they create various kinds of situations around the dying man to make sure he gets the worst possible suffering or the worst possible hell. They want you to get the worst accommodation down there (laughs).

If loved ones are there, if spiritually aware people are there, they try to create a different kind of atmosphere for the last moment of death. That is there in every culture, isn't it?

These days you think a good atmosphere means your wife, husband or child hugging you, kissing you; but you should not die with your family, really. In India, when people who are a little aware want to die, they always go away from their family. They want to die in a space of non-attachment. They want to die in a way that has nothing to do with their body, their attachments, their struggles and their things. They want to die in a space which is more spiritual in nature. Dying with your family is not a great way to die. Some amount of love is good, but there are so many attachments. The last moment of your life, if you look at your son, your daughter, your wife or husband, not just love will come. So many other things will come along with it, isn't it? Yes? Their faces are a reminder of many, many things in your life, not just of love, because the relationship has not been just about love. It has been so many things and all that will come. So always, at the moment of death, it is suggested in India that you should not be with the family. I know it's unthinkable for you Westerners. You have always thought that dying means die with the family. This is not out of love, it's out of fear. Do you understand? Because there is a deep fear, you want someone you know around you.

SEEKER: *What other rites are performed for the dead in India? Would you talk about them, Sadhguru?*

SADHGURU: Every culture in the world has its own type of rituals for the dead. Generally, a lot of it is to settle certain psychological factors that will anyway come with the death of the dear and near ones; but in some way most cultures have known certain rituals which actually have a certain relevance and science behind them. Probably no other culture has such elaborate methods as the Hindus have. Nobody has looked at death with the kind of understanding and depth that this culture has. Right from the moment that death occurs, or even before it occurs, in yoga there are whole systems as to how to help a person die in the most beneficial way. The Hindu way of life, having thousands of years of background behind it, is very cunning. They want to extract something out of everything. Even if death is going to occur, even that they want to make use of in some way. So they have rituals for the dying, and rituals for the dead.

Now when the moment of death is approaching, those who are aware of this generally move the dying person out of the house and keep them in a north-south alignment with the head to the north. If death is certain and they want it to happen with ease, they take the body outside because if the body is still in the house, inside constructed atmospheres, the being does not leave the body with ease. So they want the body to be outside a constructed atmosphere and placed in a north-south alignment because it further eases the disentanglement of the being from the body.

Even after clinical death has occurred, still the prana is not completely gone from the physical body. The physical body is not totally broken. So the being still tends to hover around the body; but if you place it in a north-south alignment, the being will be pulled away from the body because of the magnetic pull. Certain changes happen in the physiology, or certain changes happen quickly within the body that has been discarded, so that the being realizes that it is futile to hang around that particular body, because it can no more access it once it is placed in the north-south direction. A certain distance arises between the being and the body. Because most people live totally identified with the body, as far as you're concerned, death has happened, but as far as the dead person is concerned, he has just slipped out of the body. All his life he lived being identified with the physical body. Suddenly he is out of it, which leaves him bewildered and he does not realize that it's over. So he tends to make attempts to get back into the body, which is unfit to sustain life. This can lead to a certain energy in that place which is neither good for him nor good for the people who are living around that space. So placing the body north-to-south is one precaution;

it distances the being from the body.

Another thing that is known in India is, when a person dies, the first thing is they tie the toes together, because if the toes are not tied together, the remaining aspect of the prana tends to leave from the Muladhara, and it also tends to become a passageway for the being to again enter the body in a partial way, if the Muladhara is open. If the anal outlet is left open, then the being will make an attempt to re-enter from this lower passage, which is not at all good for that being, nor is it good for the situation in which the living still exist. It can cause a very negative situation, so the toes are always tied together so that the Muladhara is closed. If you put your toes together, you will notice that your anal outlet is always tightly shut and that's the precaution that you are taking when you're doing the yoga kriyas. When you put your toes together, your anal outlet gets naturally closed. The same thing is done with the dead, so that this play of trying to get in and repossess the body cannot happen. This wanting to possess the body through the Muladhara, or the anal passage, need not necessarily be by the being or the person who left the body. There are other beings who will seek such a passage.

If somebody wants to do certain occult practices where freshly-dead bodies are used, it's always the Muladhara which is made use of because that's the easiest passage. Other passages will not be easily available. So if you leave their legs open, one thing is, the body tends to become distorted and the legs will naturally spread across, spread wide when death happens. So putting them together – one thing is, not to distort the body, another thing is to ensure that the anal passage is properly closed so that it cannot be misused by any other hovering spirits which are always looking for such a possibility. It can also be misused by people who are into occult practices. They can use that body for other purposes, which would bind that being in so many ways. Whenever a person dies in this culture, a certain atmosphere is created. Certain mantras are chanted, and certain care is taken to ensure that people who are into these practices, who are always looking for the freshly-dead, cannot make use of the body of your loved ones for such purposes. So the moment it is identified that the person is dead, the feet are tied together, or the toes are tied together so that such misuse will not happen.

SEEKER: *It is generally said that the body should be burned in the next four hours. Is it so, Sadhguru?*

SADHGURU: This is because until the body is destroyed, there is a tendency for the being to hang around and not proceed. What should happen will not happen, simply because the being is still not aware that it is over. So as quickly as possible, the body should be burnt. In ancient times, the rule was that within an hour and a half after death, the body should be burned.

When that was so, certain mistakes were made sometimes because, unlike today, there were no doctors to exactly say that somebody is dead, and there have been instances when they were put on the pyre, when the fire touched them, people sat up. Once, a funeral service was held in a synagogue for a woman who just passed away. At the end of the service, the pallbearers were carrying the casket out when they accidentally bumped into a wall, jarring the casket. They heard a faint moan, so they opened the casket and found that the woman was actually alive. She went on to live for ten more years and then died. A ceremony was held again at the same synagogue and at the end of the ceremony the pallbearers were again carrying the casket. As they were walking, the husband cried out aloud, "Watch out for the wall!" So later on they extended it to four hours to ensure that the dead are really dead and then they burn it as quickly as possible. Today, because of your attachments, you are keeping the body for days on end which is not a good thing, neither for the dead nor for the living.

SEEKER: *Sadhguru, in other cultures they keep it for three days before burying it. The Christians...*

SADHGURU: That's because of Jesus. They're hoping that after three days they'll get up.

SEEKER: *What about the ashes, Sadhguru? Is there any significance to what happens to the ashes?*

SADHGURU: It is forty days after the conception that the being enters the body. Similarly, up to forty days, the being still takes time to completely leave the body. When I say completely leave the body, even if you have burned the body, it will look for certain elements of the body like the ash or anything else, something that belongs to them, maybe their used clothes. If you do not know this, in the Hindu families, the moment the person dies, all the clothes that the person used, especially those clothes which touched the person's body, like underclothes, are all burned. This is because the being still looks for elements of the body, maybe the sweat, maybe the smell of the body, maybe something for which it seeks again, because still the realization has not come that it's over. All that is there. They want to just get rid of it. If you keep the ashes in one place, there is a tendency for the being to look for that. So they are put in a river where they are spread, that way they cannot be found. It's all gone. Everything possible is being done to make the being understand that it's over, and it's also for the living to understand that it is all over.

SEEKER: *Sadhguru, why do they offer food on the third day?*

SADHGURU: On the third day after death, there is a tradition or a ritual to offer milk and water to the grave. One thing is that there is a psychological need in you to still feed them, still take care of them, though they are dead, though you can't do anything. All the milk and water or food, whatever you can offer, only a body can consume. One who is bodiless has nothing to do with all this. It has a very deep

Body's Plight

psychological implication for the living. The other aspect of it is that the one who has left the body, the dead – this is not true with everybody who dies, but with certain people – when he dies in a certain unfulfilled way, or if he dies without running the course of his prarabdha karma or the allotted karma for this life, such a person could be quenched by making certain offerings. This is not always true. In some cases it's true, so they just made that a general ritual so that in case the dead in your house has such a requirement, it is taken care of. Above all, it quenches the psychological thirst in you, wanting to do something for somebody that you care for; and generally, when they were living maybe you were not on talking terms. Maybe when they asked for a glass of water you did not bring it, but now you want to do it. All this knowledge has come out of people's awareness of experiencing those dimensions which are beyond the body very clearly. They have been established in the Indian culture, but over a period of time, they get distorted and people start doing very silly things, not realizing exactly why certain things were said.

SEEKER: *Sadhguru, are there words that you can convey that will help me understand what the 'nothingness experience' is like?*

SADHGURU: There is no experience. When you do not exist, where is the experience? All experiencing stops. Only because you are experiencing you exist, isn't it? When you are asleep you don't exist because you are not experiencing. Your existence itself is just a certain level of experiencing. Suppose we compare you to insects, birds or other animals; your levels of experiencing are different from what they experience. So your experiencing is a huge deception. We want to take away the deception.

It happened like this: there is this old priest who got sick of all the people in his parish who kept confessing to infidelity. One Sunday, on the pulpit he said, "If I hear one more person confess to infidelity, I'll quit!" Everyone liked him very much, so they came up with a code word. Someone who had committed an infidelity would instead say they had fallen. This seemed to satisfy the old priest and things went well, until the priest passed away at a ripe old age. A few days after the new priest arrived, he visited the mayor of the town and seemed very concerned, "Mayor, you have to do something about the sidewalks in town; when people come into the confessional, they keep telling me they have fallen." The mayor started to laugh, realizing that no one had told the new priest about the code word, but before he could explain, the priest shook an accusing finger at him and shouted, "I don't know what you are laughing about because your wife has fallen three times this week!"

See, if we take away the deception, there is nothing to experience and nobody to experience it. It's over. You just blew a bubble and you believe it is real. If you just prick the bubble, what are you going to get? Will something else fall out of it? Nothing else will fall out of it. It will just disappear, that's all.

SEEKER: *So where is the energy, Sadhguru? The energy still stays, correct?*

SADHGURU: But that is not you. There is no such specific thing as 'you' as energy. It's just a vast energy. Let us understand this right now in a more limited way. Right now, your body is sitting here. It can experience many things, the body itself, isn't it? It can experience light, it can experience sound, it can experience touch, smell and taste. Now if you die, you leave this body. It falls here and becomes a part of this earth. So where is your body now?

SEEKER: *In the earth.*

SADHGURU: Nothing like that. It has become earth. It was earth to start with. It was just a piece of earth that stood up and pranced around a little bit and again fell back. The same thing happens with your energy also, on a different level. What you call as 'my being' is also a certain amount of energy. Just like your body came out of the earth and played a game and fell back into the earth, similarly energy came out of the unboundedness and played a little game and fell back. Spirituality means you realize that you are just a little bit of energy caught in your karmic structures. Just remove the karma and the energy falls back to what it was. It has always been that. Even today, even now, that's what it is. You imagine it is something else. You think it's you. There is no such thing. It's just the same energy playing a game. So you put it back where it belongs. You return the loan. You settle your debts and there's nothing left. You do not like it. You still want to go to heaven and be there and look down upon us, because they told you God would be waiting there with a long white beard. He will welcome you and treat you well. That's a fairy tale! It's like this: once, Jesus was strolling through heaven when he saw an old man with a long white beard sitting on a cloud and staring into the distance. "Old man," said Jesus, "This is heaven! Why are you so sad?" The old man did not bother to turn as he said, "I have been looking for my son and have not been able to find him." Jesus said, "Tell me about it." "Well," the old man said, still gazing at the sunlit horizon, "On earth, I was a carpenter, and one day my son went away. I never heard from him again. I was hoping I would find him here in heaven." His heart pounding suddenly in his chest, Jesus bent over the old man and said, ever so softly, "Father!" The old man turned and cried, "Pinocchio!"

SEEKER: *But Sadhguru, they talk about heaven in religion. Would that be liberation, while incarnation is hell?*

SADHGURU: When you talk about heaven, there must also be a hell, isn't it? Or if there is a hell, there must be a heaven. So heaven and hell are part of the duality and duality can only exist as long as you're identified with the physical. Once the physical is completely dissolved, once the deeper modifications of your mind are completely dissolved, there is no question of duality. Once there is no duality, there is no possibility of heaven or hell.

SEEKER: *Sadhguru, when we die and are not liberated, if we don't go to a heaven or a hell, what happens? Is it either a heaven-ish or hell-ish state before rebirth?*

SADHGURU: I don't know how it is exactly described in your Lebanese culture. I think it has just been mentioned as different kinds of pleasures or sufferings. In India, there's a whole lot of description about different types of hells, different types of heavens one can go through. See, going to heaven or hell is not a destination, it's just a certain state. If you die and are in a certain state of pleasantness, we say that you're in a heaven-ish state. If you're in a state of unpleasantness, we say you are in a certain type of hell. Any experience is either pleasant or unpleasant when you are in duality. Isn't it? So when you are still experiencing, it's either pleasant or unpleasant, cool or hot, light or dark. It's always like this.

You are bound to be somewhere, either a mild or a deep hell. Or it can be a mild heaven or a high heaven. So the question is just the intensity. Unless one dies with a certain sense of awareness, where they have maintained a certain sense of conscious choice even as a disembodied being, only then they have a certain amount of choice; but still they are in pleasantness or unpleasantness. Others go just by their tendencies. See it is all a comparative experience. I have a joke for you.

General Eisenhower, being the man who brought World War II to a decisive end, went to heaven. One day he said, "I want to visit hell." God asked, "Why?" He said, "I want to see what kind of suffering Adolf Hitler is in." So they gave him a pass and he went to hell. He asked the guards there, the devils, which way to Adolf Hitler's torture chamber. They guided him and he went to the chamber. There Eisenhower saw that Adolf Hitler was standing in a septic tank up to his neck in shit with a big grin on his face. Eisenhower first noticed only the shit and he was happy and said, "You deserve it, man." Then he noticed that Adolf Hitler was grinning. "You shameless creature, standing there in such filth; what are you grinning about?" he asked. Adolf Hitler laughed and said, "I'm standing on Mussolini's shoulders!" (Laughs). So, pleasantness and suffering is comparative, you know?

Afterword

When we embarked on the mission of compiling these monumental pages of intense interactions with Sadhguru, it was not without an element of mischief. Over the years, we had seen many people approach Sadhguru with questions. Questions of any and every kind: some casual and curious, some intense, profound, and burning: some cynical and skeptic, some mischievous and malicious. Yet, each received fittingly... What inspired us most was the oft-repeated scene where multitudes came with their lives and inner energies knotted up and left with their faces and lives lit-up by just this one sathsang. Then there were those who were stunned and stupefied, and kept coming back again and again, until a point arrived where they had no need to ask to know. All in all, it was always an intense process that witnessed the flowering of many, even those unwary questioners.

Sadhguru has often said he never answers the question, but always the questioner. His answers are never meant to edify the asker, but to unblock his inner energies so as to dissolve the question. With these pages we hoped to let loose a whirlwind upon the world that would suck, twist and turn people in large numbers in a tempestuous process of the Self.

To our surprise, at a Book Reading Sathsang at the Yoga Center, shortly after the release of the first edition of this book, Sadhguru, who had concluded the earlier book *Encounter the Enlightened* by saying "The gloriousness of the written word is but the excreta of the deluded mind...", revealed that the mystical aspects of the current book were not just in the contents alone but in the form as well, making it a potent and

Afterword

formidable concoction. The written word herein was hence carefully crafted to function as a *yantra*, offering the reader keys to deeper dimensions of life.

In Sadhguru's own words:

When you labor through 500 pages of word, we want to provide you certain keys – keys to the Existence, opening a certain dimension of life which is not in normal access to people. If you are open to it, it will do things. But if we talk about it, then people try to use it in certain ways and it won't work.

The only book where every part of it is a key is the Yoga Sutras. *Every part of it – that's dangerous. That's very dangerous. That's why Patanjali took enormous care in using the language in a particular way. His mastery of language is not just scholarly; his mastery of the language is something that is not normally considered human. Because of that kind of mastery over language, he dared to write the sutras in such a way that every part of it is like a yantra.*

Logically, they don't mean much, but experientially if you imbibe it, if you receive it, then it's an explosive possibility. There is a yantra involved in it. If you allow it, it is another big dimension opening up within you.

You don't have to read it; you don't have to know the language. You can do Braille on Yoga Sutras'. Even if you don't know Sanskrit language, you just touch it with your fingers; it will still do things to you. Some parts of Mystic's Musings *– I won't tell you which ones – are made like that, just to intrigue.*

Those parts, which need not necessarilly emotionally and intellectually mean something to you, but when you read them, set forth a certain experience in you.

Probably a spoken book likes this, a book that was spoken and not written – like Mystic's Musings *– that too in English language, has never happened before. The language has never been used in this context. I don't think so. I have not seen any.*

Hence, it is our sincere hope that these musings from an unfathomable mystic transport you, in many ways, into the overwhelming sacred space of a Guru.

Isha Foundation

Isha Foundation is a non-religious, not-for-profit, public service organization that addresses all aspects of human well-being. From its powerful yoga programs for inner transformation to its inspiring social and environmental projects, Isha activities are designed to create an inclusive culture as a basis for global peace and development.

This integral approach has gained worldwide recognition, reflected in Isha Foundation's Special Consultative Status with the Economic and Social Council (ECOSOC) of the United Nations. Hundreds of thousands of volunteers support the Foundation's work in over 200 centers across the globe.

Sadhguru

A profound mystic and visionary humanitarian, Sadhguru is a spiritual Master with a difference. An arresting blend of profundity and pragmatism, his life and work serve as a reminder that inner sciences are not an esoteric discipline from an outdated past, but vitally relevant to our times.

With speaking engagements that take him around the world, Sadhguru is widely sought after by prestigious global forums such as the United Nations Millennium Peace Summit, the Australian Leadership Retreat and the World Economic Forum.

Isha Yoga Programs

Isha Yoga offers a unique possibility for individuals to empower themselves and reach their full potential. Designed by Sadhguru to suit individuals from every social and cultural background, Isha Yoga programs extend a rare opportunity for self-discovery and inner transformation under the guidance of an enlightened Master.

Isha Yoga Center

Isha Yoga Center, founded under the aegis of Isha Foundation, is located at the Velliangiri Foothills amidst a forest reserve with abundant wildlife. Created as a powerful center for inner growth, this popular destination attracts people from all parts of the world.

Dhyanalinga Yogic Temple

The Dhyanalinga is a powerful and unique energy form, the essence of yogic sciences. The Dhyanalinga Yogic Temple is a meditative space that does not ascribe to any particular faith or belief system nor require any ritual, prayer or worship. The vibrational energies of the Dhyanalinga allow even those unaware of meditation to experience a deep state of meditativeness, revealing the essential nature of life.

Isha Rejuvenation

Isha Rejuvenation offers unique, carefully scientifically structured programs designed by Sadhguru to bring vibrancy and optimal balance to one's life energies, thus facilitating healthy living as well as the prevention and uprooting of chronic ailments.

Action for Rural Rejuvenation

Action for Rural Rejuvenation (ARR) is a holistic social outreach program whose primary objective is to improve the overall health and quality of life of the rural poor.

Dedicated teams of qualified and trained personnel operate ARR's Mobile Health Clinics, which currently provide free basic health care to more than 4,000 villages in South India.

Project GreenHands

Project GreenHands (PGH) is an ecological initiative of Isha Foundation to prevent and reverse environmental degradation and enable sustainable living. The project aims to create 10% additional green cover in Tamil Nadu. Drawing on the participation of a wide cross-section of people, 114 million trees will be planted by the year 2010.

Isha Vidhya – An Isha Education Initiative

Isha Vidhya provides affordable, high quality primary school education to villages across South India's Tamil Nadu state. Over the coming years, Isha Vidhya will set up 206 schools designed specifically to create confident, English-speaking, computer literate children. Students will graduate prepared to pursue higher education.

Isha Home School

Isha Home School, set in the tranquil surroundings of the Velliangiri Foothills, offers a stimulating environment for the inner blossoming of each child. Isha Home School helps each student reach his or her true potential and enhances his or her natural and latent talents while maintaining high standards of academic excellence.

Isha Business

Isha Business is a venture spearheaded and promoted by Isha Foundation to bring a touch of Isha into people's lives through numerous products and services, such as architectural and interior design, construction, furniture, crafts, clothing and much more. The proceeds benefit the poorest of the poor through Action for Rural Rejuvenation.

Contact Us:

INDIA
Isha Yoga Center
Velliangiri Foothills
Semmedu (P.O.)
Coimbatore-641 114, India
Tel. +91-422-2515345
info@ishafoundation.org

USA
Isha Foundation Inc./Isha Institute of Inner Sciences
951, Isha Lane
McMinnville, TN-37110, USA
Tel: +1-866-424-ISHA (4742)
usa@ishafoundation.org

UNITED KINGDOM
Isha Institute of Inner Sciences
PO Box 559,
Isleworth, TW7 5WR, UK
Tel: +44-7956998729
uk@ishafoundation.org

For more information and your local center please visit our website:
www.ishafoundation.org

Dhyanalinga – The Silent Revolution

This richly illustrated book presents a deeper definition of yoga and its metaphysical essence. It culminates in the presentation of the Dhyanalinga.

Encounter the Enlightened – Conversations with the Master

This book captures interactive moments with the Master. It is an invitation to the reader to go beyond words and experience the wisdom of the boundless.

Eternal Echoes – The Sacred sounds through the Mystic

A compelling and provocative collection of poetry by Sadhguru. This book of high artistic merit moves us into the timeless, eternal reality of an enlightened being.

Flowers on the Path

A compilation of articles created by Sadhguru for the Speaking Tree column of the Times of India. These articles bring infusions of beauty, humor, clarity and insight into our lives.

Midnights with the Mystic – A Little Guide to Freedom and Bliss

Presented in a series of conversations between seeker, the co-author Cheryl Simone, and enlightened Master, Sadhguru, this captivating book challenges us to embrace the possibility of a higher reality, a peak of consciousness. Available at bookstores and online booksellers such as amazon.com and Barnes & Noble.

Find further inspiration in Sadhguru's profound insights on a variety of life-relevant topics, combined in pairs of two to the following revealing books:

- Enlightenment: What It Is & Leave Death Alone
- Dissolving Your Personality & Good and Bad Divides the World
- Ancient Technology for the Modern Mind & Culture of Peace
- Dimension Beyond the Physical & Circus of the Intellect
- Living Life to the Fullest & Unleashing the Mind
- Is Spirituality a Science & Isha: Sacred Space for Self Transformation

Glossary

abhisheka	Sprinkling or pouring of water, milk etc. Often used in religious, yogic or ceremonial contexts, particularly in tantric rituals. A ritual of empowerment also used to denote initiation in general.
adi	The first or fetal; primordial or embryonic, the beginning.
agnihotri yagna	Vedic ritual using the elemet of fire.
ajna chakra	Lit. command wheel. The sixth of seven major energy centers of the human body. Physically, located between the eyebrows, it is also known as the 'third eye'. Derives its name from the fact that it is an able receiver of the Guru. Hence, it is also called 'Guru-chakra'.
akka	Lit. sister – a respectful way of addressing a woman, in the Tamil language. Here, it refers to a saint popularly known as Akka Mahadevi – a 12th century queen in Karnataka, who renounced everything to go in search of Shiva, her celestial husband. Akka is known for her spiritual couplets, which are revered even today as classic poetry.
amavasya	The new moon – the darkest night of the month. The planetary positions of the earth and moon have long been made use of by spiritual seekers in India to enhance their spiritual practices.
amma	Mother – a reverential way of addressing a woman.

amman temple	Refers to temples which have feminine deities, a place of worship of Kali or Shakthi. Often used in occult practices.
Anahatha chakra	The fourth chakra, known as the 'lotus of the heart' or the 'heart chakra', it has been recognized as a special locus of the sacred within the human body. Celebrated as the seat of the Divine, the center is related to emotion and love.
ananda	Bliss, unconditional joy.
Ananda Tirtha	Gautama's elder cousin, who eventually became a disciple
anandamaya kosha	The innermost body or the bliss body.
anatma	Lit. the soul-less one.
anga	A limb, or aspect of yoga.
anga mardhana	Mardhana' means to kill – 'anga mardhana' means killing of the limbs of the body – the means to experience bodiless-ness.
annamaya kosha	Food-formed sheath or the gross body (sthula sharira), made up of the five gross elements or bhoothas – earth, wind, water, fire, ether – which are resolved again into their initial states after death.
aradhana	Lit. adoration.
Ardhanarishwara	Another manifestation of Shiva, beyond duality, in the form of half man and half woman.
Arjuna	Hero of the great epic Mahabharatha, to whom Krishna imparted the Divine message of the Bhagavad Gita.
asana	Lit. seat. Generally referring to yogic postures, or postures that lead one's energies to liberation. One of the eight limbs of yoga.

Glossary

ashram	Sacred dwelling of spiritual seekers under the guidance of a Guru, or spiritual Master.
Ashtanga Yoga	The eight limbs, or disciplines, of yoga: yama, niyama, asana, pranayama, pratyahara, dharana, dhyana, and samadhi, as described by sage Patanjali.
Ashtavakra	One with eight deformities. An ancient spiritual master par excellence.
Assam	Indian state in the northeast region of the country.
Atharva Veda	Last of the four Vedas, that expounds the technology of using physical energy to one's advantage.
Atma	Individual spirit, the supreme soul or Bhrahman.
baba	Lit. father. Common term used to address any elder, especially in the religious communities.
Badrinath	A holy place in the Himalayas – the holiest of shrines for the Vaishnavaites (followers of Lord Vishnu). This temple was established by Adi Shankara, one of the foremost scholars of South India, around the ninth century A.D.
Bala Krishna	Lord Krishna, as a child.
bala yogi	Child yogi. Refers to someone who attains Enlightenment at an early age and usually does not retain the body for long thereafter.
Bhaghirathi	River Ganga at its origin, where it melts its way out of the 'ice cave' called Gomukh.
Bhairava	A fierce form of Shiva.
bhaktha	A devotee.
bhakthi	Devotion. Refers to the spiritual path of Self-Realization through love and devotion. Intense desire and will for union with one's chosen deity.

Bhava Spandana program	"Bhava" means sensation or feeling. "Spandana" "Spandana" means to resonate, or emphatic vibration. This four day high intensity residential program is offered as a part of Isha Yoga programs, to experience levels of consciousness that take one to an experience beyond the limitations of body and mind.
Bhojpur	A town in Madhya Pradesh, Central India.
bhootha	Ghoul or a ghost. Also refers to the five primary elements of nature – earth, wind, fire, water, and ether.
Bhoothnath	Master of the five elements – another form of Shiva.
Bhramha	The Creator in the classic trinity of Hinduism, the other two gods being Vishnu and Shiva.
bhramhachari	'Bhraman' means divine and 'charya' means path. One who is on the path of the Divine. Usually refers to one who has formally been initiated into monkhood through a certain energy process.
bhramhacharini	A female bhramhachari.
bhramhacharya	The path of the divine. A life of celibacy and studentship on the path of spirituality moving towards the highest modifications of the senses. The first of four stages of life as per the Varnashrama Dharma.
Bhramhin	Member of the priestly Hindu caste, which is the highest in the Indian caste system.
bodhi tree	The sacred tree under which Buddha attained enlightenment.
Buddha	One who is above buddhi (intellect). Generally used to refer to Gautama the Buddha.
buddhi	Faculty of discrimination, analysis, logical and rational thought; the intellect.
budubuduku	A traditional gypsy soothsayer in Karnataka.

Glossary

chakra	Lit. wheel. Here, it refers to the seven junctions of nadis in the pranic body. Though seven major chakras are associated with the human body, there are a total of 114 chakras, of which two are outside the body. Each chakra has a distinct color, form, sound and quality associated with it.
Chakreshwara	One who has attained mastery over all the chakras.
Chamundi Hills	A famous pilgrimage center on the outskirts of Mysore, India, which was patronized by the Maharajas of Mysore. Also the place where Sadhguru had a deep experience of the Self at the age of twenty-five.
Coimbatore	A major industrial city in Tamil Nadu, a South Indian state.
Cudappah	A small town in the state of Andhra Pradesh, India.
deva	A generic term used to describe a class of celestial beings. Also referred to as God in Hindu mythology.
devi	Goddess, the feminine aspect of the Divine.
dhamma	Spiritual path set forth by Gautama, the Buddha.
dharana	Maintaining mental focus. One of the eight limbs of yoga.
dharma vada	Theological debate.
Dronacharya	The royal tutor of the Pandavas and Kauravas, princes of the Indian epic Mahabharatha.
dhyana	Meditative state. One of the eight limbs of yoga.
Dhyanalinga	A powerful energy form consecrated by Sadhguru exclusively for the purpose of meditation, at Isha Yoga Center.

dosha	Defect or blemish. Specifically refers to defects in the physical, mental or energy bodies.
Dostoevsky	A well known Russian author and philosopher who lived in the nineteenth century.
Dussehra	A traditional Indian festival of color, dance and music that lasts nine days, culminating in the celebration of the victory of good over evil. The celebration of this festival in Mysore attracts thousands of people from all over the country.
Essenes	Ancient Jewish sect of ascetics and mystics which existed from the second century B.C. to the second century A.D. A secret school of mysticism which is known to have aided Jesus during his life.
Forest Flower	Quarterly newsletter published by Isha Foundation.
gandharva	A class of celestial beings who are usually gifted with extraordinary talents such as music and dance.
Gandhi	Refers to Mahatma (great soul) Gandhi, an Indian nationalist leader, considered the father of the freedom movement. His peaceful, non-violent methods of protest were revolutionary, and brought an element of spirituality into public life.
Ganga	A major Indian River. Originating in the Himalayan glaciers, it is held extremely sacred. The legend says that it is a heavenly downpour routed through the locks of Shiva. Water from this river is carried to all parts of the country for religious rituals, including those of birth and death. It is also customary to cremate the dead on the banks of the river Ganga or immerse the bodies in the river itself.
Gangotri	Place of origin of the river Ganga in the

Glossary

	Himalayas.
Gita	Lit. song. Refers to the Bhagavad Gita, one of the most sacred teachings of the Hindus. This central episode of the epic Mahabharatha is a dialogue between Lord Krishna and his chief disciple Arjuna, on the battlefields of the Kurukshetra. Krishna imparts to the warrior-prince Arjuna his knowledge on yoga, asceticism, dharma and the manifold spiritual path.
gnana	Knowledge, perception, discrimination. One of the four kinds of yogas.
Goa	An Indian state on the western coast known for its pristine beaches.
Gomukh	Lit. cow-face. A place in the upper Himalayas, the location where the glacier forms the river Ganga. The glaciatic form has melted in such a way that it resembles the face of a cow.
Goraknath	A great spiritual master who was one of the disciples of Matsyendranath. He is believed to have lived sometime between 900 and 1225 A.D.
gowripeeta	The base or the feminine portion of a linga.
grihastha	A householder, the second of the four stages of life as per the Varnashrama classification of the stages of life.
guna	Lit. quality or attribute. Refers to the three qualities of mind: tamas (inertia), rajas (activity) and sattwa (purity).
guru	Lit. dispeller of darkness. A spiritual Master; a Realized being who guides spiritual seekers towards liberation.
Guru pooja	Invoking the Grace of the Guru.
Hatha Yoga	Physical form of yoga involving different bodily postures and practices. Used as both a

	purificatory and preparatory step for meditation and higher dimensions of spiritual experience.
Himachal Pradesh	A North Indian State in the Himalayan region.
Himalayas	Lit. the abode of ice and snow. Range of mountains in the north of India which plays an important part in Indian history, mythology, art and spirituality.
Ida	One of the major pranic channels in the body. Located on the left side of the body, is feminine (intuitive) in nature.
Indra	The chief or the king of the Gods in Indian mythology.
Isha	Formless Divine energy. Also the name chosen by Sadhguru for the Foundation created to offer the ultimate spiritual possibility to all mankind.
Isha Yoga program	Refers to the foundation level program offered all over the world by Isha Yoga Center, wherein Yoga is experienced as a living science. Sadhguru's provocative questions compel one to look deeper within oneself and bring the necessary awareness to find experiential answers about life itself.
Ishwara	The supreme Lord. Another name of Shiva.
jala	Water, one of the five elements of nature.
Janaka	An ancient Indian King and an enlightened disciple of Sage Ashtavakra, Janaka was known for his extraordinary wisdom.
Jyotir Linga	Lingas of special importance to the Shaivaites. There are twelve Jyotir Lingas in India which are a part of the mandatory pilgrimage of any Shiva devotee.
Kaivalya	Aloneness, oneness or absolute. A state of

ultimate oneness. Patanjali used the name Kaivalya to describe the goal and fulfillment of Yoga, the state of complete detachment from transmigration. Virtually synonymous with mukthi, Kaivalya is the highest condition, resulting in liberation.

Kaivalya padha The fourth and final part of Patanjali's Yoga Sutra, dealing with absolution.

kaka pranayama Kriya involving a sound like a bird call, which makes one less available to gravity. Taught in Isha Yoga programs.

Kali A powerful goddess; a form of Shakthi in a fierce aspect. She signifies annihilation through which the seed of life emerges. She inspires terror and love at the same time.

Kanti Sarovar A serene lake in the Himalayas, considered to be the abode of Shiva.

kapala-bhati Lit. skull-brightening. A certain powerful yoga kriya which is taught in Isha Yoga basic programs.

karma Refers to the volition with which one performs action. Karma is the mechanism by which relative existence maintains itself. Referring to past action, the cause of all bondage. That which binds one to the body and creates tendencies that rule one's life. Law of cause and effect.

karma kanda The region of karma.

karma yoga The path of selfless service.

Karthikeya Another name for the second, six-faced son of Shiva. He has six faces.

kaya Body or sheath.

kechari mudra Mudra consisting of turning the tongue backwards so that the 'nectar' flowing down from the Sahasrar, after the rise of Kundalini,

Kedar	is arrested. Short for Kedarnath – a pilgrimage place in the Himalayas.
khanda	Region.
Kaanphat	Lit. torn ear. A spiritual sect in Northern India, who are so called because of their tradition of piercing their ears.
kosha	Lit. sheath, vessel, layer.
Krishna	Divine incarnation of Lord Vishnu, historically over 3500 years ago, Krishna is one of the most popular gods of the Hindu pantheon. A Yadava prince and the central character of the epic Mahabharatha, His discourse to his chief disciple Arjuna in the form of the Bhagavad Gita is the most sacred of Hindu scriptures.
Krishnamurti, Jiddu	Twentieth century spiritual Master of great repute.
kriya	Lit. act, rite. Refers to a certain class of yogic practices. Inward action as opposed to karma, or external action.
krodha	Anger, aversion.
Kukkarahalli	A beautiful lake at the Mysore university that has been an inspiration for many poets and writers.
Kumara Parvat	A mountain peak in the Western Ghats – a powerful spiritual destination. Samadhi of Subramanya the six faced yogi, son of Shiva.
kumbha	An earthen pot. Storage or fullness.
Kumbha Mela	A major spiritual and religious festival on the banks of river Ganga. During this time millions of spiritual aspirants converge on the banks of the river Ganga and take a ceremonial dip. A nexus of cosmic energy every twelve years, celebrated at Allahabad and other places in

	India by a gathering of sages and mystics.
kumbhaka	Breath retention during yogic practice, especially in the practice of pranayama.
kumkum	Vermilion or red powder made of turmeric and lime worn by the Hindus at the point of the third eye on the forehead.
Kundalini	Lit. serpent power. Cosmic energy which is depicted as a snake coiled at the base of the spine (Muladhara chakra) and that eventually, through the practice of yoga, rises up the Sushumna nadi. As it rises, the Kundalini awakens each successive chakra, until it reaches the Sahasrar. The manifested Kundalini becomes Kula, the all-transcending light of consciousness.
laddu	A popular Indian sweet, in the form of lemon-sized balls.
lakh	One hundred thousand in the Indian number system.
Linga	Lit. the first form; the primordial form. An energy form consecrated for worship, generally associated with Lord Shiva.
maha	An adjective or prefix meaning great, mighty, powerful, lofty, noble.
Mahabharatha	One of India's great national epics, which revolves around the conflict between two royal families, the Pandavas and Kauravas, in the great battle of Kurukshetra, approximately 1424 B.C. The plot illustrates simple truths and ethical principles.
Mahadeva	Great God, a common epithet for Shiva.
Mahadevi	Great goddess, a common epithet for Parvathi, the consort of Shiva.
Mahanadi	A major Indian river flowing through central India, known for its devastating floods.

Mahaparinibbana	Buddhist term for Mahasamadhi, or Nirvana, the complete dissolution of the Self, the ultimate goal of spiritual seekers.
Maharaj	Lit. great king, a respectful form of address for an Indian monarch or spiritual leader.
Maharishi	Great seer, a title of respect for an adept yogi.
Mahasamadhi	Complete dissolution of the Self also known as Nirvana, and Mahaparinibbana in other spiritual traditions. The dropping of the physical body in full awareness.
Mahashivarathri	An important festival in India, celebrated on the night before the new moon in the month of Magha, or February-March, each year. On this night spiritual seekers observe an all-night vigil filled with chanting and meditation, keeping their spines upright to support the upsurge of spiritual energy. At Isha, this night is colorfully celebrated in the presence of Sadhguru, drawing thousands of meditators from all over the world.
mahatma	Lit. great soul. Title of respect given to people held in high esteem, especially saints.
Maheshwara	The Great Lord, another name of Shiva, the destroyer in the classic triad of Hinduism, the other two gods being Bhramha and Vishnu.
Mahishasura Mardhana	The killing of a certain asura or demon in Indian mythology.
mala	Garland or necklace.
mandala	Refers to a region, an area within the body or the cosmos. Also represents consecrated space and is thought to be the body of one's chosen deity. The mandala is used to worship that deity and, through complex visualization practices, to

	become one with it. Also refers to the physiognomic cycle, a time period of forty days, the natural period of many physiological processes in the body.
Manipuraka chakra	The third chakra, located a little below the navel. It provides the whole body with the vital energy needed for survival.
mantra	A sound, syllable, word or phrase endowed with special power. Mantras are most effective on the path of liberation when given by the preceptor through initiation.
mantric	Of mantra; one who is an adept in the use of mantras.
Matsyendranath	Lit. Lord of the Fish. A yogi of celestial proportions who lived around the tenth century A.D. The Guru of Goraknath, he is believed to have been an incarnation of Shiva himself.
maya	Delusion, the veil of illusion which conceals one's true nature, or conceals reality. It is used in contrast with the absolute reality.
mela	A large, colorful festival.
Mirabai	A Rajput princess of the medieval period who, intoxicated by her devotion for Lord Krishna, spent most of her life as a wandering saint, singing praises of the Lord. A poetess and mystic, her life story and bhajans are extremely popular even today.
Mizoram	An Indian state in the north-eastern region.
mukthi	Release, liberation, final absolution of the Self from the chain of death and rebirth. The highest goal of all spiritual seekers.
muladhara chakra	The first chakra, the psychoenergetic chakra located at the perineum. Source of the central channel (Sushumna-nadi) of the life force.

nadha	Sound, tone, vibration, music.
nadi	Channel through which the life force, or prana, flows in the energy body. There are 72,000 nadis interconnecting the chakras. The three main nadis are named Ida, Pingala, and Sushumna.
naga	Lit. serpent. Symbol of the Kundalini coiled at the base of the spine; one of the secondary types of life forces (prana).
Naga Babas	People belonging to a certain spiritual sect in North India, who are known to wander naked in the Himalayas with just vibhuthi smeared on the body, even during the coldest winter seasons.
naga dosha	Condition in which a diembodied snake possesses a human being.
Namaskar	Traditional salutation which acknowledges the divinity within a person.
naraka	Equivalent to the Western term Hell. Nether world.
Naren	Childhood name of Swami Vivekananda.
nari	Woman.
neem	A common deciduous evergreen tree (Azadirachta indica) which grows in India, known for its extremely bitter leaves, fruits and flowers. Used extensively for its innumerable medicinal qualities, neem is sometimes called 'the village pharmacy'. Over 100 pharmacologically active substances have been identified in this plant.
nethi	Lit. 'not this'. A way of cleansing oneself of illusions or wrong identities.
Nilgiri	Lit. blue peaks. Refers to a certain hilly district located north of Coimbatore, known for its rich wildlife.

Glossary

Nirguna	Devoid of any quality, untainted and beyond duality.
Nirmana-kaya	A created body. Adept yogis are known to have created and possessed physical bodies for themselves to fulfill certain special purposes.
Nischala	Unshakeable, unwavering.
Nishkarma	Karmically unaffected by one's actions.
Nityananda, Swami	A reclusive South Indian yogi and an extraordinary mystic who lived in the twentieth century and spent the later part of his life near Mumbai in Maharashtra. The Guru of many disciples, including Swami Muktananda.
ojas	Subtle energy.
Orissa	An Indian state on the East coast.
Palani	A South Indian town that is famous for its Murugan (son of Shiva) temple.
pancha bhootha	The five primary elements of nature – earth, wind, fire, water, and ether.
Paramahamsa	Lit. supreme swan. An honorific term applied to an adept who enjoys liberation or Enlightenment.
parikrama	Outer periphery of a temple.
Parvathi	One of the many names for the Universal Mother, and consort of Shiva.
Patanjali	Lit. one who fell (pat) into the palm (anjali). Refers to an ancient spiritual Master of extraordinary understanding, considered the father of yogic sciences. Believed to be an incarnation of Ananta, or Shesha, the thousand-headed ruler of the serpent race, Patanjali is best known for his work Yoga Sutras. The Yoga Sutras have been disclosed in a manner that cannot be understood by a superficial perusal of the text. Rather, it has

	been attributed the quality of being an encrypted code intended for the spiritual Masters who have the necessary understanding to properly impart the veiled practices.
peyi-pishachi	A phrase used to denote ghosts and spirits.
Pindari	A community of bandits.
Pingala	One of the major pranic channels of the body. Located on the right side of the body, it is masculine in nature
Pongal	A South Indian delicacy made of boiled rice, gram and pepper corns. Also, a very popular Tamil festival. It marks the change in the tilt in the Earth's axis of rotation.
Pooja	Worship, a Vedic ritual for the invocation of Divine energy and Grace.
Prakrithi	The feminine aspect of life. Refers to Nature or Creation.
prana	Fundamental life force; vital energy.
pranamayakosha	The energy sheath or body.
pranayama	A powerful yogic practice that uses certain breathing techniques to generate and direct the flow of prana in the human body.
pranic	Of prana.
prarabdha	The karma allotted for this lifetime.
prasada	Blessed food.
Prathishta	Process of consecration or energizing an object with Divine energies. These processes are mainly of two kinds – mantra prathishta, through chanting of appropriate mantras and performing of rituals and prana prathishta, through a direct process involving the consecrator's own prana shakthi – life energies.
pratibha	Lit. luster. One who has the needed qualities

Glossary

for initiation or Enlightenment.

pretha	A kind of ghost or spirit.
pungai tree	Pongamia pinnata. A tropical medicinal tree native to India, known for its shade giving and oxygen generating capabilities. The oil of the pongam seeds is traditionally used in oil lamps.
purana	Mythological texts.
purusha	The masculine aspect of life. Also refers to man.
Raigarh	A town in the Central Indian state of Madhya Pradesh.
Rajasthan	Indian State in the western region, known for its desert terrain.
Rama	The hero of the epic Ramayana, believed to be an incarnation of Lord Vishnu.
Ramakrishna Paramahamsa	A mid-nineteenth century spiritual Master who lived mostly in Calcutta. A devotee of Goddess Kali, he frequently went into ecstatic states of samadhi. One of his best-known disciples is Swami Vivekananda, who established and propagated the Ramakrishna Order, which has a world wide following today.
Ramana Maharshi	Early twentieth century spiritual Master who lived in the hills of Tiruvanamalai near Chennai, in South India. His teachings revolve around self-inquiry. He is believed to have enlightened not only humans, but also a cow and a crow.
Ramanashram	An ashram located in Tiruvanamalai, established by Ramana Maharshi.
Rameshwaram	A sacred coastal town in South India, the closest point in India to the neighboring country, Sri Lanka. Figures in the epic Ramayana, where Rama built a bridge from India to Sri Lanka to enable his army to cross

	the ocean.
rasa	Lit. juice, the essence.
rudhraksha	Sacred beads. Seeds of a tree (glaeocarpus ganitrus Roxb) found mostly in the Himalayan region. According to the legend, a tear from Lord Shiva fell to Earth and from it grew the Rudhraksha tree. Known to have many medicinal and transcendental qualities, a rudhraksha mala is one of the few possessions of an Indian spiritual seeker.
sadhaka	A spiritual seeker who has undertaken spiritual disciplines, usually under the guidance of a master.
sadhana	Spiritual practices which are used as a means to realization.
Sadhananda	Lit. the one forever in bliss. One of the names of Shiva.
sadhguru	A spiritual teacher who is Enlightened, or has Realized the Self, whose knowledge or realization comes from within rather than from any teachings learned outside.
sadhu	An accomplished spiritual seeker. Sadhus usually have no fixed abode and travel from one place to another, most often living on alms. There are countless sadhus on the roads, byways, mountains, riverbanks and caves of India who, by their very existence, have a profound effect on the consciousness of the world.
Sahasrar chakra	Lit. thousand-spoked wheel. The seventh and highest chakra of the human system corresponding to the crown of the head.
sakshi	Lit. witness, a common way of describing the Self. Witness consciousness.
samadhi	Deep state of equanimity; one of the eight

Glossary

	limbs of yoga. Greatly celebrated in the lore, experience of samadhi is immensely therapeutic and deeply transformative in nature.
Sambalpur	A small town in the state of Orissa, India.
samsara	The world, the existence, the domain of karma, protracted delusion of the mind. The cycle of birth, death, and rebirth.
samskara	Ritual, in the general sense. Denotes rites such as the birth ceremony, tonsure, marriage, cremation, etc. In yoga, it stands for the indelible imprints in the subconscious left behind by our daily experiences.
Samyama	A confluence of the states of dharana, dhyana and samadhi. Here, it refers to the eight-day meditation program conducted by Sadhguru, where one is transported into explosive states of meditativeness. This program is an opportunity to shed lifetimes of karma and experience deep states of meditativeness and samadhi.
sanchita karma	The total accumulated karma of a person.
Sangamitra	The daughter of the great king Ashoka and a disciple of Buddha.
sankalpa	Resolve.
Sanskrit	An ancient Indian language specially designed to suit expressions and transmission of the spiritual experience.
sanyas	On the path of spirituality, the fourth of the four stages of life as per the Varnashrama Dharma. The spontaneous withdrawal from the world in search of Self Realization.
sanyasi	An ascetic, a renunciate. One who has irrevocably renounced worldly possessions and relationships to seek Divine awakening, Self

	Realization.
sathsang	Lit. in the company of Truth; a congregation of seekers.
shaiva	Lit. of Shiva; worshipper of Shiva.
Shakthi	Lit. power. Divine consort of Shiva. The Creation is envisioned as a play of Shiva and Shakthi which symbolizes the duality of existence, or the Yin and Yang.
shakti moola	Energy source.
Shambho	Another name for Shiva, which denotes his loving nature.
Shankara	Lit. the benevolent; one of the many names of Shiva. Also refers to Adi Shankaracharya, the celebrated ninth century teacher of Advaita Vedanta and the founder of neo-monastic orders. In his life of thirty-two years, he traveled several times throughout India and was responsible for the renaissance of the Hindu tradition.
Shankaran Pillai	Refers to the hero in many of Sadhguru's jokes and anecdotes. He is usually a frail man whose idiocies are typical of the common man.
Shanmugha	Lit. six faced; one of the sons of Shiva.
Sharada Devi	Wife of Shri Ramakrishna Paramahamsa.
shavasana	Lit. corpse posture. One of the over six hundred asanas in the classical yogic tradition. Practiced intermittently between other asanas, it is known for its rejuvenating effect on the system.
shishya	Lit. pupil or disciple. One who has submitted himself to a teacher or a Guru.
Shiva	Lit. that which is not. The Great Lord; the Destroyer in the trinity.
Shiva linga	Symbol of Shiva traditionally used in worship.

Glossary

Shivayogi	A name borne by Sadhguru in one of his previous lifetimes.
Shoonya	Lit. emptiness. An effortless process of conscious non-doing, Shoonya meditation is an extremely powerful and unique form of meditation taught by Sadhguru in a live form in the Isha Yoga programs.
Shrimath	Short for Shrimath, a respectful title for a man.
shuddhi	Lit. purification A basic component of spiritual life.
shudra	Member of the fourth and lowest Hindu caste, that of menial laborers.
siddha	One who has attained perfection or mastery over a certain mystical aspect of life.
siddhi	Power; paranormal or supernormal accomplishment.
smaran	Remembrance, usually, of the Divine. One of the aspects of bhakthi yoga.
spandana	To resonate; empathic vibration.
Subramanya	Son of Shiva. Also refers to Kukke Subramanya, a town at the Foothills of Kumara Parvat, in the coastal region of Karnataka state.
Suka	A well known sage of the yogic lore.
sukha pranayama	A yogic practice of balancing the prana in the Ida and the Pingala nadis.
Surya	The sun.
Sushumna	The central channel in the energy body which conducts the Kundalini, or spiritual force.
Swadisthana chakra	Lit. abode of the self, the second of the seven chakras of the human body. Situated just above the genitalia.
swami	He who knows or is master of himself. A respectful title for a Hindu monk, usually a

	sanyasi, an initiate dedicated wholly to spiritual life.
tantra	The science of using mantra, the sound, and yantra, the form. Refers to an esoteric Indian spiritual tradition.
tantric	Of Tantra; a practitioner of Tantra.
Tapovan	A place above Gomukh, on the banks of Gangotri, the glaciatic origin of the river Ganga.
tathwa	Element, as in the five elements; principle or philosophy.
Thai Poosam	An important festival held on the day of pushya nakshatra of the Tamil month of Thai (near the full moon day of January-February). Celebrated with great intensity and fervor, it is a day on which many South Indian sages have chosen to leave their body.
thali	A large dinner plate.
Thiruvanaikaval	A town near Trichy in South India.
turya	Beyond the three states of waking, dreaming, and sleeping. A transcendental state of awareness and bliss.
Ujjain	The capital of the ancient kingdom of Magadh and one of the seven sacred Hindu cities. Also a great center of learning and scholarly pursuits. Located in present day Madhya Pradesh.
Upanishads	Sacred texts in the Hindu culture.
vada	A popular south Indian savory made of ground lentils and deep fried.
vaidhya	Traditional doctor; also refers to traditional system of medicine.
vajrasana	Lit. diamond posture. One of the dynamic yogic postures, through which the practitioner

	imbibes the hardness and the brilliance of a diamond.
Vajreshwari	A place in the state of Maharashtra.
Vanashree	Lit. the deity of the Forest. Name of the feminine deity in the form of a tree at the Dhyanalinga temple.
vasana	Tendencies or desire; subliminal trait left behind in the mind by action and desire.
Veda	Refers to the oldest portion of the Hindu scriptures.
Vedanta	Lit. end of perceivable knowledge; the philosophy or teachings of the Vedas.
vibhuthi	Sacred, consecrated ash. Applied to different parts of the body, makes one more sensitive to subtle life forces. Application to the upper chakras activates the chakras and makes them more receptive. Some sects of Shaivites also smear vibhuthi all over the body to sensitize the system and ward off cold.
Vishuddhi	One of the seven chakras, is the center of power and vision. Located at the pit of the throat.
vishwa rupa darshana	An experience of the vastness of the existence. Also, a rare Cosmic Vision of the Master granted by the Master to the deserving disciple.
Vivekananda	The best known of the disciples of Ramakrishna Paramahamsa, Vivekananda is often considered as a role model for Indian youth.
Vyasa	An ancient sage with legendary powers of vision, one who documented the epic Mahabharatha.
yagna	Sacrifice, one of the main pillars of the Vedic ritual system.

yaksha	Celestial disembodied beings who are believed to inhabit secluded places.
Yama	The Lord of Death, the ruler of the nether world. Riding a buffalo, his vehicle, a visit from Yama means the time of death for a person has come. Also refers to the first limb of Yoga, used along with the second limb, niyama, to codify the 'do's and don'ts' of Yoga.
yatra	Travel, journey, pilgrimage.
yogini	A female practitioner of Yoga.
yoni	Lit. the source, origin. Refers to the female genitalia.

Index

A

acceptance, 196
action, 131-138
  vs. desire, 153-154
  and disease, 209
  and neuroses, 209
  internal and external, 273
Adam and Eve, 172-174
Adi Shankara, 95
Akka Mahadevi, 84,85, 88
aloneness, 115
anadamaya kosha, 257
anatma, 268
anger, 125, 148, 154-158
animals, compassion for, 170-171
anxiety, 4
Arjuna, 182
  tales of, 35-37
ascetic path, 95-98, 150
ashram, 105, 226
Ashtavakra, 70-72
Auschwitz, 92
awareness, 77, 137-139, 148, 169, 198
  and disease, 241
  cultivating, 151-152, 180
  vs. mental alertness, 198, 281-282

B

Badrinath, 15, 178
beyond, the, 256
bhakthi, 88-89, 123
  Raigarh birth of, 75

Bhava Spandana, 48, 88
bhramacharis, Isha, 128
  and activity, 209-210
bhramacharya, 162
bliss body. see anadamayakosha
blocks, inner. see bondage, types
  of bodies (koshas), 198, 240, 255-267
  physical and subtle, 271
  subtle, at time of death, 281
body, 206-295
  and entry of prana, 260
  closed condition of, 177-179
  everything as, 256
  identification with, 223, 248
  karmic choice of, 259
  mortality of, 143-145
  time of leaving as possibility, 151
bondage, types of, 176-180
breath, : see also pranayama 59
Buddha vs. Buddha-hood, 87
Buddha, Gautama, 30, 108, 121, 184, 255
  teachings of, 42, 68, 87, 91-92, 256, 268

C

cause and effect, 240
  and choice of parents, 158
  and karma, 182-183
  compulsion to bear, 222-227
  death of, 139, 143-145
  individuality of, 260-262

choice, conscious vs.unconscious, 148-151
compassion, 81-84
compulsion, 148, 222-223
conception, entry of being after, 259-261, 289-290
cow, 167
crow, 167

D

Darwin, Charles, 175-176
Death Meditation, 255
death, 282-291
   accidental, 259
   and desire, 285
   and spirituality, 251-253
   curses at time of, 285
   fear of, 247-254
   preparation for, 275-277
   relationships continuing after, 283-284
deception, self, 89-90
desire, 181
   directing, 125-127
   vs. action, 153-156
destiny, 159-162
Devil, 12, 13, 173
devotion, 44-45
Dhronacharya, 35-36
Dhyanalinga consecration, 244
   and health of Sadhguru, 255-256
Dhyanalinga, 230
disease, 206-222, 255, 276-278
   and activation of energies, 226-232
   and awareness, 241
   and fear of death, 247-254
   and incapacity, 211-212
   healing of. see healing
   in family, 216-220
   reasons for, 240-243

dispassion, 220-221
dissolution, 282
Divine, 173-174
drugs, 94-96
dryness, 97
duality, 293

E

ego, 24, 48-49, 116
   social, 142
emotions, 177-179, 211-212, 241, 266
energy, 217, 292
   and healing of disease, 226-232
   closed, 177-180
   direction of, 122, 125
   knowledge on level of, 191-193
   nature of, 194-195
   raising, 33-35
   recording on, 207-208
   and those close to them, 68-72
   meeting with Sadhguru in vegetable market, 253
   with physical afflictions, 274
   see also bala yogis
Enlightenment, 125
   at time of death, 275-278
   foregoing, 283
   possibility of, 10, 17-19, 31, 67-72
   preparation for, 244, 249
   vs. Realization, 267
Essenes, 246
evolution, spiritual, 163-176
exclusion, karma of, 145, 156
   nature of, 79, 94-95, 140, 275
   levels of, 190
   vs. intellectual understanding, 203-204

Index

F
feminine and masculine, 230
five bodies, 198
formlessness, 153
Freud, Sigmund, 185-186, 233

G
Gandhi, Mahatma, 134
gnana, 123
God, 118, 170
   and the Devil, 8, 173-174
   and spirituality, 252-253
   as lover, 85-86
   as stillness, 106
   relationship with, 100-101
   response from, 56-59
good and bad, 15-18, 173-174
Grace, 95
   presence of, 137
gratitude, 91
growth, 91-92
gunas, 136
Gurdjieff, George Ivanovitch,
   teachings of, 253
Guru pooja, 90
Guru, 26-29, 95, 213
   access to, 66, 68
   and energy bonds, 70
   and saint, difference between, 85
   and spiritual transformation, 65
   as vehicle, 110
   attachment to, 162
   finding one's, 64
   need for, 61-62
   role of, 257
Guru-disciple relationship (Guru-shishya paramparya), 64, 101, 131-132
   carried through lifetimes, 73-74

H
healing, 206, 240
   karmic substance, 245-246
   and Yoga kriyas, 245
   pranic, 240-245
Heaven and Hell, 49, 293
Hell, 285
Himalayas, 15, 59, 66,
Hitler, Adolf, 132
hope, 93-103

I
Ida and Pingala, 143, 269
identifications, 155
   dropping, 229
   and spirituality, 19-21
   rites for the dead in, 286-291
Indra, 160-161
initiation, 192
inner being, 117
intensity, 133
Isha Yoga programs, 206
Isha Yoga, 48, 78, 88 140, 173, 181, 193, 206, 234, 238, 256

J
Jesus, 157, 246, 290
   teachings of, 143

K
kaka pranayama, 284
kapala-bathis, 266
karma yoga, 131
karma, 22, 46, 130, 204-205, 211, 234, 273
   among generations, 145
   and rebirth, 163
   and thoughts, 181

good and/or bad, 136, 138-140, 174, 180-181, 184
  law of, 78
  past, 75
  sanchita, 279
karmic substance, 260
  and individuality, 282
Kedarnath, 27, 62
Krishna, 217
  teachings of, 181, 203
krodha ; see also anger 157
Kumbha Mela, 27
Kundalini, 24, 94, 172

L

laxity, 103-104
'let go' philosophy, 42-44
liberation. see Enlightenment
life, recreation of, 269
likes and dislikes, transcending, 29
limitations, 14
Linga, 14
logic, 132, 227
longing, 66
love, 99-100, 211, 214
  and lust, difference between, 239
  nature of, 79, 94-95
  needed for growth, 101-102

M

Mahasamadhi, 264-265
Mahishasura, 124
mantra, 94, 96-97
maya, 202-203
meditation, 33, 106, 146, 237
mental illness, 229, 232-240
  and ego, 235-236
  and physical activity, 236-238
  treatment of on spiritual path, 235

Mirabai, 84-85, 88
mukthi, 53, 167, 197
  see also enlightenment
muladhara, 288

N

Naga Babas, 27
naraka, 52
Naren. see Vivekananda, Swami
Native Americans
  customs of, 142
nethi, nethi, nethi, 156
nischala tathwam, 216
nishkarma, 182
nothingness, 199, 290-291

O

offering, 134
ojas, 51
original mind, 83, 84

P

and establishing Isha sanyas, 126-127
passion, 124-125
past lives, 183-190
  teachings of, 83-84
peace, inner, 234
personality, 79
  attachment to, 253
physical, going below or above, 112-113
Pillai, Shankaran (jokes), 9, 26, 51, 144-145, 148, 149, 166, 199, 202-203
'plugging the holes', 170
  Guru, 90
population growth, 267-268
positive thinking, 195-196
prana, 205, 207, 256, 267
  vibrancy of, 260, 265, 268-269
pranamayakosha, 281

Index

pranayama, 97, 259, 284
  as preparation for death, 275-276, 281
prarabdha karma, 113, 151, 164-165, 262, 280, 291
  and death, 277
  as cause of disease, 206-210
prayer, 7
  vs. prayerfulness, 111
privacy, 115-118
psychic surgery, 240-241
Punarapi Jananam, Punarapi Maranam, 170

R

Raigarh, 75
Ramakrishna Paramahamsa, 68, 274
  teachings of, 119-120
Ramana Maharshi, 167, 274
regression therapy, 185-186
relationships, 4-7, 99-100
  and understanding, 6-7
responsibility, 220
rigidity, teachings to break, 21

S

sacrifice, 134
sadhaka, 133
sadhana, 23, 24, 28, 93-102, 106-107, 135, 170, 209, 266
  reason for, 280
Sadhguru Shri Bhramha, 61
  daughter of, 145
  his help at time of death, 277-78
  initiation by, 67
  life tales of, 67
  mother of, 218-19
  overwhelmed by presence of, 228-29
  past lives of, 74

sathsangs of, 35-36
  stillness and urgency of, 103-106
  teachings of, 23-26
Sahasrar, 94
Saint Suka and Saint Vyasa, 78-79
sakshi, 194, 198, 200-201
samadhi, 23, 263
Samyama, 48, 49, 88, 184-85, 187-190, 195-96
sankalpa, 107
sanyas, 126-129, 162
sathsang, 35-36, 296
science, 10-11, 88, 134 190, 196 207
scriptures, 98
  Bhagavad Gita, 141, 216
self-image, transforming, 46-48
Shankara, Adi, 95
Shiva, 14, 29, 85, 94, 109, 123, 125, 173
  and drugs, 95
Shoonya meditation, 111, 182, 197, 199, 253-54
smaran, 91
Snake and Ladder game, 168
snakes, 166-167
  and soul's evolution, 171
  symbolism of, 171-176
soul, 256
spiritual path, 124
  and family, 29-31, 140
  confusion on, 38-42
  fear and insecurity on, 2-3
  obsession with 31
  pain on, 53-54
  progress on, 55
spiritual practices, 33
spirituality, 59, 62, 121, 213-14
  and education, 17-18
  and other life forms, 163-169

stillness, 266
  vs. stagnation, 106
suffering, 206-210
  conscious vs. unconscious, 40
  responding to, 216-220
surrender, 189
Swami Nityananda, 60

T

tangle, ego as a, 117
teachers, three types of, 120
teaching, as tool for growth, 83
thought, creating karma, 157
trust, 37-38, 99-100
truth, 64

U

Ultimate Nature, 198
understanding, intellectual, 158

V

vasanas, 124, 164-65, 178
Vedanta, 202-204
vibhuthi, 191

Vivekananda, Swami, 69, 134
volition, 147

W

and spirituality, 87-88
childless, in India, 224-226
work situations, 6-8

Y

Yama, 113, 271
yoga asanas, 21
yoga kriyas, 21, 33, 88, 146, 180, 206, 259, 273
  and rejuvenation, 262
yoga, 47
  and enhancing performance, 10-11
  involvement in, 78
  meaning of, 10-11
  types of 12-13
young in spirit, remaining, 14-16
  tales from, 128
  teachings of, 38